UNDERSTANDING SUICIDE TERRORISM

UNDERSTANDING SUICIDE TERRORISM
Psychosocial Dynamics

Edited by
Updesh Kumar
Manas K. Mandal

 www.sagepublications.com
Los Angeles • London • New Delhi • Singapore • Washington DC

Copyright © Updesh Kumar and Manas K. Mandal, 2014

All rights reserved. No part of this book may be reproduced or utilized in any form or by any means, electronic or mechanical, including photocopying, recording, or by any information storage or retrieval system, without permission in writing from the publisher.

First published in 2014 by

SAGE Publications India Pvt Ltd
B1/I-1 Mohan Cooperative Industrial Area
Mathura Road, New Delhi 110 044, India
www.sagepub.in

SAGE Publications Inc
2455 Teller Road
Thousand Oaks, California 91320, USA

SAGE Publications Ltd
1 Oliver's Yard, 55 City Road
London EC1Y 1SP, United Kingdom

SAGE Publications Asia-Pacific Pte Ltd
3 Church Street
#10-04 Samsung Hub
Singapore 049483

Published by Vivek Mehra for SAGE Publications India Pvt Ltd, Typeset in 10/12 Sabon by SwaRadha Typesetting, New Delhi, and printed at Sai Print-o-Pack, New Delhi.

Library of Congress Cataloging-in-Publication Data Available

ISBN: 978-93-515-0034-6 (HB)

The SAGE Team: Rudra Narayan, Alekha Chandra Jena, Nand Kumar Jha, and Rajinder Kaur

To
*His Holiness Sri Sri Ravi Shankar Ji,
the Founder of Art of Living*

Thank you for choosing a SAGE product! If you have any comment, observation or feedback, I would like to personally hear from you. Please write to me at contactceo@sagepub.in

—Vivek Mehra, Managing Director and CEO,
SAGE Publications India Pvt. Ltd, New Delhi

Bulk Sales

SAGE India offers special discounts for purchase of books in bulk. We also make available special imprints and excerpts from our books on demand.

For orders and enquiries, write to us at

Marketing Department
SAGE Publications India Pvt. Ltd
B1/I-1, Mohan Cooperative Industrial Area
Mathura Road, Post Bag 7
New Delhi 110044, India
E-mail us at marketing@sagepub.in

Get to know more about SAGE, be invited to SAGE events, get on our mailing list. Write today to marketing@sagepub.in

This book is also available as an e-book.

Contents

List of Abbreviations ix

Foreword xi
Professor Ariel Merari

Preface xiii

Section I
Suicide Terrorism: A Phenomenon

1. Suicide Terrorism: Delineating the Construct
   Swati Mukherjee, Updesh Kumar, and Manas K. Mandal   3

2. Suicide Terrorism Explained: A Psychosocial Approach
   Luis de la Corte Ibáñez   18

3. Evolutionary Psychological Science of Suicide Terrorism
   James R. Liddle and Todd K. Shackelford   42

4. Suicide Terrorism as Social Noise: A Communicative Perspective
   Jonathan Matusitz   60

5. 'Mumbai Style': Exploration of a Concept
   Mark Dechesne   76

6. Suicide Bombings: Homicidal Killing or a Weapon of War?
   Riaz Hassan   93

Section II
Suicide Terrorism: A Process

7. The Psychology of Suicide Terrorism
   Jerrold M. Post, Farhana Ali, Schuyler W. Henderson, Stephen Shanfield, Jeff Victoroff, and Stevan Weine   117

8. The Militant Jihadi Ideology of Martyrdom as Short-lived Psychological First Aid for Trauma and Loss
   Anne Speckhard   147

9. Are Suicide Terrorists Suicidal?
   Bruce Bongar, Uri Kugel, and Victoria Kendrick   173

10. The Role of Military Psychologists and Psychiatrists in Understanding Suicide Terrorism
    Uri Kugel, Laurie Black, Joseph Tomlins, Elvin Sheykhani, Bruce Bongar, Morgan Banks, and Larry James   192

11. The Use and Abuse of Children/Youth in Terrorism and Suicide Bombing
    Edna Erez and Anat Berko   213

12. Deterring Suicide Terrorism
    Dushyant Singh   231

About the Editors and Contributors   257
Author Index   268
Subject Index   274

List of Abbreviations

ASVAB	Armed Services Vocational Aptitude Battery
CHF	Congestive heart failure
CNN	Cable News Network
DIPR	Defence Institute of Psychological Research
DoA	Department of the Army
DoD	Department of Defense
DRDO	Defence Research and Development Organization
GIGN	Groupe d'Intervention de la Gendarmerie Nationale of France
GSG 9	Grenz Schutz Gruppe 9 of Germany
HADD	Hypersensitive agent detection device
IDF	Israel Defense Forces
IED	Improvised explosive devices
ISI	Inter-Services Intelligence
JCS	Joint Chiefs of Staff
JI	Jemaah Islamiyah
LET	Lashkar-e-Taiba
LTTE	Liberation Tigers of Tamil Eelam
MCI	Minimally counterintuitive
MMPI-2	Minnesota Multiphasic Personality Inventory
MOS	Military Occupational Specialty
NCTC	National Counterterrorism Center
PA TV	Palestinian Authority Television
PIJ	Palestinian Islamic Jihad
PTA	Prevention of Terrorism Act
PTSD	Posttraumatic stress disorder
SERE	Survival, evasion, resistance, and escape
SES	Socioeconomic status
SF	Special Forces
SFAS	SF Assessment and Selection
SO	Special Operations
SOCOM	Special Operations Command
SOF	Special Operations Forces
USSOCOM	United States Special Operations Command
WMD	Weapon of mass destruction
WW-II	World War II

Foreword

From a historical perspective, terrorism is, arguably, the oldest form of violent struggle. Long before there were rules of war and large organized military formations, tribal wars were fought in ways that would readily fall under most of the current definitions of terrorism. It is therefore surprising that, strictly defined, suicide attacks are a relatively new method of terrorism. As a planned, systematic terrorist tactic, suicide attacks appeared as late as in the 1980s. Older cases of terrorist campaigns, especially the Jewish Sicarii of the first century CE and the Muslim Assassins of the eleventh to thirteenth centuries, which are often mentioned as ancient examples of suicide terrorism, cannot be regarded as genuine cases of suicide, because the perpetrators did not kill themselves.

Historically, new terrorist methods were often associated with technological developments, such as the invention of dynamite in the nineteenth century, which made the construction of bombs easier, or the proliferation of commercial aviation, which made the hijacking of airliners an attractive terrorist tactic in the 1960s and 1970s. Interestingly, this was not the case with suicide attacks. The hardware for these attacks—explosive devices, cars, and airplanes—had been used by terrorists long before it was utilized for suicide attacks. The novelty of this method was entirely in the mental aspect—the willingness of the suicides to cause their own death, the willingness of the organization to sacrifice them, and, often, the support, sometimes enthusiasm, of their social milieu for this form of terrorism. Thus, psychological and social processes, which are the subject of this book, are the basis of the phenomenon of suicide terrorism.

Although suicide attacks are an extreme form of terrorism, they did not attract much academic attention during the 1980s and 1990s, perhaps because the number of attacks in that period was small—less than 150. The number of scholarly publications grew in the wake of the dramatic attacks of 9/11 (2001), and continued to grow in the following years, which have been marked by a huge proliferation of suicide attacks and an expansion of their geographical spread. Still, similar to the general literature on terrorism, only a small minority of the growing body of works on suicide terrorism have specifically focused on psychological aspects of this phenomenon. Most of the literature on suicide terrorism has emphasized the political and religious aspects of conflicts that generated these attacks and on the motivation of the perpetrating organizations. The disciplines of psychology and sociology have been greatly under-represented in the academic literature on suicide terrorism. Thus, this book is an important addition to our body of knowledge.

The book reflects the complexity and diversity of suicide terrorism. While the first two chapters offer an overview of the main factors and processes involved in this phenomenon, other chapters discuss specific types of motivation that influence the decision of groups to resort to suicide attacks and the willingness of individuals to undertake them. Two chapters analyze central issues that pertain to society's response to this extreme form of terrorism: the legal perspective and the heavy question of deterring this seemingly undeterrable tactic. Altogether, this volume is a highly significant contribution toward a better understanding of this multifaceted form of malevolent human behavior.

Ariel Merari, Ph.D.
Professor of Psychology
Tel Aviv University
Israel

Preface

Terrorism to the extent of immolating oneself to kill others is one of the greatest dangers to humanity. Given its inherently fatal nature and the immense impact it makes on the victims as well as spectators, it has achieved an incomparable status in intriguing the researchers of terrorism phenomena, as well as policymakers looking for security solutions. Use of suicide tactics by various terror organizations has tended to make increasingly vast impact due to the diverse nature of geo-political conflicts and increasing polarizations in the modern world. This ultimate form of terrorism has evoked apprehensions, fear, and vulnerability across the globe and has forced the entire world to be on guard constantly. The sheer unpredictability and ingenuity of methods employed by the perpetrators have mandated the security establishments to devise ways to defend itself and the potential victims under all circumstances. The phenomenon has also compelled terrorism research to focus on it with concentrated effort and invigorated zeal.

Although the little existing literature on *suicide terrorism* provides myriad of research perspectives and interdisciplinary viewpoints offering varied explanations and proposing different pathways of understanding, a lot remains to be explored, understood, and explicated of the issues involved both as a phenomenon and as a process. Varied theoretically, complex viewpoints of different scholars pose it as a challenge to enable an objective-scientific perspective of the entire issue. The current volume *Understanding Suicide Terrorism: Psychosocial Dynamics* attempts to take on this challenge by delineating the research perspectives from prominent scholars and researchers in the field and by sifting through the overt and obvious to uncover the psychosocial dynamics lying beneath. The volume progressively deals with these dormant issues and generates a discourse that leads one beyond the mundane and clichéd dictums. The volume incorporates 12 chapters authored by prominent scholars and researchers in the field across the globe. To amalgamate and synthesize the common focal viewpoints, the volume has been divided into two sections—the former delineating on *suicide terrorism as a phenomenon* and the latter delineating on *suicide terrorism as a process*. The sections have been well balanced by having six chapters in each.

The first section focusing on *suicide terrorism as a phenomenon* concisely puts together the scholarly views that provide a scientific framework to the conceptual understanding of this phenomenon. The second section's scholarly impetus is on uncovering the underlying operative dynamics and to make the reader understand *suicide terrorism as a process* rather than one independent act. The volume opens up with the chapter titled 'Suicide terrorism: Delineating the construct' wherein Swati Mukherjee, Updesh Kumar, and Manas K. Mandal attempt to unearth the contentious issues involved in defining the construct of suicide terrorism. Emphasizing upon suicide terrorism as a multifaceted phenomenon, the authors skim through the existing information frameworks and utilize theoretical, developmental, sociocultural inputs for developing the construct of suicide terrorism. Beginning with the issues in definition, the chapter wades through the multiplicity of views in the field. Though the authors endeavor to satisfy the reader's enthusiasm of thorough conceptual understanding of suicide terrorism, multiple related questions still remain unanswered being beyond the scope of the chapter.

The volume steps forward to address the raised questions. Ibáñez, in the second chapter, puts efforts toward *explaining suicide terrorism* from *a psychosocial approach*. The chapter critically reviews several hypotheses about the nature and causes of the phenomenon and offers a characterization of suicide terrorism from a psychosocial point of view. A detailed discussion is included based on the conceptualization of suicide terrorism as more than a symptom of social or psychological disorders and suicide campaigns as instrumental but not entirely rational acts toward the achievement of set targets. The author traces the development and sustenance of the phenomenon as a social construction in which matters of social identity play a dominant role. Further, the author delineates on the multidimensional dynamics inherent to the development of suicide terrorist campaigns and provides an insightful discussion on the risk factors related to the strategic shift toward suicide terrorism and those associated with the processes of polarization and radicalization that sustain suicide campaigns as a viable strategy. Moving ahead in a systematic manner, the *evolutionary psychological science of suicide terrorism* has been well documented upon in the third chapter by Liddle and Shackelford who urge the readers to view the suicide terrorism phenomenon through the lens of evolutionary theory and lead them through the journey toward exploring hidden causes going beyond the obvious proximate explanations. The chapter reviews key concepts and misconceptions related to evolutionary psychology and proceeds to argue that there is a significant overlap between suicide terrorism and religious commitment. Based on the premise, the authors explicitly review the evolutionary psychological theories and associated empirical research related to religious belief, and examine the phenomenon of suicide terrorism in the light of this. They further highlight several promising directions for future research on suicide terrorism from an evolutionary psychological perspective and discuss broader implications of applying evolutionary psychology to suicide terrorism.

Taking the volume forward, Jonathan Matusitz provides *a communicative perspective* and explains *suicide terrorism as social noise* in the next chapter. Herein, the author examines the phenomenon from the particular perspective of communication, as social noise. The author conceptualizes the attention grabbing property of the suicide terrorist acts through noisy, graphic, provocative, or controversial acts intended to create change in the audience's attitudes or opinions. The chapter puts forth a model of the concept as a specific form of communication in the context of martyrdom in Islamist terrorism. The conceptualization of suicide terror as a form of communication, the roles and different types of the audiences in the context that perpetuate the phenomenon and lead to the ultimate consequence of public disorder are the points of author's discourse and have been supported by the provision of a specific case study.

Exploration of the concept with specific emphasis on *Mumbai Style* is the focal point of the fifth chapter wherein Mark Dechesne builds on an argument to consider 'Mumbai Style' or fidayeen terrorist attacks as a specific category of suicide attacks. The horrific Mumbai attacks of 26/11 characterized by perpetrators seemingly randomly killing until they get caught or killed by security forces do not find any match in the formal theorizations of suicide terrorism. Providing a detailed and engaging account of the Mumbai attack, the chapter utilizes this instance as a case study to analyze suicide terror tactics in broader perspective. Uniquely characterizing 'Mumbai Style' in terms of conviction, combinations of weapons, coordination, and communication, the author attempts to set apart the 'Mumbai Style' suicide attacks. The section of explaining suicide terrorism as a phenomenon comes toward an end by scholarly article on 'Suicide bombings: Homicidal killing or weapons of war?' authored by Riaz Hassan. Hassan critically examines the distinction between war and terrorism and argues that both of these kill civilians and insert the coerciveness of precaution in the daily rhythm of social life. The argument has been well supported by discussion of Palestinian and Sri Lankan as incidences as case studies. Using evidence from ethnographic studies on the nature of war and homicide, the chapter concludes that suicide bombing attacks, because of the principle of *substitutability* which characterize war killing, could be regarded as a weapon of war. But given that they are characterized by willful killing of civilians, they could be regarded as 'War Crimes' under the Fourth Geneva Convention. As an eminent scholar, the author emphasizes that exploration of the meanings of the suicide terror acts requires critical theoretical, conceptual, and hermeneutical tools which do not distort their meanings.

After the seemingly apt efforts put in the first section to arrive at a comprehensive understanding of suicide terrorism as a phenomenon, the volume uncovers the second section to delve upon *suicide terrorism as a process*. Having a concise focus on the theme, this section also includes six chapters by prominent scholars in the field. The section delineating upon the process of suicide terrorism opens up with the seventh chapter authored by Jerrold M. Post and his colleagues, and is aptly titled as 'The psychology of suicide terrorism.' The authors of the article attempt to provide a comprehensive review of the current understanding of suicide terrorism from a mental health perspective. The chapter discusses the key concepts and definitions, and reviews individual and group-level models to explain the processes involved in the development of suicide terrorism. Uncovering many of the psychological processes underlying suicide terrorism, Post and his colleagues emphasize the need for a multidisciplinary approach for attaining a holistic comprehension of suicide terrorism. The next chapter in the section continues the discourse by conceptualizing *the militant jihadi ideology of martyrdom as short-lived psychological first aid for trauma and loss*. Anne Speckhard, the author, conceptualizes militant jihadi ideology as providing short-term psychological first aid in conflict and non conflict zones where deep psychological vulnerabilities exist among Muslims and converts to Islam—temporarily attending to the psychological needs of the person following it. The chapter further discusses the consequences of exposure to violent conflict as posttraumatic stress disorder and traumatic dissociation, and traces the development of allegiance to jihadi ideology as a search for redressal of these traumas. It is posited that the process develops especially powerful in societies where other types of psychological assistance are either not available or stigmatized.

The process underlying the phenomenon of suicide terrorism further raises an ever essential question—*Are suicide terrorists suicidal?* An effort has been made by Bruce Bongar, Uri Kugel, and Victoria Kendrick to answer this question in the ninth chapter. The authors attempt to answer the question by presenting the current literature and analyzing suicide terrorism from several different perspectives such as the act itself, motivational background of suicide bombers, the organizational component of suicide terrorism, and the psychological profiles of the suicides. The classical categorization of suicides as egoistic, altruistic, and anomic provided by Durkheim has been discussed in order to debate similarities and dissimilarities between the suicidal processes and suicide terrorism. The chapter asserts the multidimensional and multidetermined nature of suicide attacks and the process leading up to it, and emphatically distinguishes these from other acts of suicide. Extending the discourse on similar lines, in the next chapter, Uri Kugel and associates attempt to specify *the role of military psychologists and psychiatrists in understanding suicide terrorism*. The authors put forth that suicide terrorists materialize from a psychological commitment to a specific cause, along with group influences, and the crucial role of training and selection. The chapter addresses a crucial need in comprehending suicide terrorism by exploring what military psychologists and psychiatrist, with their knowledge of training and selection criteria, can bring to the current understanding of the recruitment, training, and deployment of suicide terrorists. The authors interestingly compare and contrast the selection, recruitment, training, and motivation of Special Forces personnel with that of the suicide terrorist and show both commonalities and extreme differences to make the understanding of the reader more convenient.

As the volumes shape toward the end, the 11th chapter deals with the sensitive issue of *the use and abuse of children/youth in terrorism and suicide bombing* wherein Erez and Berko provide a comprehensive review of the ways children are used and abused in war and terrorism. The functions that children serve for military and terrorist organizations, the reasons for the recruitment of them, and the benefits of using them over adults in suicidal operations have been discussed in detail by the authors. Taking the Israeli–Arab/Palestinian conflict as a case study to highlight the methods of indoctrination employed to influence children to join terrorism and suicide missions, and the way in which participating children view and evaluate their experiences, the authors elaborate upon the adverse effects of living in conflict areas and being involved in armed hostilities have on children. Policy implications for needful social and political actions have been discussed in brief. The final chapter of the book sums up the entire discourse by coming to the crux of the matter of and the most essential aspect of 'Deterring suicide terrorism.' The author, a security expert, Major General Dushyant Singh joins the quest for evolving workable counterterrorism strategies against suicide terrorism and proposes that a specific deterrence strategy developed using cumulative deterrence appears to work best against suicide terror. The chapter builds the argument for deterrence based on the elaborate database of Chicago Project on Security and Terrorism and identifies key elements in deterrence. Finally, the author summatively puts forth specific points of intervention at individual, familial, organizational, and societal levels that might prove effective in deterring suicide attacks.

Suicide terrorism involves highly complex subject matter and simultaneously it incorporates a vast and varied area of scholarly expertise as well as a crucial part of security policy. Editing a volume on suicide terrorism has been a quite formidable exercise. It has been an effortful and enlightening experience for us to put together in a synthesized form such expert views and scholarly opinions as this volume contains. We hope that this effort fructifies not merely by adding a multidisciplinary perspective to the ocean of literature on the issue, but by taking us all a step closer to rational analysis of the enigmatic issue of suicide terrorism and by helping us arrive at a comprehensive understanding of its underlying psychosocial dynamics.

Any venture of this intensity can never be undertaken or accomplished all alone. There have been people around us who have provided the encouragement, understanding, and undeterred support through the task. We extend our gratitude to one and all who have helped and facilitated us. We are grateful to our institute, Defence Institute of Psychological Research (DIPR) and our mentors at the Defence Research and Development Organization (DRDO) for providing us with all kinds of support and encouragement. It has indeed been a rewarding experience to edit a volume in which eminent scholars brought in not only diverse disciplinary knowledge but also their diverse cultural experiences. We extend our heartfelt thanks to all the contributors in the volume and look forward to continued association with them in developing an interface between research and policy in a manner to be able to evolve effective deterrence against terrorism. We will always be indebted to our beloved family members who always encouraged us and provided us with their complete care and support to complete this volume in a short span of time. We are also obliged to acknowledge the effort put in by the anonymous reviewers of the order of distinguished professors. Without their involvement, the volume would not have materialized in the present form. We hope that this volume will serve to help the reader in multiple ways and will promote a higher sense of security by means of making people aware of the dynamics of the acts of terror.

Updesh Kumar
Manas K. Mandal

Section I

Suicide Terrorism: A Phenomenon

Section 1

Suicide Terrorism: A Phenomenon

1

Suicide Terrorism: Delineating the Construct

Swati Mukherjee, Updesh Kumar, and Manas K. Mandal

Terrorism is the biggest political and strategic challenge of our times. A major variant of the modern-day terrorism is suicide terrorism in which the perpetrators create threat by killing themselves and inducing in mass damage. It is different from the conventional terrorism but executed with the very purpose of creating mass hysteria and threat to normalcy. Suicide terrorists have specific personal, social, and environmental compulsions and they pose a challenge to scientists in terms of description, assessment, and prediction of such behavior. The phenomenon has defied an explanation so far, despite engaged efforts at political, strategic, and scientific levels. There are single-factor explanations that prove grossly inadequate, and there are multicausal approaches emphasizing presence and dynamic interaction of several causal variables, yet do not succeed in answering the persistent contentious issues. Integrative theoretical frameworks that take account of individual attributes, organizational dynamics, as well as the structural or environmental variables have not been able to withstand the test of predictability.

Though terrorism manifests and is usually conceptualized in the form of a political issue, the problem "stripped to the basics—is one of atypical human behaviour" (Victoroff, 2005, p. 4), it has been emphasized that developing effective management strategies that reduce the threat of terrorism depends on gaining an understanding of the terrorist mindset (Clayton, Barlow, & Ballif-Spanvill, 1998; Wardlaw, 1989). Terrorism is a tool in the hands of its perpetrators that is utilized for creating a fear in the mind of the target so as to disable them of making objective risk assessments (Schmid, 2005), and in this sense is the most potent weapon of psychological warfare that incapacitates the target by precluding predictability. The suicide terrorist has a manifold effectiveness in this context as the motivations, intentions, and strategies behind the act of giving up one's life in order to damage or terrorize the target have never really been understood in their totality.

DEFINITIONAL ISSUES

The issue of defining terrorism has not been beyond controversies and contentions. Similarly, a review of the published literature on suicide terrorism reveals the contentiousness involved (Crenshaw, 2007). Crenshaw, while reviewing 13 books by prominent scholars in the field, brings out the sheer lack of consensus in defining suicide terrorism. She asserts that most disagreements on definition stem from the uncertainties involved in using the label of terrorism; however, the term suicide also has been avoided by many researchers who view the act in the cultural perspective of specific societies (e.g., assumption of martyrdom associated with Islamic notions of *Istishhad*—an act of martyrdom in fulfillment of religious commands). The act of suicide might not necessarily be considered courageous or even desirable in a particular society, and hence the attacks on the enemy that cause the perpetrator to lose one's life may not be viewed as suicide at all. The apparent failure of the United Nations to come up with a definition of the phenomenon acceptable to all member nations (O'Connor, 2011) reflects upon the value-laden nature of terrorism. Terrorism *per se*, and concomitantly suicide terrorism being value-laden terms, cannot be defined in a politically neutral manner. And, this very nature of the phenomena adds to the variations in how different researchers view the acts of suicidal terror, provide a definition, and attempt at prediction depending upon their own location and value positions they prefer in the specific contexts they choose to study.

Deriving from the commonalities and variance in the literature, suicide terrorism can summarily be defined as a politically motivated violent attack deliberately carried out in full awareness and knowledge of one's own death. However, as emphasized by scholars (e.g., Bloom, 2005; Crenshaw, 2007), suicide terrorism is not a uniform phenomenon, and there are variations in the extent to which 'the knowledge and intent of dying in the act' are considered core of the phenomenon. While some scholars assert that inevitability of the death of the perpetrator for success of the mission is essential for labeling the act as suicidal attack (e.g., Ganor, 2007), others like Merari (1990, p. 192) do not propound such strict stance and capture the suicidal intent within such attacks merely as "the readiness to die in the process of committing a terrorist act." The definition one accepts, thus, determines the range of attacks falling in the purview of the concept of suicidal attack or suicide terrorism. There are value judgments involved on at least three levels: (i) deciding to term a particular act as an act of terror, (ii) determining whether the attack was indeed suicidal based on the intentionality involved, and (iii) accepting these attackers as suicidal.

Use of one's life as the ultimate weapon to cause gross damage to the enemy is not new. Throughout history, it has been the most deadly weapon in the hands of the weaker party in a conflict that was financially or technologically asymmetrical. It provided the weaker with an edge over the mighty opponent and created an illusion of invincibility. As Atran (2003, p. 1534) says, "Suicide attack is an ancient practice with a modern history"; there are ample examples around the world in varied cultures that have used and have faced suicide attacks. Ancient examples that are often cited are those of the Jewish sect of Zealots (*sicari*) in Roman-occupied Judea and by the Islamic Order of Assassins (*hashashin*) during the early Christian Crusades (Lewis, 2002). Lesser known examples are of the suicide squads raised by Chera kings in eleventh-century India in order to counter the superior military might of a rival Chola empire (Menon, 1967). Beginning from the ancient through the medieval till the modern times, history is replete with instances of use of life as a weapon. Incidences of Dutch soldiers blowing up their posts along with themselves and the aggressors during a war to gain control over Taiwan in 1661 have been documented (Yonghe, 2004). The Japanese 'Kamikaze pilots' during World War II and the Viet-minh 'death volunteers' post World War II who blew up enemy tanks using long stick like explosives are well-known examples. Beginning in early 1980s, in the Middle East, the suicide attacks have gained global spread in past two decades. With organizations like Hezbollah, Liberation Tigers of Tamil Eelam (LTTE), Hamas, and Al-Qaeda opting for suicidal attacks in an increasingly polarized world post 9/11, efforts to delineate the phenomenon have definitely been intensified.

VARIED PERSPECTIVES

Different perspectives have provided different levels of analysis to the phenomenon; for example, tracing the motivation for launching a suicidal campaign would require a strategic analysis, as opposed to analysis of factors that motivate the individuals to volunteer for such campaigns that would need a structural analysis at the individual level (Ismayilov, 2010). Similarly, the attempts to explain suicide terrorism either view the phenomenon as a rational choice under the given circumstances or attempt to explain it away as an irrational behavioral aberration. The varied and multifaceted nature of the phenomenon has often led the scholars to assert that psychological profiles of suicide attack perpetrators are not possible (Merari, 1990). Another common assumption is that the characteristics that mark suicidal individuals are not applicable to the suicide attackers (Israeli, 1997). However, such assumptions have been challenged (e.g., Lester, Yang, & Lindsay, 2004) asserting the inadequacy of data on which such conclusions have been drawn, and anecdotal nature of most evidence in the area.

Are Terrorists Suicidal?

A pertinent question often raised is whether the perpetrators of suicidal attack are indeed suicidal. As Lester et al. (2004) point out there is obvious difficulty involved in ascertaining existence of suicide risk factors among these individuals, as their very act extinguishes their lives. Moreover, it has not been very feasible to obtain extensive life history data from the perpetrators who are apprehended before committing the attack, and as a result there are very few insights gained into the psychological processes involved. A probable means of overcoming this lacuna might be provided by studying behaviors that do not involve suicide attack, but are closely associated.

One such behavioral aberration that has been studied extensively is homicide–suicide that involves occurrence of both the destructive acts in close succession involving the same individual. Both these behaviors are "antagonistic expressions of human aggression" (Liem & Nieuwbeerta, 2010), and provide an opportunity to understand the dynamics of both. Though in the Western cultures, most homicides involve a single victim, usually an intimate partner or family member, multiple homicides are not uncommon in most societies. Homicidal behaviors occurring in different cultures, involving violent outbursts have been described by Cooper (1934), such as 'amok' in Malaysia, 'Wihtico psychosis' among the Cree Indians, 'jumping Frenchman' in Canada, and 'imu' in Japan. The typical psychological profile of the perpetrator in cases of homicide–suicide appears to be "that of a passive–aggressive, young adult, with poor self-esteem, insecure, and socially inadequate, who occasionally uses drugs and alcohol and exhibits proneness to explosive behaviour. The background frequently includes a dysfunctional family, including sexual abuse as a child" (Palermo, 2007, p. 10). Palermo (1994) views homicide–suicide as extended suicide. Similarly, Freud (1920/1961) viewed both suicide and homicide as expressions of aggression, and conceptualized suicide as an impulse to kill another turned inward on the self. The frustration–aggression hypothesis (Dollard, Doob, Miller, Mowrer, & Sears, 1939) construes aggression as an outcome of frustration due to thwarted efforts of goal attainment. The aggressive behavior has the possibility of manifesting in the form of hostile aggression or instrumental aggression (Feshbach, 1964). Hostile aggression is primarily aimed at destroying or causing harm to the target, whereas instrumental aggression is characterized by its orientation for attaining a desired goal, aggression being merely instrumental for neutralizing the agents that are perceived as blocking the path toward the desired goal. Dollard et al. (1939) assert that such aggressive behaviors might be directed at the source of frustration or might get displaced to substitute targets. The aggressive behaviors are heightened or diminished based on the perceived intentionality and legitimacy of the blocking agents (Berkowitz, 1989).

Sole reliance on such explanations based on individual psychological processes, without incorporating the larger sociocultural dynamics, however might prove grossly inadequate for understanding the complex phenomenon of suicide terrorism. The task of understanding (suicide) terrorism begins with a search for the questions of whose goals are thwarted by whom, by what methods, whose stance is perceived as legitimate in the global scenario, and the dynamics of power involved among nation states or non state groups need to be answered if a meaningful picture is to be made. Such attribution decisions bring in the issues of political motivations, sociocultural influences, value judgments that characterize political violence, in general, and suicide terrorism specifically.

Attempting a Neurobiological Explanation

With huge advancements made in the field of genetics and neurological sciences, a moot point arises if suicide attacks or political violence in general could be explained and predicted based on these predispositions. Despite the potency of sociocultural explanations of suicide terrorism, they fail to tell the entire story (Post, 2005a). It remains to be answered as to why only a handful of individuals among the many in a society facing oppression, conflict, or perceived injustice choose to act in fatal or altruistic manners, giving up their lives to save others or to damage the enemy. A neurobiological approach that would work in tandem with the existing approaches adds to the preventive potential of the efforts by helping identify the individuals who are most vulnerable in the given environments. Hatemi and McDermott (2012) propose an individual level of analysis in order to have obvious advantage over the socioenvironmental and anecdotal methods of analysis and decision making. They advocate the use of a model based in neurobiology and behavior genetics for understanding political violence and site the following advantages they envisage: (i) quantifying the effects of genes, environments, and their interaction on behavior; (ii) identifying specific genetic and environmental contexts that lead to such behavior; (iii) developing a comprehensive model of the biological and social pathways to political violence; (iv) identifying populations under specific circumstances which pose a higher or lower prevalence for any specific genes, neurobiological or environmental mechanisms which pose an increased liability for political violence; (v) developing mechanisms to identify individuals within given populations who are most at risk for committing violence, as well as those most resistant to such action; and (vi) creating environmental responses which can mitigate risk among those individuals.

Early explorations into the individual factors implicated in propensity for political violence focused on individual psychopathology (e.g., Post, 1998). However, over the years it was made apparent that no obvious psychopathology is involved in most cases of political violence, be it terrorism or suicide terrorism (e.g., Atran, 2003; Ruby, 2003). Explorations of individual level variables beyond psychopathology that increase the propensity for engaging in acts of terror or suicide terrorism have not been taken up so far. In the absence of direct empirical evidence, it would be only speculative to discuss the nuances of neurobiology or behavioral genetics involving violent behavior in specific contexts of terrorism.

The evolutionary behavioral perspective on suicide that benefits the group one belongs to was propounded by de Catanzaro (1986, 1991, 1995) who asserted that self-destructive behavior under certain circumstances ensures one's genetic legacy by ensuring survival of one's in-group. Sacrifice by selected few members of the group may be the evolutionary way of ensuring that the larger group has an enhanced defense or has its burden reduced. Future researches from the perspective might provide answers to many questions that have intrigued scholars in the field of suicide terrorism.

The Social Context of Suicide

A closely associated proposition of 'altruistic suicide' provides support for the evolutionary perspective. This sociological proposition that is often seen to have a bearing on the understanding of suicide terrorism is the construal of suicide as an act rooted not within the individual, but in the societal processes (Durkheim, 1897/1951). Durkheim asserted that occurrence of both suicide and homicide is determined by the degree of cohesion and social regulation in a society. Enhanced impulsivity in disorganized societies in the times of rapid social change causes "a state of irritated weariness" (p. 257) at the individual level that gets turned toward self (constituting suicide) or the other (constituting homicide). The typology of suicide proposed by Durkheim (1897/1951) proposes four categories of suicide, egoistic, anomic, altruistic, and fatalistic. Though Durkheim did not conceptualize the eventuality of using one's life as a weapon to kill others, Pedahzur, Perliger, and Weinberg (2003) argue that the last two of the above categories, that is, altruistic and fatalistic suicide can make important contributions to comprehension of the phenomenon of suicide terrorism.

Durkheim specifies altruistic suicide as the act of giving up one's life in order to ensure betterment of the group to which the person belongs. In this sense, an absolute integration of the individual in the group or society is an essential precondition for altruistic suicide to occur so that suicide is perceived as a social duty. Johnson (1979) emphasizes that the integration of the individual in the collective must be complete so as to make the individual perceive his/her life as secondary to the interest of the collective. Stack (2004, p. 10) describes four key features of altruistic suicide: a context of abnormally excessive societal integration; it is generally marked by support from public opinion; it benefits the society materially or culturally; and it is often marked by positive emotionality. Altruistic suicides are a hallmark of traditional societies going through political, social, and economic transitions (Johnson, 1979) and the concept has been aptly used to explain the rising incidence of suicide bombing in the Palestinian society (Brynen, 1995; Riemer, 1998; Sirriyeh, 2000). Durkheim (1897/1951) also provides subtypes of altruistic suicide: obligatory, optional, and acute. Obligatory altruistic suicide is dictated by the norms of the society and is seen as a cultural duty; optional altruistic suicide, though not perceived as a duty, is still supported or encouraged by the society under certain conditions; acute altruistic suicide precludes any notion of compulsion and is committed by the individual willingly in order to fulfill a goal larger than self. Scholars (e.g., Pedahzur et al., 2003; Stack, 2004) view the typology of acute altruistic suicide aptly fits the characteristics of contemporary suicide terrorist, with their total submergence in the group (Young, 1972) and carrying oneself to death in a surge of faith and enthusiasm on their own volition (Pedahzur et al., 2003). Scrutiny of the world over events of suicide terrorism and profiles of the perpetrators reveals that the organizations responsible for such attacks are organizations with a collective culture that subsumes the individual identity. The religious/cultural beliefs subscribed by the members make them believe in the glory of death for the betterment of the collective and promise of a glorious afterlife (Stack, 2004). Such beliefs coincide with the propositions of acute altruistic suicide, where the act of suicide is voluntary and committed not in melancholy, but with a positive motivational conviction of betterment for the group.

Along with altruism involved in suicide attacks, Stack (2004) also implicates the fatalistic element. Fatalistic suicide is an outcome of situations of continuous oppression from which no escape is apparently possible (Johnson, 1979; Taylor, 1982). Stack (1979, p. 162) notes:

Fatalistic suicide . . . results from excessive regulation, such as that of persons with futures blocked, aspirations choked by oppressive discipline, and persons living under physical or moral despotism.. . . Fatalistic suicides involve an escape from a normative situation from which there is no appeal.

According to him, such totalitarian environments provide an added impetus to the individuals toward suicide.

Contrary to initial beliefs, looking at the trend of strategic use of suicide attacks against key targets it has become apparent that suicide terrorism is an organized and organizational phenomenon (Merari, 1990). Implicating fatalism at the level of the individual would be akin to labeling the perpetrators as deviants and summarily explaining away their acts as aberrations. However, a sense of fatalism at the group level given the conflict with a powerful enemy in an asymmetrical war, coupled with a strong sense of collective brought about by sociocultural circumstances and certain religious beliefs (e.g., belief in an afterlife, giving up one's life in service of God or Allah) makes the framework of altruism–fatalism applicable to incidents of suicide terrorism. Moreover, it cannot be denied that under circumstances of instability and upheaval that characterize most locales where there is a concentration of suicide attacks, increasingly higher number of individuals would succumb to fatalism. Terrorist organizations with a strategy to recruit appropriate members would have ample opportunity to prepare and use such vulnerable individuals as perpetrators of suicide attacks by providing a sense of belonging and hope. Pedahzur et al. (2003) in their extensive empirical analysis of suicide terror cases in Palestine propagate and confirm the hypothesis that most cases represent a combination of the two typologies involving altruistic as well as fatalistic motivations. As Young (1972, p. 106) puts it:

These two types should be treated as twin sisters nursed in the same type of sociocultural system. Their differences can be sought only from the subjective meaning of the suicidal action. If a person commits suicide to fulfil his duty, his psychological state may either be one of serene conviction (altruism) or it may be one of extreme fear and despair (fatalism) or a combination of both.

Being Prepared to Die and Suicide: Are They the Same?

A perusal of the sociocultural interpretations of causes increasing the propensity of violent acts involving the destruction of self and the other establishes suicide terrorism as a value-laden construct. Scholars delineate the issues involved depending not only upon the theoretical positions they ascribe to but such explanations are also rooted in the political value positions they choose for themselves. The mainstream literature on the issue of self-inflicted death for the cause of meeting group goals labels such acts as suicide, at best terming these as 'altruistic suicide' (Abdel-Khalek, 2004). Abdel-Khalek (2004, p. 100) details the difference in perspective that the Western literature propagates and the Islamic perspective that views such acts as martyrdom. Drawing from him, the term suicide is used to denote the act of self-inflicted intentional death that is motivated primarily by an inner state such as psychological disorder, attention seeking, blaming, expressing anger, or escaping an intolerable situation (Campbell, 1996). Suicide is viewed largely as a personal matter resorted in response to experiences of personal distress. In contrast and as asserted by Abdel-Khalek martyrdom is the act of defending one's homeland/group at the cost of one's life by inflicting damage to the enemy, and involves subsuming of individual life for the attainment of group goals. The fundamental difference between the two acts is emphasized by asserting a group-oriented perspective of the suicide attacker, as he is perceived to be giving up his life for the greater good of his brethren.

Most of the recent discourse on martyrdom has concentrated on Islamic notion of jihad (holy war with religious underpinnings); however, the notion of martyrdom has existed in various groups, communities, religions, and across nations since antiquity. Most of the Third World nations that fought colonialism have a history of dedicated young men and women who fought against the might of the colonial masters, many of them sacrificing their lives in acts of bringing damage or death to the oppressors. It is not uncommon to find tales of unmatched heroism during modern military operations, where a single individual gives up his life in order to save his buddies, or as a method of achieving the goal that appears impossible otherwise. It has been emphasized that the mainstream Western literature often views the acts of terror in an antagonistic manner that precludes a comprehensive understanding of the issues involved (Brannan, Esler, & Strindberg, 2001). Suicide terrorism is conceptualized as an act of deviance or aberration in motivation by the Western literature (Kruglanski & Fishman, 2006), or as a product of deviations at the societal or religious levels. However, the suicide attackers have not been found to display signs of depression, psychoticism, or sociopathy (Abdel-Khalek, 2004). On the contrary, a heightened sense of purpose, group allegiance, and task focus (Lester et al., 2004) has been a mark for them. In this context, the entire issue can be viewed as a socioculturally constructed discourse (Hafez, 2007) in which one man's terrorist becomes the other man's freedom fighter. The self-perceptions of suicide attackers as selfless righteous individuals (Stevens, 2005) apparently arise as a result of indoctrination into dichotomous ways of perceiving the world (Silberman, Higgins, & Dweck, 2005) encouraged by a totalitarian social arrangement and sanction, even encouragement, by subjective interpretations of religious doctrines (Lester, 2004). The authoritarian societies, especially when marred by an environment of perpetual conflict and upheaval, provide a limited scope of identity explorations to its youngsters, leading to premature foreclosure of identities and uncritical commitment to goals construed desirable by the social environment. Such foreclosure of identity has been linked with rigid and unequivocal commitments (Marcia, 1967) and provides the foundation for dichotomized thinking. Such individual with diffused foreclosed identities are likely to place the dichotomies created by their colored perceptions at the core of their sense of self (Lester et al., 2004; Post 2005b). It is likely that such individual vulnerabilities are then utilized by the organized terror groups and propel the person toward identifying with the group goal, perceiving it as valuable to the extent of devaluing his/her own life, and committing oneself with apparent zeal and utmost motivation. Discussing the rise of suicide attacks in Iraq, based on his extensive review of audio and video recordings and online pictures associated with suicide terror attacks posted by terror groups, Hafez (2007, p. 96) brings out the larger discourse associated with 'martyrdom mythology' and the culturally constructed narratives of

unmerciful humiliation and suffering inflicted on Muslims in Iraq and throughout the world, ... the impotence of existing

Muslim regimes and their collusion with the West, ... [and] inevitability of Muslim victory because pious and heroic cadres have stepped forward to redeem the suffering and humiliation of their fellow Muslims through faith in God, sacrifice on the battlefield, and righteousness in their cause.

Such discourses of humiliation, impotence, and redemption are evoked and perpetuated using the mass media with the purpose of sustaining a culture that promotes martyrdom and honors the martyrs, thereby ensuring a supply of enough young and dedicated lives for the cause.

AND THE QUESTIONS REMAIN ...

Any deliberation on suicide terrorism is bound to raise more questions than be able to provide answers. The multidimensional nature of the phenomenon and complexity of the factors involved make it veritably difficult to come up with an answer that could be acceptable to all without any contentions. Genesis of the present volume lies in the idea of bringing together the multifarious theories, evidences and perspectives, not in search of any absolute answers, but in an endeavor to build a single platform where all these voices could be heard, combined, and integrated to make the answers more plausible to achieve. Beginning with divergence over definitions of terrorism, delving over the biological processes implicated in propensity for self-destruction in order to achieve group goals, unearthing the psychological roots and exploring the sociocultural processes associated with the phenomenon, the raging debates in the area have been fashioned in the form of the subsequent chapters. A conclusive comment would probably be unwarranted, given the fluid nature of evidences generated by narrow and restrictive perspectives adopted by most studies so far. The current effort, thus, envisages to act as a catalyst in generating multiple questions from multiple perspectives, and contributing to the search for the multiple subjective truths, a concurrence of which may provide a solution to the human menace of terrorism.

REFERENCES

Abdel-Khalek, A. M. (2004). Neither altruistic suicide, nor terrorism but martyrdom: A Muslim perspective. *Archives of Suicide Research, 8*(1), 99–113.
Atran, S. (2003). Genesis of suicide terrorism. *Science, 299*(5612), 1534–1539.
Berkowitz, L. (1989). Frustration-aggression hypothesis: Examination and reformulation. *Psychological Bulletin, 106*(1), 59–73.
Bloom, M. (2005). *Dying to kill: The allure of suicide terror.* New York: Columbia University Press.
Brannan, D. W., Esler, P. F., & Strindberg, N. T. A. (2001). Talking to "terrorists": Towards an independent analytic framework for the study of violent substate activism. *Studies in Conflict and Terrorism, 24*(1), 3–24.
Brynen, R. (1995). The dynamic of Palestinian elite formation. *Journal of Palestinian Studies, 24*(3), 31–43.
Campbell, R. J. (1996). *Psychiatric dictionary,* 7th ed. New York: Oxford University Press.
Clayton, C. J., Barlow, S. H., & Ballif-Spanvill, B. (1998). Principles of group violence with a focus on terrorism. In H. V. Hall & L. C. Whitaker (Eds.), *Collective violence* (pp. 277–311). Boca Raton, FL: CRC Press.
Cooper, J. M. (1934). Mental disease situation in certain cultures: A new field for research. *Journal of Abnormal Social Psychology, 29*(1), 10–17.
Crenshaw, M. (2007). Explaining suicide terrorism: A review essay. *Security Studies, 16*(1), 133–162.
de Catanzaro, D. (1986). A mathematical model of evolutionary pressures regulating self-preservation self-destruction. *Suicide and Life Threatening Behaviour, 16*(2), 166–181.
de Catanzaro, D. (1991). Evolutionary limits of self-preservation. *Ethology and Sociobiology, 12*(1), 13–28.
de Catanzaro, D. (1995). Reproductive status, family interactions, and suicidal ideation: Surveys of the general public and high-risk groups. *Ethology and Sociobiology, 16*(5), 385–394.
Dollard, J., Doob, L., Miller, N., Mowrer, O. H., & Sears, R. (1939). *Frustration and aggression.* New Haven, CT: Yale University Press.
Durkheim, E. (1951). *Suicide: A study in sociology* (J. A. Spaulding & G. Simpson, Trans.). New York, NY: Free Press (Original work published 1897).
Feshbach, S. (1964). The function of aggression and the regulation of aggressive drive. *Psychological Review, 71*(4), 257–272.

Freud, S. (1961). Beyond the pleasure principle. In J. Strachey (Trans. & Ed.), *The standard edition of the complete psychological works of Sigmund Freud* (Vol. 18, pp. 7–64). London: Hogarth (Original work published 1920).

Ganor, B. (2007, March 21). The rationality of the Islamic radical suicide attack phenomenon. In Countering terrorism at institute for counter terrorism. Retrieved from http://www.ict.org.il/Articles/tabid/66/Articlsid/243/currentpage/15/Default.aspx

Hafez, M. M. (2007). Martyrdom mythology in Iraq: How jihadists frame suicide terrorism in videos and biographies. *Terrorism and Political Violence, 19*(1), 95–115.

Hatemi, P., & McDermott, R. (2012). A neurobiological approach to foreign policy analysis: Identifying individual differences in political violence. *Foreign Policy Analysis, 8*(2), 111–129.

Ismayilov, M. (2010). Conceptualizing terrorist violence and suicide bombing. *Journal of Strategic Security, 3*(3), 15–26.

Israeli, R. (1997). Islamikaze and their significance. *Terrorism and Political Violence, 9*(3), 96–121.

Johnson, K. (1979). Durkheim revisited: Why do women kill themselves? *Suicide and Life-Threatening Behaviour, 9*(1), 45–53.

Kruglanski, A. W., & Fishman, S. (2006). The psychology of terrorism: "Syndrome" versus "tool" perspectives. *Terrorism and Political Violence, 18*(2), 193–215.

Lester, D. (2004). Altruistic suicide: A view of the issues. *Archives of Suicide Research, 8*(1), 37–42.

Lester, D., Yang, B., & Lindsay, M. (2004). Suicide bombers: Are psychological profiles possible? *Studies in Conflict and Terrorism, 27*(4), 283–295.

Lewis, B. (2002). *The assassins*. New York: Basic.

Liem, M., & Nieuwbeerta, P. (2010). Homicide followed by suicide: A comparison with both homicide and suicide. *Suicide and Life-Threatening Behavior, 40*(2), 133–145.

Marcia, J. E. (1967). Ego identity status: Relationship to change in self-esteem, "general maladjustment," and authoritarianism. *Journal of Personality, 35*(1), 118–133.

Menon, S. (1967). *A survey of Kerala history*. Kerala (India): Sahitya Pravarthaka Co-operative Society [Sales Department]; National Book Stall.

Merari, A. (1990). The readiness to kill and die: Suicidal terrorism the Middle East. In W. Reich (Ed.), *Origins of terrorism* (pp. 192–207). Washington, DC: Woodrow Wilson Center Press.

O'Connor, T. (2011, July 17). Definitions and typologies of terrorism. *Mega links in criminal justice*. Retrieved from http://www.drtomoconnor.com/3400/3400lect01.htm

Palermo, G. B. (1994). Murder suicide: An extended suicide. *International Journal of Offender Therapy and Comparative Criminology, 38*(3), 205–216.

Palermo, G. B. (2007). Homicidal syndromes: A clinical psychiatric perspective. In Richard N. Kocsis (Ed.), *Criminal profiling: International theory, research, and practice* (pp. 3–26). Totowa, NJ: Humana Press.

Pedahzur, A., Perliger, A., & Weinberg, L. (2003). Altruism and fatalism: The characteristics of Palestinian suicide terrorists. *Deviant Behaviour, 24*(4), 405–423.

Post, J. M. (1998). Terrorist psycho-logic: Terrorism as the product of psychological choices. In W. Reich (Ed.), *Origins of terrorism* (pp. 25–40). Washington, DC: Woodrow Wilson Center Press.

Post, J. M. (2005a). Psychological operations and counterterrorism. *Joint Forces Quarterly, 37*, 105–110.

Post, J. M. (2005b). The new face of terrorism: Socio-cultural foundations of contemporary terrorism. *Behavioral Sciences and the Law, 23*(4), 451–465.

Riemer, W. J. (1998). Durkheim's "heroic suicide" in military combat. *Armed Forces and Society, 25*(1), 103–120.

Ruby, C. L. (2003). Are terrorists mentally deranged? *Analyses of Social Issues and Public Policy, 2*(1), 15–26.

Schmid, A. (2005). Terrorism as psychological warfare. *Democracy and Security, 1*(2), 137–146.

Silberman, I., Higgins, E. T., & Dweck, C. S. (2005). Religion and world change: Violence and terrorism versus peace. *Journal of Social Issues, 61*(4), 761–784.

Sirriyeh, H. (2000). Democratization and the Palestinian national authority: From state in the making to statehood. *Israel Affairs, 7*(1), 49–62.

Stack, S. (1979). Durkhiem's theory of fatalistic suicide: A cross-national approach. *The Journal of Social Psychology, 107*(2), 161–168.

Stack, S. (2004). Emile Durkheim and altruistic suicide. *Archives of Suicide Research, 8*(1), 9–22.

Stevens, M. J. (2005). What is terrorism, and can psychology do anything to prevent it? *Behavioral Sciences and the Law, 23*(4), 507–526.

Taylor, S. (1982). *Durkheim and the study of suicide*. London: Hutchinson.

Victoroff, J. (2005). The mind of the terrorist: A review and critique of psychological approaches. *Journal of Conflict Resolution, 49*(1), 3–42.

Wardlaw, G. (1989). *Political terrorism, theory, tactics, and countermeasures*. Cambridge: Cambridge University Press.

Yonghe, Y. (2004). *Small sea travel diaries*, trans. Macabe Keliher, Taipei: SMC Publishing Inc.

Young, L. (1972). Altruistic suicide: A subjective approach. *Sociological Bulletin, 21*(2), 103–121.

2

Suicide Terrorism Explained: A Psychosocial Approach

Luis de la Corte Ibáñez

A suicide attack is an offensive operation whose execution depends upon the death of the perpetrator. Suicide attacks have become a modality of terrorism of growing application among extremist groups. As some experts have said, suicide attacks are the newest stage in the development of bombing attacks, which have been used by terrorists for many years (Ganor, 2001). For others, suicide attacks are the "defining act of political violence of our age" (Gambetta, 2006). Anyway, during the last three decades, this phenomenon has emerged in many countries around the world, including Lebanon, Israel, Sri Lanka, Iraq, the United States, Spain, the United Kingdom, Afghanistan, Pakistan, India, Algeria, Morocco, Turkey, Chechnya, Uzbekistan, etc.

Scholars have approached this subject from different scientific disciplines and theoretical perspectives. Accordingly with a previous and general understanding about terrorism (De la Corte, Kruglanski, De Miguel, Sabucedo, & Díaz, 2007), in this chapter I outline a psychosocial explanation of suicide terrorist attacks. I develop this explanation in two consecutive stages. First, I offer a characterization of suicide terrorism from a psychosocial point of view. Second, I address the multidimensional dynamic which is inherent to the development of any organized suicide terrorist campaign. For this, I try to answer three critical questions: why terrorist organizations move their tactics to a martyrdom strategy; why individuals may radicalize their attitudes at the point to become a suicide bomber; and why people would support suicide tactics.

SUICIDE TERRORISM AS A PSYCHOSOCIAL PHENOMENON

More than a Symptom of Social or Psychological Disorders

Kruglanski and Fishman (2009) have pointed out that the syndrome view is implicit in many treatments of terrorism. From that point of view, suicide attacks are like a syndrome which prompts the search for some definite causes: internal (e.g., personality traits) and/or external causes (e.g., poverty, political oppression). In other words, suicide terrorism can be seen as a direct effect of some social or psychological disorders. The empirical research, however, did not reveal any distinctive psychological disturbance in suicide attackers and their leaders. Profiles of both are not informative enough to give a serious explanation of their behavior. Finally, there are also serious doubts about the impact of social or situational so-called 'root causes' on suicide terrorism. Therefore, suicide terrorism is unlikely to emerge as an inevitable consequence of some root cause, such as poverty or political oppression (Krueger & Maleckova, 2002). An alternative perspective views terrorism, including suicide terrorism, as a tool: a means to an end and a tactic of warfare that anyone could use. That assumption is congruent with evidence regarding a variety of extremist groups that have perpetrated suicide attacks in order to attain different goals. Terrorism as a tool view is also coherent with a typical psychosocial conception about behavior and social interaction.

According to a classical definition, social psychology is the scientific study of the way in which people's thoughts, feelings, and behaviors are influenced by other people. The phenomenon of social influence is at the very heart of social psychology. Sometimes, this influence happens in a nondeliberated or nondirect way. But other times, individual and groups deliberately try to change another person's behavior. There are a variety of tactics that people apply to influence other people. Terrorism involves the use of force or violence in order to instill fear as a means of coercing individuals or groups to change their political or social positions which means that social influence is the ultimate goal of terrorism. Obviously, we could say the same about suicide terrorism.

Suicide Campaigns: Instrumental but Not Entirely Rational

In opposition to some stereotypes, suicide terrorism involves some degree of rationality. According to the most influential theoretical model in contemporary social sciences, individuals, organizations, and social movements usually behave like rational actors (Coleman, 1990; Rosenberg, 1995). A rational actor only develops actions that are considered the most effective means to attain his objectives or satisfy his preferences. In other words, rationality is related to instrumental or goal-oriented actions, which is coherent with the terrorism as a tool view. The thesis of instrumental orientation of suicide behavior is supported by two main reasons. First, the fact that most of suicide attacks do not constitute isolated incidents but are grouped in campaigns, according to a precise schedule and guidelines. Second, the groups and leaders that promote suicide attacks select this method among others in order to achieve certain strategic goals. The arguments that jihadi leaders and ideologues employ to justify suicide bombings and the analysis of the evolution of most terrorist organizations that have conducted suicide attacks campaigns make evident the instrumental meaning of such violent activity (Pape, 2005). Volunteers may not be willing to blow themselves fully aware of it but their deaths usually serve a plan designed to attain certain strategic, operational, and tactical goals.

The main strategic goals associated with suicide are the expulsion of foreign occupying forces, national independence, destabilization or replacement of a political regime, intensification of a violent conflict in progress, or interruption of some process of peaceful solutions for a political, ethnic, or religious conflicts (Bloom, 2005; Ganor, 2001; Gupta & Mundra, 2005; Moghadam, 2007; Pape, 2005). Moreover, there are several tactical and operative advantages. The most important are the following: higher lethality, intense psychological and social impact, attract wide media coverage, communication of relevant messages to target audiences (determination, commitment to escalate, deterrence of neutral observers, shaming the enemy, solicitation of recruits [Hafez, 2007]), access to well-protected and high-value targets, independence from remote controls systems to activate explosive devices, no required escape plan, no chance to capture the attackers, etc. (Bloom, 2005; Ganor, 2001; Hafez, 2007; Moghadam, 2007; Pape, 2005). Considering all these advantages and so far rationality involves instrumental motivation and a calculus of the benefits and costs of an action, "it is evident that committing a suicide attack is an outcome of a rational decision" (Ganor, 2001). But, is it completely rational?

Although most researchers would agree that suicide terrorist campaigns follow an instrumental logic at the strategic level, there are several reasons to assert that pure rationality cannot give a complete explanation of the phenomenon. There is a wide variety of motives that seem connected to suicide terrorism beyond rational considerations. It is important to underline the influence of not 'outcome-oriented' motivations that have encouraged people to become a suicide bomber or support suicide terrorism (Kruglanski et al., 2009). Thus, emotions related to pain and personal loss, humiliation, hate or vengeance can play a decisive motivational role (Bloom, 2005; Ricolfi, 2005). But norms can also be crucial. For instance, based on information extracted from interviews, Atran (2006) has suggested that deep sense of obligation to become 'martyrs' proves the prevalence of non instrumental motivations among religious-oriented suicide bombers.

Another argument against the view of suicide terrorism as entirely rational could be deducted from the own limitations of the rational choice theory. In its earlier version, rational choice theory assumed that human rationality tends to be almost perfect. However, psychological research has shown that the rationality of human beliefs and choices is bounded and imperfect because of the own cognitive limitations of the human mind and its interferences with emotion and motivation (Kahneman, 2011; Simon, 1995). A psychosocial approach to explaining any terrorist behavior has to bear in mind the principle of bounded rationality. This approach is coherent with the following consideration from Elster (2006):

> *In itself, there is nothing irrational in the willingness to sacrifice one's life for a cause, an even less in the willingness to send others to their death for it ... nevertheless in some case suicide attacks fall short of being fully rational due to the instability of the underlying motivations or also because some attackers are subject to irrational belief formation.*

The Social Construction of Suicide Bombers

Social psychological perspective tends to explain the psychological characteristics of individuals as a result of processes of social interaction. Since there is no unique typical profile, the previous psychosocial assumption could be useful for tracing the origin of the willingness to perpetrate a suicide attack. The pathway toward the participation in a suicide mission can be analyzed as the result of an accumulation of socialization processes that can be accounted for by classic social psychological mechanisms. This is congruent with the empirical evidence about how the process of joining a terrorist group usually is heavily influenced by the prevailing political and social environment shared by friends and relatives. Several studies conclude that becoming a terrorist is basically an issue of socialization (Fields, 1979; Silke, 2006). Radicalization and engagement in violent activities are facilitated by contacts and links with people who already have embraced an extremist ideology. Social interaction is the vehicle through which individuals receive the 'reasons' that motivate and 'justify' their desire to give up their lives to carry out a terrorist attack. As a condition of integration in a terrorist group, social interaction also makes possible that people who choose to participate in a suicide mission put this willingness into practice.

The interaction between the would-be suicide bombers and members of radical networks or extremist organizations could follow two patterns of social influence. The first is a bottom-up pattern in which the would-be suicide attackers take the initiative of joining a radical network or terrorist organization. The studies conducted by Sageman (2004, 2008) have shown the importance of this pattern for the engagement of people in the so-called global Salafi-Jihadis movement. Sageman (2004) has stated that joining this violent movement that supports and promotes suicide terrorist attacks is, in essential, a bottom-up activity. On the one hand, Al-Qaeda, because it is a more prominent organization, does not have top-down formal recruitment program. On the other hand, because the reaction to 9/11 attacks provoked the operational dead of Al-Qaeda and, as a result, the groups that continued perpetrating suicide attacks in the name of Al-Qaeda were not formally subordinated to Al-Qaeda top leadership, but a group of friends who get together and after been inspired by Al-Qaeda's discourse decided to do something (Sageman, 2004, 2008). Although the Sageman point of view has been strongly criticized by other experts, we should retain his emphasis on how pre-existing social bonds (kinship, friendship, and later informal cliques) facilitate the radicalization of individuals and groups who meet in their neighborhoods and on the Internet and plot violent actions, including suicide attacks.

The second pattern of influence through social interaction that contributes the making of suicide bombers is a top-down or vertical one. This pattern involves initiatives promoted by leaders and members of terrorist organizations in contacting and relating to the would-be suicide attackers, as well as recruiting, indoctrinating, and training them. So far, suicide attacks are rarely perpetrated by individuals acting on their own, but by people who become members or organizations, groups, or cells attached to a larger network, this type of influence processes should not be underestimated for understanding suicide terrorism. As Hafez (2007) claims, terrorist groups and organizations play the role of mobilization structures that facilitate the engagement of new volunteers for sacrificing their lives on behalf of a political or religious cause. On the other hand, some studies have detected significant similarities between the indoctrination methods applied by sectarian groups and those that are used inside terrorist organizations (Della Porta, 1995; De la Corte, 2006; Sageman, 2004). In any case, there is no doubt that the activities and lifestyle adopted within terrorist organizations shape the mentality of its members, intensifying their commitment to such organizations, and preparing them to participate in violent activities as suicide attacks. Typical organizational practices in which would-be suicide bombers are stimulated to participate, like binding or religious rituals, making written or videotaped statements a few days before the mission, and their integration in tightly knit units seem designed to sustain the ephemeral state of mind required to detonate themselves (Gambetta, 2006; Merari, 1990).

Social Identity Matters

William James (1891) stated in his pioneering book *Principles of Psychology* that the way that people define themselves is central for explaining their mental states, their feelings, and their behaviors. Social psychology and other social sciences recovered that principle focusing on the social aspects of identity, that is, the attributes of the self-concept that individuals share with other people, allows to define themselves as members of a social group or community. The study of social identity (or collective identity, as many sociologists and political scientists prefer to say) has opened a window to understanding how psychological processes interact with social and political processes in the causation of human social behavior and collective action. Consequently, it is not rare that many social scientists consider social identity a particularly relevant phenomenon to study terrorism (De la Corte, 2006; Taylor & Louis, 2003). Actually, the mechanisms and experiences of collective identification play a central role in the emergence, activity, and evolution of every type of political or religious movement or organization, including extremists and terrorist cases. Moreover, this appears to be particularly clear in the case of suicide terrorism, no matter if we focus on meanings that human bombers give to their actions or the support that terrorist attacks could receive in some societies.

Research on radicalization indicates that involvement in suicide terrorism often begins with individual's need to find or restructure a meaningful identity (Dalgaard-Nielsena, 2010; Mursheda & Pavan, 2011). Membership of supportive social groups can reduce uncertainty and enhance an individual's self-esteem, thus treating some of the wounds caused by difficult personal experiences. Particularly, terrorist organizations offer an ideology with a strong moral component, profound meaning, and an optimistic vision of the future.

It is not a coincidence that suicide terrorist organizations tend to describe themselves as the champions of their own national, ethnic, or religious groups, volunteers for suicide missions consider their death as a sacrifice for the sake of their own community, and terrorist propaganda try to promote this idea among their own reference community. So it is also normal that nationalist and religious motivations, feelings and arguments appear connected to suicide terrorism. Pape (2005) has stated that nationalism is the 'taproot' of modern suicide terrorism. This author defines nationalism as "the belief among members of a community that they share a distinct set of ethnic, linguistic, and historical characteristics and are entitled to govern their national homeland without interference from foreigners." In part, Pape (2005) also attributes certain influence to religion on suicide campaigns when it appears attached to nationalism, which is supported by his own analysis of the universe of cases in which a democratic state controlled the homeland of a distinct national community for the period 1980 to 2003. Thus, 49 of 58 cases were congruent with a nationalist theory of suicide terrorism which predicts the occurrence of suicide campaigns as a result of a combination of two factors: the existence of a violent organized resistance ('rebellion') and the existence of a religious difference between the foreign occupier and the local community. According to Pape (2005), those factors are crucial because suicide terrorism campaigns require significant community support and foreign occupation and religious differences favor the identification of a local community with a local terrorist organization. Anyway, it is true, as Pape (2005) also states, that martyrdom (death for the sake of one's community) is a social construct and it is the reference community of the terrorist that judges whether the self-sacrifice of specific individuals meets the requirements for the special status of martyr. However, other authors consider that Pape's nationalist theory of suicide terrorism underestimates the influence of religious identity on the perspective, motivation, and behavior of suicide organizations and their volunteers and supporters. This seems true if we observe the evolution of suicide terrorism during the last years, a period in which global jihadism has become the main inspiration for suicide attackers all over the world. Since, during the 1980s and 1990s, the vast majority of attacks took place in only a handful of countries like Israel, Lebanon, Sri Lanka, and Turkey, the emergence of the threat represented by Al-Qaeda showed that suicide terrorism also could be a method used by religious but non nationalistic terrorist organizations. Next, when suicide attacks perpetrated by jihadist networks, groups, and organizations in Iraq and other Muslim countries increasingly targeted Muslim people, it became clear that suicide campaigns could be adopted as part of a strategy not only to gain a national homeland but also to depose political regimes (in those cases, regimes regarded as un-Islamic, according to the jihadist view; see Moghadam, 2007). Moreover, the experience of suicide terrorism in Iraq since 2003 exemplify perfectly that nationalism is not the main driver of suicide terrorism, considering that it corresponds to an Arab-occupied country with the highest rate of suicide attacks for several years most perpetrated not by Iraqis suicide volunteers but by foreign religious fanatics from jihadi Salafi networks, and not against foreign forces but directed at Iraqi security forces and local population (Hafez, 2007).

In sum, extremist goals linked to collective identities frameworks, as much nationalist or ethnic as religious, may give rise to suicide violence. Our understanding of this relationship could significantly improve if we take a psychosocial approach. In this sense, it is worth to remember that most of terrorist phenomena have their roots in a radicalization process of some pre-existing political or religious movements. Therefore, there exists an important parallel between the way ordinary social movements and terrorist movements emerge and escalate (De la Corte, 2006; Della Porta, 1995; Hafez, 2007). As research demonstrates, no political or religious movement would emerge or persist without the chronic psychological activation of a more or less sustained sense of shared identity among his members, collaborators, and supporters (see Simon & Klandermans, 2001). This is much more important in the case of movements whose aim is to defend the supposedly threatened values and interests of a certain national, ethnic or religious community (Castells, 2004), as represented by radical organizations underpinned by ethno-nationalistic or religious ideology. The individuals making them up define themselves as members of a much broader community, which they consider oppressed or humiliated, and whose collective interests and values are perceived to be threatened. The terrorists' ideology usually provides the content for these representations about their threatened social identity and maintains their feelings of identification psychologically accessible with the community of reference: for example, the Tamil community for the Tiger Tamils in Sri Lanka, the Palestinian people for Hamas, or the *Umma* or Muslim community for Al-Qaeda. As we suggest before, terrorist organization's disposition to identify itself with a certain reference community makes more attractive the option of joining the organization in the eyes of that community's members. Furthermore, two prominent social-psychological theories like the social identity theory (e.g., Tajfel & Turner, 1986) and self-categorization theory (Turner et al., 1987) predict other complementary and no less important ways in which the self-identification of suicide terrorists as members of an organization and defenders of a much larger community can contribute to further the dynamics of suicide terrorism. At least, we should consider the following four psychosocial effects (De la Corte, 2006; De la Corte et al., 2007):

1. *Depersonalization:* The terrorists tend to perceive themselves as interchangeable members of their own group or organization.

As a result of that, they could give preference to the interests and goals of the organization against their personal needs and goals, which is a requisite for involving in suicide operations.

2. *Social cohesion:* The identity share by terrorists promotes positive relationships among them, increasing intragroup cohesion and cooperation, which facilitate the preparation and execution of suicide missions. No less important, social psychological research has shown that excessive group cohesiveness leads to group polarization effects, that is, a propensity for groups to develop attitudes and make decisions that are more extreme than the mean of individual members' initial positions (Gill, 2007).

3. *In-group influence effects:* The more intense become the identification from a terrorist with their group, the greater influence the group would exert on him. The group influence effects provoked by group identification are several: obedience to the order of group leaders, majority influence (yield the majority opinion), normative influence (private and public agreement with the normative structure of the group and the norms which rule their member's behavior).

4. *Manichean worldview and intergroup bias:* Identification with their group and reference community motivates terrorist to develop negative stereotypes and prejudices about people from other communities. The world is divided between us and them. The responsibility of problems and injustices suffered by the terrorist's reference community may be attributed to another community who could play a scapegoat role. This perspective tends to reinforce the agonistic worldview and negative emotions (humiliation, resentment, hate) that usually inspire terrorists.

A Multidimensional Approach

At the first sight, only one thing could be needed for a suicide terrorist attack to happen: the existence of an individual willing and capable to die to kill others. However, the majority of terrorist suicide attacks are perpetrated by militants of any more or less organized group. Finally, as Lankford (2010, 2011) puts it, social approval of any activity increases the likelihood that people will engage in it, and suicide terrorism is no exception. Indeed, we have seen before that it is difficult to explain the prevalence of the majority of suicide campaigns without taking into account the support that these activities received from certain communities or audiences. So, generally speaking, the explanation of suicide terrorism raises different questions that correspond to three levels of analysis: why and how organizations promote suicide attacks (organizational level), why and how individuals agree to become human bombs (individual level), and why suicide terrorism received support from certain audiences (societal level) (Moghadam, 2007; Pape, 2005). It is not possible to develop a complete understanding of suicide terrorism without investigating the phenomenon on those three levels.

Suicide Terrorism as a Process

As we mentioned before, contrary to other psychological perspectives, social psychological approaches focus not on the individual and their presumed psychological qualities, but on the process variables such as the changing context that the individual operates in, and also the relationships between events and the individual as they affect behavior. Taylor and Horgan (2006) have argued that adopting that view may lead to better conceptual development in analyses of terrorist behavior.

It should be noted that the emergence of suicide terrorist campaigns tends to occur at a final point in the escalation processes in which terrorist organizations attack evolves toward greater levels of destructiveness (Bloom, 2005). Most terrorist organizations use other modalities of attacks before they begin to perpetrate suicide missions (Moghadam, 2007). It suggests that suicide terrorism involves a specific dynamic. Inspired by Pedahzur (2004), we can assume the emergence of a suicide campaign needs to cover two phases. The initial phase would be the result of what we could name a strategic or tactic shift. During this phase, calculations and strategic and tactical discussions are made inside a terrorist organization provoking the decision to engage in suicide attacks. The second stage involves more or less simultaneous activation of two psychosocial processes needed to start and continue a suicide campaign. The first would be a radicalization process by which a number of individuals begin to sympathize with the aims and political or religious ideology of the insurgents, motivating to integrate in a would-be suicide terrorist organization and become volunteers to carry out suicide operations. Nevertheless, many authors agree that the movement from radicalization to action for the sake of a collective cause usually needs the intervention of some selective incentives. Once again, we should remember that probably the most influential selective incentive to become a suicide bomber is the belief that he will be celebrated as a martyr. Nevertheless, this only can arise as a result of the political or religious polarization, that is, a process by which the political or religious attitudes of a given community or audience going to extremes in a direction of supporting suicide terrorist activities.

Based on previous accumulated research about our topic, the last part of this chapter identifies several variables which could contribute to activate and accelerate the three aforementioned processes involved in the dynamics of suicide terrorism. Since any of these variables guarantee by itself the emergence or prolongation of a suicide terrorist campaign, we proposed interpreting them as risk factors, that is, as single conditions which can increase the likelihood that a terrorist network, group, or organization resort to suicide violence or prolong a suicide terrorist campaign (De la Corte & Giménez-Salinas, 2009).

VARIABLES OR RISK FACTORS RELATED TO THE STRATEGIC OR TACTIC SHIFT TOWARD SUICIDE TERRORISM

Each strategic goal that can motivate suicide terrorism could be pursued through other means. Thus, it seems reasonable to think that a strategic or tactical shift toward suicide terrorism should be contingent on some circumstances that make salient some potential benefit that could be followed from carrying out a campaign of suicide bombings. The decision to promote a suicide campaign becomes more likely due to the intervention of one or more of the following variables:

Asymmetric Conditions

Very often, suicide missions are carried out by the weaker side in conflicts characterized by a patent asymmetry in terms of military force (Atran, 2006; Gambetta, 2006; Merari, 2005; Pape, 2005). Therefore, a real or perceived great imbalance of power between the terrorists and their adversaries could intensify the motivations to incorporate suicide methods into their repertory of action.

Feeling of Stagnation, Crisis, or Failure in the Use of Other Terrorist or Insurgent Methods

Sometimes, the leadership or some factions of a terrorist organization can get the impression that they are arriving at a point of stagnation or crisis, as a consequence of the ineffectiveness of strategies, tactics, and methods previously employed (Pape, 2005). This impression can lead terrorists to consider suicide operations as an alternative method which could help to overcome the perceived state of stagnation, crisis, or failure.

Coexistence of Several Terrorist or Insurgent Groups

Suicide operations attract more attention than any other terrorist method; the organizations that promote them send a message of determination, and the suicide bombers appear the most dare and heroic. These qualities could become powerful incentives to deploy suicide attacks if several terrorist organizations operate in the same territory, pursuing equivalent goals, and trying to capture the attention and gain the support of the same community or audience. According to Bloom (2005), different historical examples confirm that suicide tactics can emerge where multiple organizations with increasing degrees of lethality try to distinguish themselves from their competitors. In fact, the shift toward suicide violence can intensify the escalation, especially in environments where domestic communities begin to support suicide bombings, encouraging the non suicide organizations to adopt the same tactic.

Cognitive Accessibility and Pre-existence of a Suicidal Terrorist Activity

A first, condition to make the decision of employing suicide operations is to know and think about them (Elster, 2006; Kalyvas & Sánchez Cuenca, 2006). In part for this reason the exposure to examples or information about suicide mission perpetrated by one or more organizations sometimes can further inspire other groups to emulate the former. This can occur in a single environment marked by competition among different terrorist organizations, and also it can provoke the diffusion on suicidal tactics from one context to other. However, insofar suicide terrorism would be the consequence of a strategic or tactic shift, the contagion effect only will take place under a particular condition, that is, the exposure to examples (models) or information about suicide attacks to attribute suicide attacks a major tactic effectiveness in comparison to conventional terrorism. This is consistent with a central postulate from the social learning theory which states that people usually need having a good reason to imitate others and that reason usually results from the association of some (observed or presumed) reward to the behavior that could be imitate (Bandura, 1979). From this very point of view, Bandura adds that the more similarities (attitudes, traits, or values) an observer attribute to other people, the more likable will be that the former imitate the successful behavior of the latter. On the other hand, social movement theories postulate that the transference of new strategies and tactics also can be facilitated by situational similarities. In this sense, Della Porta and Diani (2006) point out that perceptions of common circumstances enable activists to adopt methods from different countries or regions because they see a 'functional equivalence' between the transmitters and adopters of innovation. At the same time, Hafez (2007) puts that the exposure to examples of suicide attacks executed by others not only favors the diffusion of suicide tactic because it appears successful but also seems legitimate in the eyes of potential imitators.

VARIABLES OR RISK FACTORS RELATED TO THE PROCESSES OF POLARIZATION AND RADICALIZATION

Political or religious polarization and radicalization processes related to suicide terrorism are closely related. Both phenomena have a similar psychosocial outcome, for example, a positive attitudinal change toward suicide violence and suicide organizations. As research has showed, the personal and collective attitudinal change in favor of the use of suicide terrorism can be facilitated, at least, by the subsequent factors:

Intractable Conflicts and Conflictive Ethos

Experts characterize intractable conflicts as protracted, irreconcilable, violent, of a zero-sum nature, total, and central, with the parties involved having an interest in their continuation, and seemingly irresolvable (Kriesberg, 1998). It is interesting to consider the psychological consequences of intractable conflicts. According to Bar-Tal (2000, 2007), since intractable conflicts are painful, stressful, exhausting, disturbing, and costly both in human and material terms, society members or human groups involved tend to develop a set of share attitudes and cognitions that provide a dominant orientation and ethos that enable them to cope successfully with the conflict situation. In attitudinal terms, this 'psychological infrastructure' can include elements as devotion to the own country, ethnic or religious community, high motivation to contribute, persistence, readiness for personal sacrifice, unity, solidarity, determination, courage, and maintenance of the society's or community objectives. These attitudes normally are complemented by a core of central shared beliefs. Among the several shared beliefs suggested by Bar-Tal (2007) as elements of this conflictive ethos, we would emphasize the following: beliefs about justness of one's own goals that lead to conflict, beliefs of positive self-image concerning the ethnocentric tendency to attribute positive traits, values, and behavior to one's own society or community, beliefs of one's own victimization concerning self-presentation as a victim, focusing on the unjust harm, evil deeds, and atrocities perpetrated by the adversary, beliefs of delegitimizing the opponent, beliefs of patriotism and unity which generate attachment to their own country or community by propagating loyalty, love, care, and sacrifice and refers to the importance of ignoring internal conflicts and disagreements in order to unite the forces in the face of external threat. Needless to explain how the conflictive ethos resulting from this shared beliefs and their corresponding attitudes can create a propitious environment to engage in extreme practices like suicide bombing for the sake of their own community or to support them.

Apart from creating a particular conflictive ethos, sustained or intractable conflicts impact upon the states of mind of individuals and collectives in other forms that also can facilitate radicalization process and increase the support to violence, including suicide violence. Particularly, we focus on two effects: mortality salience and personal or proximal trauma.

Mortality salience

Unquestionably, sustained conflict brings a sense of threat to the fore. An increased awareness of one's eventual death—mortality salience—becomes an important element of that intense sense of threat. Psychosocial research has shown that mortality salience and fear of death stimulate an array of relevant psychological consequences that can contribute to involve in suicide violence and support suicide terrorist organizations. First, when a sense of threat or their own death becomes salient positive feelings toward one's belief system and those holding similar beliefs arouse. As a result of that, it is highly likely that people bolster their own worldview, engaging in a so-called 'worldview defense,' while they also increase connections with one's in-group and negative feelings toward those perceived to be a threat. Besides, Greenberg et al. (1990) have showed a significant link between the fear of death and what Kruglanski and Fishman (2009) identify as the 'deep theme' that underlies most of numerous surface differences terrorists' motivation: the quest for personal meaning and significance. Put in the words of the authors, generally the awareness of the own mortality and the fear of living a life that is insignificant motivates people to be 'good' members of society. But when the group faces a severe perceived threat to its existence, the ultimate 'goodness' would be sacrificing one's self for the sake of the larger group. Moreover, besides the group first is highly valued, it could bring the promise of immortality by becoming a martyr engraved forever in the group's collective memory (Kruglanski & Fishman, 2009).

On the other hand, more experimental evidences indicate that threat salience increases reliance on stereotypes to characterize the threatening out-group (Arndt, Greenberg, & Cook, 2002; Schimel et al., 1999). Studies also have found a positive correlation between threat salience, the likelihood of resorting to authoritarian modes of thinking (Gill, 2007; Greenberg et al., 1990; Lavine, Lodge, Polichak, & Taber, 2002) and the need for strong leaders to lessen the anxiety produced by the situation (Montuori, 2005), including leaders who espouse authoritarian values and symbolic narratives perceived to be legitimate and aggressive toward those who cause the threat and anxiety. Gill (2007) has emphasized the relevance of the aforementioned experimental data to understand the process whereby audiences become susceptible to the influence of narratives and leaders that promote suicide terrorism.

Personal or proximal trauma

Some traumatic events frequently operate as death reminders, helping to activate the effects linked to mortality salience. Apart from that, relationship between frustrating or traumatic experiences and aggressive behavior is a classical topic for social psychologists. This idea, which is consistent with commonsense has been proposed by several writers to explain the origins of volunteerism for suicide attacks (Speckhard & Akhmedova, 2005). Given that many suicide bombers have not been personally traumatized, not to mention that most of the traumatized people do not involve in terrorism and vast majority of terrorists do not suffer from mental disorders, we cannot support the trauma theory as a general explanation. However, if we review the list of catalysts that usually precipitate the compulsion to become a suicide bomber, we can see that several involve some kinds of traumatic incidents like personal suffering, experiencing of humiliation, exposure to acts of violence by opposition forces, torture or death of some friend or family member (see below), imprisonment, restrictions on movement, frustration of personal goals, etc. (Gill, 2007). It should be noted that, some of these traumatic experiences can be relatively frequent among individuals who belong to a discriminated minority or people who live in societies undergoing violent conflicts.

Implementation of Bloody Counterterrorist Strategies

The correlation between overreactions to terrorism and the increase of terrorist activity has been noted on several occasions. That premise can be applied to suicide terrorism. Percentages of support for suicide attacks are higher in countries or regions where potential sympathizers and reference community of terrorist groups have suffered severe repression perpetrated by security or foreign forces. According to Bloom (2005), Palestine, Chechnya, and Sri Lanka provide empirical regularity about suicide bombers who lost a family member to the 'unjust state' and resolve to participate in suicide missions to express their outrage (Ricolfi, 2005). In addition, suicide organizations can try to recruit people who have lost relatives as a consequence of counterterrorism. Nevertheless, although there are examples of counterproductive effects of hard counterterrorism operations in terms of increase in suicide terrorism, we also can find cases where suicide campaigns have been developed during a period of a decrease of hard counterinsurgent operations (Pape, 2005).

Wide (Real or Attributed) Difference between Terrorists and Their Adversaries and Targets

Social psychologists know that the larger differences aggressors attribute to their victims, the greater levels of violence would be used. This principle is also useful for explaining propensity to launch suicide attacks or support them. As it was previously suggested in other terms, the people who identify suicide organizations and their militants as members of their own group or community are more disposed to support them than others. Actually, the support can be higher when the terrorist's reference community perceives clear differences between them and the targets of the attacks. Although Pape's study apparently confirms that such contrast can be mainly or exclusively based on nationality or religion, other differences matter too, for example, differences on political attitudes or even profession (remember that suicide attacks against military personnel or senior officials usually get a stronger social support than those attacks carried out against civilians). Anyway, none of those characteristics are necessary conditions for involvement in suicide terrorism or support it. Indeed, often the most influential unique differences that separate the identity of terrorists from their victims depend on stereotypes and biased beliefs rather than on nationality, religion, or profession. These stereotypes and beliefs, which constitute essential elements of the ideology, discourses and propaganda of suicide terrorist organizations, shape an image of the targets of terrorist attacks as enemies, frequently characterized with subhuman or demoniac attributes (Bandura, 1998). Stigmatization, dehumanization and demonization discursive, and propaganda strategies are employed in order to exclude the victims from the ordinary sphere of morality. As Opotow (1990) explained, people who are morally excluded are perceived as nonentities, expendable, or undeserving; consequently, harming or killing them appears acceptable, appropriate, or even just. Indeed, along with the spread of a culture of martyrdom (see below), the derogation of the victims can further suicide terrorism through a redefinition of that practice as morally acceptable actions.

Dissemination of a Culture of Martyrdom

The diffusion of a culture that frames the death of human bombers as an altruistic and venerable action for the sake of their own community (i.e., the meaning of martyrdom operations) is probably the most important accelerant of radicalization, mobilization, and polarization that stimulate suicide terrorism.

The promotion of a culture of martyrdom requires in first place the selection and exploitation of texts, traditions, myths, symbols, and rituals extracted from the culture or the religion that suicide promoters share with their constituency of supporters, no matter if it is local community or a transnational distributed constituency connected via Internet. That selection of arguments and symbols enables to create the contents of a cultural or martyrdom: basically, an agonistic narrative and rhetoric that heightens the sense of threat among the members of their own constituency and imbue suicide attacks with morality, besides demonizing the targets of suicide attacks. The culture of martyrdom that promotes jihadist leaders and organizations adds a significant religious appeal for suicide terrorism through linking 'martyrdom operations' to some heavenly rewards as the atoning for previous sins or to attaining paradise.

After creating its own culture of martyrdom, terrorist organization tries to spread it, resorting to an array of means: preaching, propaganda, discourses of charismatic leaders and epistemic authorities, agency-laden institutions, indoctrination, etc. Finally, the adoption and diffusion of a culture of martyrdom has the main effect of creating a state of moral disengagement (Bandura, 1998), that is the suspension of ordinary ethical standards that usually refrain people from committing or supporting murder and suicide (Hafez, 2007).

CONCLUSION

In some critical aspects, suicide terrorism is not so different from other social behaviors. First, suicide attacks and campaigns share with others social behavior the same goal of influence people to change their (political) attitudes and behaviors. Similar to other social phenomenon, suicide terrorism results from a combination of instrumental and non instrumental motivations, including strategic, operational, and tactical goals as much as emotions and social or cultural norms. Social interaction and social identification processes are the bridges through which some individuals and militants become volunteers for suicide operations.

After discussing this psychosocial characterization of suicide terrorism, this chapter has developed a comprehensive explanation on three levels: organizational, individual, and social. The development of any suicide attack's campaign involves critical processes. At the organizational level, a strategic shift in favor of suicide violence is needed. At the individual level, an extreme radicalization experience should take place before individuals and militants decide to become suicide bombers. Finally, at the social level, a polarization effect at the core of the terrorist's reference community could be necessary to increase the popular acceptance of suicide terrorism and the support to suicide organizations. The likelihood that a terrorist network, group or organization promote or prolong a suicide terrorist campaign is affected by some several risk factors intricately connected to the three aforementioned processes. Asymmetric conflicts, feelings of stagnation, crisis or failure in the use of other terrorist or insurgent methods, coexistence of several terrorist or insurgent groups, and cognitive accessibility to pre-existence of a suicidal terrorist activity are all conditions that can move terrorists to launch a suicide attack or campaign. On the other hand, our analysis on radicalization and polarization processes also stress the influence of manifold factors, including intractable conflicts and conflictive ethos, mortality salience, personal or proximal trauma, bloody counterterrorist strategies, strong perceived differences between terrorists and their adversaries, and cultures of martyrdom.

The multiple social psychological factors involved in the dynamics of suicide terrorism should be taken in account in order to confront this mortal practice. By understanding those factors, policymakers and security officials should be able to better predict when a terrorist threat could evolve to suicide violence expressions. In addition, this knowledge should guide the implementation of short- and long-term countermeasures. Our approach highlights the importance to design and implement interventions that operate at the organizational level, individual, and societal levels. That is, according to social psychological point of view, three tasks are equally relevant to prevent suicide terrorism. First: to avoid the escalation of terrorist groups and organizations toward suicide methods. Second and third: to avert circumstances, influences, experiences, and actions that could promote the emergence of individual and collective positive attitudes to suicide violence and suicide organizations.

REFERENCES

Arndt, J., Greenberg, J., & Cook, A. (2002). Mortality salience and the spreading activation of worldview-relevant constructs: Exploring the cognitive architecture of terror management. *Journal of Experimental Psychology, 13*(3), 307–324.

Atran, S. (2006). The moral logic and growth of suicide terrorism. *The Washington Quarterly, 29*(2), 127–147.

Bandura, A. (1979). The social learning perspective: Mechanisms of aggression. In H. Toch (Ed.), *Psychology of crime and criminal justice* (pp. 193–236). Prospect Heights, IL: Waveland Press.

Bandura, A. (1998). Mechanisms of moral disengagement. In W. Reich (Ed.), *Origins of terrorism: Psychologies, ideologies, theologies, states of mind* (pp. 161–191). Cambridge: Cambridge University Press.

Bar-Tal, D. (2000). *Shared beliefs in a society: Social psychological analysis*. Thousand Oaks, CA: SAGE.

Bar-Tal, D. (2007). Sociopsychological foundations of intractable conflicts. *American Behavioral Scientist, 50*(11), 1430–1453.

Bloom, M. (2005). *Dying to kill. The allure of suicide terror*. New York: Columbia University Press.

Castells, M. (2004). *La era de la información (vol. II): el poder de la identidad*. Madrid: Alianza.

Coleman, J. S. (1990). *Foundations of social theory*. Cambridge: Harvard University Press.

Dalgaard-Nielsena, D. (2010). Violent radicalization in Europe: What we know and what we do not know. *Studies in Conflict & Terrorism, 33*(9), 797–814.

Della Porta, D. (1995). *Social movements, political violence, and the state: A comparative analysis of Italy and Germany.* New York: Cambridge University Press.
Della Porta, D., & Diani, D. (2006). *Social movements: An introduction.* Oxford: Blackwell.
De La Corte, L. (2006). *La lógica del terrorismo.* Madrid: Alianza.
De La Corte, L., & Giménez-Salinas, A. (2009). Suicide terrorism as a tool of insurgency campaigns: Functions, risk factors, and countermeasures. *Perspectives on Terrorism, 3*(1), 11–19.
De La Corte, L., Kruglanski, A., De Miguel, J. M., Sabucedo, J. M., & Díaz, D. (2007). Seven psychosocial principles for explaining terrorism. *Psychology in Spain, 2008, 12*(1), 70–80.
Elster, J. (2006). Motivations and beliefs in suicide missions. In D. Gambetta (Ed.), *Making sense of suicide missions* (pp. 233–258). Oxford: Oxford University Press.
Fields, R. (1979). Child terror victims and adult terrorists. *Journal of Psychohistory, 7*(1), 71–76.
Gambetta, D. (2006). *Making sense of suicide missions.* Oxford: Oxford University Press.
Ganor, B. (2001). The rationality of the Islamic radical suicide attack phenomenon. In B. Ganor (Ed.), *Suicide terrorism: An overview.* Herzliya: Institute for Counterterrorism.
Gill, P. (2007). A multidimensional approach to suicide bombing. *International Journal of Conflict and Violence, 1*(2), 142–159.
Greenberg, J., Pyszczynski, T., Solomon, S., Rosenblatt, A., Veeded, M. Y., & Kirklan, S. (1990). Evidence of terror management theory II: The effects of mortality salience reactions to those who threaten or bolster the cultural worldview. *Journal of Personality and Social Psychology, 58*(2), 308–318.
Gupta, D. K., & Mundra, K. (2005). Suicide bombing as a strategic weapon. An empirical investigation of Hamas and Islamic jihad. *Terrorism and Political Violence, 5*(17), 573–598.
Hafez, M. (2007). Martyrdom mythology in Iraq: How jihadists frame suicide terrorism in videos and biographies. *Terrorism and Political Violence, 19*(1), 95–115.
James, W. (1891). *The principles of psychology.* London: Macmillan.
Kahneman, D. (2011). *Thinking fast and slow.* New York: Farrer, Straus & Giraux.
Kalyvas, S., & Sánchez Cuenca, I. (2006). Killing without dying: The absence of suicide missions. In D. Gambetta (Ed.), *Making sense of suicide missions* (pp. 209–233). Oxford: Oxford University Press.
Kriesberg, L. (1998). Intractable conflicts. In E. Weiner (Ed.), *The handbook of interethnic coexistence* (pp. 332–342). New York. Continuum.

Krueger, A. B., & Maleckova, J. (2002). Does poverty cause terrorism? *The New Republic*, 226(24), 27–33.
Kruglanski, A. W., Chen, X., Dechesne, M., Fishman, S., & Orehek, E. (2009). Fully committed: Suicide bombers' motivation and the quest for personal significance. *Political Psychology*, 30(3), 331–357.
Kruglanski, A., & Fishman, S. (2009). Psychological factors in terrorism and counterterrorism: Individual, group, and organizational levels of analysis. *Social Issues and Policy Review*, 3(1), 1–44.
Lankford, A. (2010). Suicide terrorism as a socially approved form of suicide. *Crisis: The Journal of Crisis Intervention and Suicide Prevention*, 31(6), 287–289.
Lankford, A. (2011). Requirements and facilitators for suicide terrorism: An explanatory framework for prediction and prevention. *Perspectives on Terrorism*, 5(5–6), 70–80.
Lavine, H., Lodge, M., Polichak, J., & Taber, C. (2002). Explicating the black box through experimentation: Studies of authoritarianism and threat. *Political Analysis*, 10(4), 343–361.
Merari, A. (1990). The readiness to kill and die: Suicidal terrorism in the Middle East. In W. Reich (Ed.), *Origins of terrorism: Psychologies, ideologies, theologies and states of mind* (pp. 192–207). Cambridge: Cambridge University Press.
Merari, A. (2005). Social organizational and psychological factors in suicide terrorism. In T. Bjorgo (Ed.), *Root causes of terrorism*. London: Routledge.
Moghadam, A. (2007). Suicide terrorism, occupation and the globalization of martyrdom: A critique of dying to win. *Studies in Conflict and Terrorism*, 29(8), 707–729.
Montuori, A. (2005). How to make enemies and influence people: Anatomy of the anti-pluralist, totalitarian mindset. *Futures*, 37(10), 18–38.
Mursheda, S. M., & Pavan, S. (2011). Identity and Islamic radicalization in Western Europe. *Civil Wars*, 13(3), 259–279.
Opotow, S. (1990). Moral exclusion and injustice: An overview. *Journal of Social Issues*, 46(1), 1–20.
Pape, R. A. (2005). *Dying to win: The strategic logic of suicide terrorism*. New York: Random House.
Pedahzur, A. (2004). Toward an analytical model of suicide terrorism. A comment. *Terrorism and Political Violence*, 16(4), 841–844.
Ricolfi, L. (2005). Palestinians: 1981–2003. In D. Gambetta (Ed.), *Making sense of suicide missions* (pp. 77–130). Oxford: Oxford University Press.
Rosenberg, S. W. (1995). Against neoclassical political economy: A political psychological critique. *Political Psychology*, 16(1), 99–136.

Sageman, M. (2004). *Understanding terrorist networks*. Philadelphia, PA: University of Pennsylvania Press.
Sageman, M. (2008). *Leaderless jihad: Terror networks in the twenty-first century*. Philadelphia, PA: University of Pennsylvania Press.
Schimel, J., Simon, L., Greenberg, J., Pyszczynski, T., Solomon, S., Waxmonsky, J., & Arndt, J. (1999). Stereotypes and terror management: Evidence that mortality salience enhances stereotypic thinking and preferences. *Journal of Personality and Social Psychology, 77*(5), 905–926.
Silke, A. (2006). The role of suicide in politics, conflict and terrorism. *Terrorism and Political Violence, 18*(1), 35–46.
Simon, H. A. (1995). Rationality and political behavior. *Political Psychology, 16*(1), 45–61.
Simon, B., & Klandermans, B. (2001). Politicized collective identity: A social psychological analysis. *American Psychologist, 56*(4), 319–331.
Speckhard, A., & Akhmedova, K. (2005). Talking to terrorists. *Journal of Psychohistory, 33*(2), 125–156.
Tajfel, H., & Turner, J. C. (1986). The social identity theory of intergroup behavior. In S. Worchel & W. G. Austin (Eds.), *Psychology of intergroup relations* (pp. 7–24). Chicago, IL: Nelson-Hall.
Taylor, M., & Horgan, J. (2006). A conceptual framework for addressing psychological process in the development of the terrorist. *Terrorism and Political Violence, 18*(4), 585–601.
Taylor, D. M., & Louis, W. (2003). Terrorism and the quest for identity. In F. M. Moghaddam & A. J. Marsella (Eds.), *Understanding terrorism. Psychological roots, consequences and interventions*. Washington, DC: American Psychological Association.
Turner, J. C., Hogg, M. A., Oakes, P. J., Reicher, S. D., & Wetherell, M. S. (1987). *Rediscovering the social group: A self-categorization theory*. New York: Blackwell.

3
Evolutionary Psychological Science of Suicide Terrorism

James R. Liddle and Todd K. Shackelford

Suicide terrorist acts, and the fatalities associated with such acts, have increased dramatically throughout the world over the last decade (Hronick, 2006). It is vital for researchers to redouble their efforts to understand why this behavior occurs, because with greater understanding comes the potential means to curtail its occurrence. Already, several attempts have been made to identify systematic psychological features of suicide terrorists or to identify the psychological factors that give rise to acts of suicide terrorism (see Borum, 2004; Hoffman, 1999; Ross, 1996), but it is ultimately the architecture of our minds that makes such behavior a possibility. Our minds must be vulnerable to being convinced to put one's ideals—often the most powerful being religious ideals—above one's own life (Dennett, 2006).

Psychologists often attempt to explain mental phenomena through proximate causes; that is, through the immediate, salient reasons for a given phenomenon (see Workman & Reader, 2008). For instance, most of us find painful experiences highly unpleasant and go out of our way to avoid them. On the other hand, we tend to pursue enjoyable experiences, such as sex, with great zeal. We can account for such behaviors through physiological means, by describing how the nervous system responds to the respective phenomena of painful stimuli and sex. Or we can ask people why they avoid pain and pursue sex, reaching an obvious conclusion: sex feels good, and pain does not. Although such proximate explanations are of interest and contribute to our understanding of human nature, they do not provide a *full* explanation. In other words, they do not account for why such behaviors exist in the first place. Why do we feel pain at all? Why are we so motivated to pursue sex?

The answer lies in that blind, unconscious, omnipresent driving force behind biological diversity on earth: natural selection. Only by looking at the mind as a product of natural selection can we arrive at a full explanation, and once we do, we can gain a greater understanding of human behavior. The pleasure derived from sexual behavior, as well as the pain derived from various harmful stimuli, is a result of specific pieces of cognitive architecture that we have inherited from our ancestors. Our ancestors are those individuals who responded to stimuli in a way that made them more likely to survive and reproduce than their conspecifics, on average. The cognitive architecture that made those responses possible, whether it be responding to sex with pleasure or to harmful stimuli with pain and avoidance, were selected for and eventually became 'universal' characteristics of the species. An evolutionary approach to psychology can thus do much more than merely catalogue psychological phenomena and describe which conditions give rise to particular mental states; it can account for why such mental states and behavioral proclivities exist in the first place.

There is no reason in principle why this approach cannot be extended to the topic of suicide terrorism, and even terrorism in general. Whatever the proximate causes of such behavior, there must be underlying evolved mechanisms that open these behaviors up to the realm of human possibility. The purpose of this chapter is to explore just this possibility by introducing evolutionary psychology to a general readership and explaining how such an approach is valuable in understanding suicide terrorism.

We argue that one of the primary, if not the most important, motivating factors underlying the occurrence of suicide terrorism is religious belief. Although we are not suggesting that *all* suicide terrorism is necessarily religiously motivated, there is significant overlap between suicide terrorism and religion, in that the vast majority of those who commit suicide terrorism espouse strong religious beliefs (see Pedahzur, Perliger, & Weinberg, 2003; Weinberg, Pedahzur, & Canetti-Nisim, 2003), often of a fundamentalist or extremist nature, most notably Islamic (Harris, 2004). This overlap suggests that understanding the evolutionary psychology of religion can provide a useful foundation for exploring the evolutionary psychology of suicide terrorism. Therefore, we begin by exploring how evolutionary psychology has begun to penetrate the root causes of religion, and then extend the current theories on religion to the phenomena of suicide terrorism.

THE EVOLUTION OF RELIGION

Religion is by no means a new topic of study within psychology (see James, 1902), and applying evolutionary theory to religious belief and behavior can be traced to Darwin (1871) himself, who proposed that, "The same high mental faculties which first led man to believe in unseen spiritual agencies, then in fetishism, polytheism, and ultimately in monotheism, would infallibly lead him ... to various strange superstitions and customs" (p. 816). But despite Darwin's laudable prescience of applying evolution to the 'mental faculties' of religious belief, an evolutionary psychological approach to religion is relatively novel and has only begun to gain momentum over the last decade.

Although there is much empirical work left to be done, the current consensus among many evolutionary psychologists and other researchers approaching religion from this perspective is that religion originated as a byproduct resulting from the interaction of several evolved psychological mechanisms, and with that initial foundation interacting with cultural evolution, religion has become what it is today (Atran, 2002; Bering, 2005; Boyer, 2001). One such psychological mechanism is the 'hypersensitive agent detection device,' or HADD, which was proposed by Guthrie (1993), although the term was coined by Barrett (2000, 2004), who also expanded upon the idea.

Humans have a tendency to detect agency in the environment even when none exists, and Guthrie (1993) hypothesized that this behavioral predisposition could have an evolutionary basis. For the majority of human evolutionary history, predators were a real threat, and successfully detecting predators meant the difference between life and death. However, our ancestors likely had to interpret ambiguous environmental stimuli often (e.g., hearing a noise in the bush). Given ambiguous stimuli, those who made a false-positive error suffered a much smaller fitness cost compared to those who made a false-negative error. In other words, misinterpreting a harmless, natural noise in the bush for a predator would at most result in wasted energy escaping from an imaginary foe, whereas misinterpreting a real predator for a harmless noise could lead to severe injury or death. Therefore, a selection pressure likely existed for hypersensitive agency detection, because those who made false-positive errors were more likely to survive and reproduce than those who made false-negative errors.

Several researchers have demonstrated that adults have a strong tendency to detect agency, even when none exists (Berry, Misovich, Keen, & Baron, 1992; White & Milne, 1999; also see Boyer, 2001 and Scholl & Tremoulet, 2000 for a review), and there is an extensive developmental literature suggesting that this tendency emerges in infancy (Bering, 2005; Gergely & Csibra, 2003; Hamlin, Wynn, & Bloom, 2007; also see Atran, 2002 for a review). This psychological mechanism may have laid the foundation for religious belief, with people predisposed to posit supernatural agents (e.g., ghosts, spirits, Gods) for certain classes of ambiguous stimuli. However, this mechanism by itself is not enough to explain the existence of complex religious beliefs.

Belief in supernatural agents may emerge as a byproduct of the HADD, but this does not explain the characteristics bestowed upon such agents by those who believe in them. In further support of the byproduct hypothesis of religious belief, it has been proposed that the design of our memory system plays an important role. More specifically, Boyer (2001) suggests that people are particularly susceptible to remembering what Barrett (2004) has labeled 'minimally counterintuitive' (MCI) concepts, and that supernatural agents are examples of such concepts. MCIs can be succinctly described as concepts in which a relatively small number of assumptions are violated, thus grabbing our attention (see Barrett, 2004, for a detailed description). However, not all MCIs are equally memorable. After conducting several experiments to determine the degree of recall among concepts of varying counterintuitiveness, Boyer (2001) explains:

> *Barrett and I also found that violations of ontological expectations—as found in the templates for supernatural concepts—are recalled better than what we called "mere oddities." For instance, "a man who walked through a wall" (ontological violation) was generally better recalled than "a man with six fingers" (violation of expectations, but not of*

those expectations that define the ontological category PERSON). (p. 80)

Additionally, these experiments found that concepts with too many assumptions violated were not recalled as well as MCIs, a finding that was replicated by Barrett and Nyhof (2001). Boyer and Ramble (2001) have provided cross-cultural support for these recall tendencies.

In summary, a condensed description of the byproduct account of religious belief focuses primarily on the HADD and MCIs. *Supernatural agents arise as a byproduct of the HADD, and the specific characteristics of supernatural agents persist in a given society because they were the easiest to remember, because one byproduct of our memory systems is the susceptibility to MCIs.* However, not all researchers studying religion from an evolutionary perspective agree with this byproduct account, and so it is only fair to provide a brief review of adaptationist hypotheses for religious belief.

Wilson (2002) has proposed that religion may be an adaptation because throughout our evolutionary history, religious beliefs allowed groups to function more successfully and 'out-compete' groups that did not hold religious beliefs. Wilson is an advocate of group-level selection, which suggests that in addition to operating at the level of individuals, natural selection can operate at the level of groups. Group-level selection was powerfully and decisively refuted by Williams (1966), and the current consensus among evolutionary researchers is that group-level selection is highly unlikely except under very specific and rare circumstances. Also, Wilson provides little empirical support for his claims, and until such empirical support is provided by Wilson or others, group-level selection will likely remain a minority view.

Some researchers have proposed that religious belief, especially church attendance, may have a positive effect on one's health (Koenig & Vaillant, 2009; Koenig et al., 1999; McCullough & Larson, 1999; McCullough, Larson, Hoyt, Koenig, & Thoresen, 2000), which would seem to support the view that religion has adaptive qualities. However, despite the positive relationships that have been found, these researchers have properly acknowledged the possibility of alternative explanations, such as one's health benefiting from the feeling of belonging and acceptance in a tight-knit group, feelings which are not exclusive to religious organizations.

For example, Park, Fenster, Suresh, and Bliss (2006) have written about the importance of general social support in facilitating positive adjustment in chronic illness populations, and they have provided evidence that social support is a significant predictor of decreased feelings of depression for those suffering from congestive heart failure (CHF). Furthermore, Murberg and Bru (2001) have shown that the perceived social isolation of patients with CHF is a significant predictor of mortality. On the other hand, positive relationships between church attendance and health have been found even after controlling for social connection variables (Koenig et al., 1999). Nevertheless, this does not address whether people belonging to certain *non*-religious groups might benefit in similar ways. Although manipulating religiosity or church attendance is not feasible, additional research must be conducted to determine whether these health benefits result from factors that are exclusive to religiosity, or if these factors exist in other contexts.

Arguably, the most compelling adaptationist account of religion suggests that religious belief leads to a greater degree of prosocial, or cooperative behavior within groups (Alcorta & Sosis, 2005, Bering, McLeod, & Shackelford, 2005; Bulbulia, 2004; Purzycki & Sosis, 2009). Although this could be interpreted as group-level selection, it could also apply to selection at the level of individuals, because individual members of a prosocial group will, on average, benefit from these prosocial tendencies. A review of the literature on religious belief and prosociality by Norenzayan and Shariff (2008) led the authors to conclude that religious belief does indeed increase prosocial behavior, but that this increase is highly context-sensitive. Specifically, religious individuals are more likely to exhibit prosociality toward other members of their group than to 'outsiders.' Also, the increase in prosocial behavior occurs primarily when the situation can affect one's social reputation in the group. Finally, increased prosociality is not reliably observed unless one's religious beliefs, particularly those regarding a morally concerned deity, are cognitively salient at the moment when prosocial behavior is possible. Taken together, these results suggest a possible adaptive role for religious belief, but they do not eliminate the possibility of religion as a byproduct. Perhaps religious belief can be best described as an exaptation (Gould, 1991; Buss, Haselton, Shackelford, Bleske, & Wakefield, 1998), originally a byproduct of the HADD, our memory system, and other psychological mechanisms, and eventually serving the adaptive function of facilitating cooperation among individuals in a group.

Finally, it is worth mentioning memetics, which is another evolutionary approach to understanding religious beliefs, but does not neatly fall into the category of byproduct or adaptation. Dawkins (1976) coined the term 'meme' and suggested that ideas, or memes, may 'evolve' in a way analogous to genes. Ideas can be thought of as competing with one another for residence in the minds of people, and those ideas that are most successful at being remembered will survive, get passed on, and possibly change (i.e., evolve) over time. Since its inception in 1976, memetics has been expanded upon by several authors (Blackmore, 1999; Brodie, 2009), and has been discussed explicitly in reference to religion by Dennett (2006). However, at this stage, memetics is still a speculative and controversial approach to understanding cultural evolution and the spread of ideas (see Aunger, 2000). Nevertheless, Fincher and Thornhill (2008) have provided some indirect support for the memetic perspective in their examination of the degree of religious diversity throughout the world as it relates to pathogen prevalence. Fincher and Thornhill hypothesized and found that pathogen prevalence is positively correlated with religious diversity. Although they were not conducting this research from a memetic perspective, their results make sense within a memetic framework. If high pathogen stress limits contact between groups, there is less direct competition between different religious beliefs, which means that these different beliefs will continue to survive. Conversely, low pathogen stress translates into greater cultural transmission, which leads to competition between beliefs, and only the 'fittest' beliefs survive.

An evolutionary psychological perspective has generated many interesting hypotheses regarding religious belief, and these hypotheses will undoubtedly be refined as additional empirical work is done. We can now turn our attention to how such a perspective can be used to examine suicide terrorism.

APPLYING EVOLUTIONARY PSYCHOLOGY TO SUICIDE TERRORISM

Like religion, suicide terrorism has been studied extensively from a psychological perspective (see Bongar, Brown, Beutler, Breckenridge,

& Zimbardo, 2007; Stern, 2003). However, the focus of this research has largely been to determine and understand the proximate causes of suicide terrorism. Although this research is important, we argue that the addition of an evolutionary psychological perspective has the potential to increase our understanding of terrorism, in general, and of suicide terrorism in particular, by explaining why the propensity for such behavior exists in the first place.

We argue that religious belief is a primary factor in the occurrence of suicide terrorism, yet it is necessary to clarify this argument before attempting to link evolutionary psychological theories of religion to suicide terrorism. We are *not* arguing that religiosity is a strong predictor of suicide terrorism, since the number of religious people in the world vastly outnumbers those willing to engage in suicide terrorism. However, there are certain religious beliefs that may facilitate such willingness (e.g., belief in the afterlife, endorsement of martyrdom, viewing one's in-group as 'the chosen people,' the vilification of heretics and nonbelievers). Although religiosity may not positively predict one's willingness to engage in suicide terrorism, the *lack* of religiosity (i.e., the lack of certain specific religious beliefs) should predict one's *unwillingness* to engage in suicide terrorism.

We are not the first to propose a link between religious beliefs and terrorism (Dawkins, 2006; Harris, 2004; Stern, 2003), but there is a lack of strong empirical data supporting this link. At the same time, data provided to disconfirm this link (Ginges, Hansen, & Norenzayan, 2009) is, as of yet, unconvincing (Liddle, Machluf, & Shackelford, 2010). People may point to the Liberation Tigers of Tamil Eelam, or the Tamil Tigers, as a disconfirmation of the link between religion and suicide terrorism because they are recognized as a secular organization. However, this label does not provide us with information about the specific beliefs of Tamil Tigers who are willing to commit acts of suicide terrorism. One can maintain supernatural beliefs without belonging to an organized religion (Zuckerman, 2008), and unless we can determine that the majority of Tamil Tigers willing to commit suicide terrorism lack the beliefs that are likely to facilitate such terrorism (e.g., belief in the afterlife), the secular identity of the organization as a whole is not a convincing argument.

As it stands, the direct link between specific religious beliefs and one's willingness to engage in suicide terrorism is open for debate, since there is no evidence strong enough to effectively confirm or disconfirm this hypothesis. Nevertheless, the theories of religion outlined earlier provide a useful illustration of the application of evolutionary psychology, and the same principles of evolutionary psychology that have begun to demystify religious belief can be applied to the issue of suicide terrorism.

As with religious belief, an evolutionary psychological perspective requires us to consider whether suicide terrorism is produced by specialized psychological adaptations or is a byproduct of other psychological mechanisms. Although at first glance such behavior would appear maladaptive, primarily because of the forfeit of one's life in the process, there are promising adaptationist hypotheses worth considering. Perhaps the most promising hypothesis is that such behavior can be maintained via kin selection.

The theory of kin selection, originally proposed by Hamilton (1964), explains how traits that are not necessarily beneficial to an organism can nevertheless be selected for. This apparent contradiction is eliminated when one switches their focus from the *individual* to the *gene*. A trait that is harmful to an individual can be selected for if it is sufficiently beneficial to the individual's relatives, because from the gene's perspective, the harm is offset by the benefits to others who are likely to carry the same gene. The use of this theory by evolutionary psychologists has been particularly helpful in providing a partial explanation for altruistic behavior (see Buss, 2004). Although altruistic behavior often entails a cost to the altruist, the psychological mechanisms that allow such behavior to occur can be selected for if the behavior is directed toward genetic relatives. The genes for altruism are likely to survive even if the altruist suffers, because those same genes are likely to be carried by the altruist's relatives who benefit from the behavior.

In terms of suicide terrorism, it is possible that such behavior persists because it provides benefits to the relatives of terrorists (Victoroff, 2009). Pedahzur et al. (2003), when examining the demographics of Palestinian suicide terrorists, concluded that these terrorists had few 'family ties' because 84.2 percent of their sample consisted of bachelors. However, 81 percent of these terrorists came from families with at least eight members (Blackwell, 2005).Therefore, even though the majority of these terrorists were seemingly unsuccessful in passing on their genes *directly*, their large families of genetic kin provided an ample opportunity for kin selection to take place, if their kin benefited from the act of suicide terrorism. In addition to the increased status and honor bestowed upon the families of these Palestinian suicide terrorists, these families have been paid between $10,000 and $25,000 by Hamas, spread out in monthly stipends of roughly $1,000 (Blackwell, 2005). Given the benefits bestowed upon the genetic kin of these suicide terrorists, and the large number of genetic kin in place to receive such benefits, the seemingly maladaptive act of suicide terrorism can prove to be adaptive through the action of kin selection. Although these data do not refer to *all* acts of suicide terrorism, they provide support for kin selection as a driving force behind Palestinian suicide terrorism, suggesting that a similar driving force may exist in other regions.

Whereas kin selection theory provides an adaptationist explanation for suicide terrorism, the same theory can also provide a useful foundation for considering byproduct explanations. One possibility is that, in cases in which genetic kin do not benefit from such terrorist acts, the same psychological mechanisms geared toward helping kin are 'hijacked.' In much the same way as altruism toward strangers may be produced by the misfiring of mechanisms designed to benefit relatives, suicide terrorism may sometimes be triggered by feelings toward one's group (i.e., terrorist organization or religious sect), despite the lack of genetic relatedness. In other words, one's group may be considered 'fictive kin,' leading to the unconscious activation of mechanisms that generate behavior normally geared toward benefitting genetically related kin.

Indeed, organizations that recruit individuals to carry out suicide terrorism promote feelings that are likely to lead to a misfiring of kin selection mechanisms. As Goetze and James (2004, p. 155) describe:

> The small, terrorist cell serves as a meaningful substitute to family and it is not surprising that members end up forming strong emotional bonds with each other as well as the typical sacrificial inclinations of close family. Leaders of terrorist organizations cultivate and manipulate these emotional bonds and steer their expression toward political goals of the terrorist organization.

Furthermore, data on 39 recruits to an organization allied with Al-Qaeda indicate that, "All believed that by sacrificing themselves they would help secure the future of their 'family' of fictive kin" (Atran, 2003, p. 1537). In addition to terrorist organizations, religious sects of would-be suicide terrorists are also prime suspects for the misfiring of kin selection mechanisms. Many religious belief systems, such as Judaism, Islam, and Christianity, rely heavily on terminology often reserved for genetic kin (Atran, 2002). In short, the idea of suicide terrorism resulting from the misfiring of psychological mechanisms deserves further empirical attention, because discovering the factors that contribute to these misfiring can help guide actions to prevent or reverse such effects.

For kin selection mechanisms to motivate suicide terrorism, whether these mechanisms are activated by expected benefits to genetic kin or fictive kin, the benefit to the survival and reproduction of one's kin must outweigh the costs to oneself. This provides another opportunity for religious beliefs to play a role in facilitating suicide terrorism. Without the belief that one's life continues after death (and the belief that martyrdom will be rewarded in the afterlife), the largely unconscious cost–benefit calculation that motivates kin selection-related behaviors would likely motivate the would-be terrorist to not follow through with a suicide act. Life after death, particularly a life of rewards in paradise for eternity, might play a large role in offsetting the costs associated with suicide terrorism, thereby 'tipping the scale' in favor of the expected benefits to one's kin. In short, even with expected kin benefits, specific religious beliefs may be a vital, but insufficient, motivating factor for suicide terrorism.

Speaking of beliefs, it is possible that, as with religion, memetics can shed light on the phenomenon of suicide terrorism. It may be the case that suicide terrorism persists because the ideas and beliefs that terrorist organizations and certain religious sects disseminate to their followers 'parasitize' the brain. As Pedahzur et al. (2003) describe, "In a society where honor is among the highest virtues, there are indeed powerful social pressures lying behind the suicide bomber's decision" (p. 420). The 'virtues' of groups that foster terrorist activity can be considered memes, with the terrorist acts serving to benefit and propagate those memes. More specifically, the belief of everlasting life in paradise can be an extremely powerful meme, which is possibly one of the main reasons that suicide terrorism is so often performed by individuals with strong religious beliefs. It is clear that a terrorist's beliefs are a crucial component when attempting to explain their actions and it is possible that these beliefs can be better understood within a memetic framework.

For example, often when confronted with stories of Islamic suicide terrorism, Muslims are quick to explain these terrorists as twisting Islamic beliefs and misinterpreting the Quran. These explanations can take on a whole new meaning from a memetic perspective. The differential survival and replication of religious beliefs (memes) should be related to which beliefs are the most 'successful' in a given environment. Islamic beliefs that promote martyrdom, condemn heresy, apostasy, and nonbelief, and highlight rewards in the afterlife for killing the 'enemies of Islam' will be emphasized by those who recruit, train, engage in, or support suicide terrorism. Likewise, these beliefs will be de-emphasized by moderate Muslims, who will instead emphasize Islamic beliefs that promote peace and tolerance of those with different religious beliefs, and condemn acts of martyrdom. Both sets of beliefs can be found in the Quran (Harris, 2004), but moderate Muslims are right to distinguish 'their' Islam from the Islam promoted by terrorists. Asking whether Islam is a religion of peace or a religion of war is the wrong type of question to ask, and memetics can illustrate why: Islam, like other organized religions, is not a homogenous set of beliefs. It has evolved into several 'subspecies' of Islam, each with their own sets of core beliefs that can be traced back to a 'common ancestor' (i.e., the Quran). These subspecies are the result of different selection pressures, in that different groups select, emphasize, and transmit those beliefs that best suit their needs. By adopting a memetic perspective, we may gain a better understanding of how and why the Islam of suicide terrorists differs so widely from the Islam of moderates, and how the emphasis of different sets of core beliefs can influence the occurrence of suicide terrorism.

DIRECTIONS FOR FUTURE RESEARCH

We have provided the theoretical groundwork for thinking about suicide terrorism from an evolutionary psychological perspective, but such an endeavor is only useful if it can open up new avenues of empirical study. We now provide some examples of how an evolutionary psychological approach to suicide terrorism can be applied to future research.

As mentioned earlier, kin selection may be a motivational force in suicide terrorism. Given the data on Palestinian suicide terrorists and the benefits received by their genetic kin (Blackwell, 2005), a next step would be to investigate whether genetic kin receive similar benefits in other populations in which suicide terrorism takes place. Are the majority of suicide terrorists in other populations bachelors? Do these individuals come from large families? Do their kin receive monetary rewards or improved status after the terrorist act? If so, do the monetary rewards or increases in status correlate with the degree of relatedness (i.e., parents and siblings of suicide terrorists receiving greater benefits than cousins)? The accumulation of data related to these questions would go a long way in determining whether kin selection plays a role in motivating individuals to engage in suicide terrorism.

In addition to (or in lieu of) benefitting genetic kin, suicide terrorists may be motivated by affiliations with 'fictive kin,' which causes kin selection mechanisms to misfire. One way to investigate this would be to question suicide terrorists directly, using surveys or interviews to determine the extent to which they view others in their organization, religious sect, society, etc. as kin, and to compare their responses to those from the population at large. However, this brings us to one of the greatest difficulties in attempts to study this population: researchers would be hard pressed to find a less amenable group to analyze than suicide terrorists, with the only ones available for questioning being those who are in training or those who were unsuccessful; and of that subgroup, those willing to respond to surveys or engage in systematic interviews may well be in the minority. Nevertheless, such interviews are possible (see Stern, 2003), but there are other options available as well.

One option is to measure the *support* for suicide terrorism among individuals who are not suicide terrorists themselves. Although people who support terrorism are not synonymous with people who *engage* in terrorism, there is likely to be some overlap in the psychology of these two groups. For example, Ginges et al. (2009) found a positive relationship between religious service attendance and support for suicide attacks, which is consistent with the possibility of misfiring kin selection mechanisms, since attending religious services can strengthen one's feeling of being connected to the community (Zuckerman, 2008). Additional research should be conducted in this fashion, comparing support for suicide terrorism and perceptions of fictive kin. This can be done through surveys, as well as other methods, such as investigating whether priming concepts of kin influences one's level of support for suicide terrorism. Clearly, studying individuals who support suicide terrorism should not be viewed as a replacement for studying actual suicide terrorists, but the former group can inform our understanding of the factors associated with suicide terrorism.

Another important avenue for future research is testing the hypothesized relationship between religiosity and suicide terrorism. Granted, there are difficulties associated with trying to empirically assess this relationship. As we stated earlier, religiosity is unlikely to have any strong predictive power because there are far more religious people than would-be suicide terrorists in the world. Nevertheless, investigating the relationship between religiosity and suicide terrorism is not a lost cause. One can generate hypotheses regarding which *specific* religious beliefs are likely to facilitate suicide terrorism. For example, belief in the afterlife is likely to have a strong impact on the (probably unconscious) cost–benefit analysis of engaging in suicide terrorism by minimizing the projected costs. Also, religious beliefs that strengthen the in-group bond and create a feeling of 'fictive kin,' coupled with beliefs that strengthen out-group hostility, may activate psychological mechanisms related to kin selection and protecting one's in-group (which consisted mostly of genetic kin throughout our evolutionary history), thus motivating behavior that is perceived to benefit the in-group and hurt the out-group, such as suicide terrorism.

A list of specific religious beliefs, like the ones mentioned above, allows us to generate more specific hypotheses. Within terrorist organizations, or among individuals who support suicide terrorism, there should be an emphasis on promoting these religious beliefs relative to other beliefs from the same religion. In other words, religious beliefs that likely facilitate suicide terrorism should be rated as more important than other beliefs within the same religion, but this pattern should not be found among those from the same population who are not supportive of, or willing to engage in, suicide terrorism. By considering specific religious beliefs, rather than religiosity in general, we may have a better chance of detecting the link between religiosity and suicide terrorism, if such a link exists.

CONCLUSION

Terrorism, in all its forms, is a phenomenon that we must try to understand as best we can, in the hopes that we can curtail its occurrence. This level of understanding can only be achieved by interdisciplinary efforts. We have reached a point at which proximate explanations of terrorism are becoming clearer, but ultimate or evolutionary explanations have yet to be pursued with similar enthusiasm. We believe that an evolutionary psychological perspective has the potential to provide such ultimate explanations.

For the purposes of this chapter, we restricted our analysis to suicide terrorism. The surge of evolutionary psychological research on religion in the last decade provides a powerful stepping off point for examining acts of terrorism that are seemingly motivated by certain religious beliefs. By reviewing some of the ways in which an evolutionary perspective has influenced current research on religion, we sought to illustrate how evolution can be a useful framework for researching suicide terrorism. Applying the evolutionary principles of kin selection, and possibly memetics, to suicide terrorism has great potential, but researching terrorism from an evolutionary perspective is by no means limited to the ideas offered here. We encourage researchers to utilize the principles of evolutionary psychology when studying suicide terrorism or terrorism in general, with the hope that such an approach will uncover valuable insights regarding such behavior.

REFERENCES

Alcorta, C. S., & Sosis, R. (2005). Ritual, emotion, and sacred symbols. *Human Nature*, 16(4), 323–359.

Atran, S. (2002). *In gods we trust: The evolutionary landscape of religion.* New York: Oxford University Press.

Atran, S. (2003). Genesis of suicide terrorism. *Science*, 299(5612), 1534–1539.

Aunger, R. (2000). *Darwinizing culture: The status of memetics as a science.* New York: Oxford University Press.

Barrett, J. L. (2000). Exploring the natural foundations of religion. *Trends in Cognitive Sciences*, 4(1), 29–34.

Barrett, J. L. (2004). *Why would anyone believe in god?* Lanham, MD: AltaMira Press.

Barrett, J. L., & Nyhof, M. (2001). Spreading non natural concepts: The role of intuitive conceptual structures in memory and transmission of cultural materials. *Journal of Cognition and Culture*, 1(1), 69–100.

Bering, J. M. (2005). The evolutionary history of an illusion: Religious causal beliefs in children and adults. In B. J. Ellis & D. F. Bjorklund (Eds.), *Origins of the social mind: Evolutionary psychology and child development* (pp. 411–437). New York: The Guilford Press.

Bering, J. M., McLeod, K., & Shackelford, T. K. (2005). Reasoning about dead agents reveals possible adaptive trends. *Human Nature*, 16(4), 360–381.

Berry, D., Misovich, P., Keen, R., & Baron, S. (1992). Effects of disruption of structure and motion on perceptions of social causality. *Personality and Social Psychology Bulletin*, 18 (2), 237–244.

Blackmore, S. (1999). *The meme machine*. New York: Oxford University Press.

Blackwell, A. D. (2005). *Terrorism, heroism, and altruism: Kin selection and socio-religious cost-benefit scaling in Palestinian suicide attack*. Poster session presented at the 17th Annual Human Behavior and Evolution Society Conference, June 1–5, Austin, TX.

Bongar, B., Brown, L. M., Beutler, L. E., Breckenridge, J. N., & Zimbardo, P. G. (2007). *Psychology of terrorism*. New York: Oxford University Press.

Borum, R. (2004). *Psychology of terrorism*. Tampa: University of South Florida.

Boyer, P. (2001). *Religion explained: The evolutionary origins of religious thought*. New York: Basic Books; Harper Collins.

Boyer, P., & Ramble, C. (2001). Cognitive templates for religious concepts: Cross-cultural evidence for recall of counter-intuitive representations. *Cognitive Science*, 25(4), 535–564.

Brodie, R. (2009). *Virus of the mind: The new science of the meme*. Carlsbad, CA: Hay House.

Bulbulia, J. (2004). The cognitive and evolutionary psychology of religion. *Biology and Philosophy*, 19(5), 655–686.

Buss, D. M. (2004). *Evolutionary psychology: The new science of the mind*, 2nd ed. Boston, MA: Allyn & Bacon.

Buss, D. M., Haselton, M. G., Shackelford, T. K., Bleske, A., & Wakefield, J. C. (1998). Adaptations, exaptations, and spandrels. *American Psychologist*, 53(5), 533–548.

Darwin, C. (2006 [1871]). *The descent of man, and selection in relation to sex*, 1st ed. In E. O. Wilson (Ed.), *From so simple a beginning: The four great books of Charles Darwin* (pp. 767–1248). New York: Norton.

Dawkins, R. (1976). *The selfish gene*. Oxford: Oxford University Press.

Dawkins, R. (2006). *The god delusion*. London: Bantam Press.

Dennett, D. C. (2006). *Breaking the spell: Religion as a natural phenomenon.* New York: Penguin Books.
Fincher, C. L., & Thornhill, R. (2008). Assortative sociality, limited dispersal, infectious disease and the genesis of the global pattern of religion diversity. *Proceedings of the Royal Society: Biological Sciences, 275*(1651), 2587–2594.
Gergely, G., & Csibra, G. (2003). Teleological reasoning in infancy: The naive theory of rational action. *Trends in Cognitive Sciences, 7*(7), 287–292.
Ginges, J., Hansen, I., & Norenzayan, A. (2009). Religion and support for suicide attacks. *Psychological Science, 20*(2), 224–230.
Goetze, G. B., & James, P. (2004). Evolutionary psychology and the explanation of ethnic phenomenon. *Evolutionary Psychology, 2*, 142–159.
Gould, S. J. (1991). Exaptation: A crucial tool for evolutionary psychology. *Journal of Social Issues, 47*(3), 43–65.
Guthrie, S. E. (1993). *Faces in the clouds: A new theory of religion.* New York: Oxford University Press.
Hamilton, W. D. (1964). The genetical evolution of social behavior, II. *Journal of Theoretical Biology, 7*(1), 17–52.
Hamlin, J. K., Wynn, K., & Bloom, P. (2007). Social evaluation by preverbal infants. *Nature, 450*(7169), 557–559.
Harris, S. (2004). *The end of faith: Religion, terror and the future of reason.* New York: W.W Norton & Company.
Hoffman, B. (1999). The mind of the terrorist: Perspectives of social psychology. *Psychiatric Annals, 29*(6), 337–340.
Hronick, M. S. (2006). Analyzing terror: Researchers study the perpetrators and the effects of suicide terrorism. *National Institute of Justice Journal,* (254), 8–11.
James, W. (1902). *The varieties of religious experience. A study in human nature.* New York: The Modern Library.
Koenig, H. G., Hays, J. C., George, L. K., Larson, D. B., Cohen, H. J., McCullough M., et al. (1999). Does religious attendance prolong survival? A six-year follow-up study of 3,968 older adults. *The Journals of Gerontology, 54*(7), M370–M376.
Koenig, L. B., & Vaillant, G. E. (2009). A prospective study of church attendance and health over the lifespan. *Health Psychology, 28*(1), 117–124.
Liddle, J. R., Machluf, K., & Shackelford, T. K. (2010). Understanding suicide terrorism: Premature dismissal of the religious-belief hypothesis. *Evolutionary Psychology, 8*(3), 343–345.
McCullough, M. E., & Larson, D. B. (1999). Religion and depression: A review of the literature. *Twin Research, 2*(2), 126–136.

McCullough, M. E., Larson, D. B., Hoyt, W. T., Koenig, H. G., & Thoresen, C. (2000). Religious involvement and mortality: A meta-analytic review. *Health Psychology, 19*(3), 211–222.

Murberg, T. A., & Bru, E. (2001). Social relationships and mortality in patients with congestive heart failure. *Journal of Psychosomatic Research, 51*(3), 521–527.

Norenzayan, A., & Shariff, A. F. (2008). The origin and evolution of religious prosociality. *Science, 322*(5898), 58–62.

Park, C. L., Fenster, J. R., Suresh, D. P., & Bliss, D. E. (2006). Social support, appraisals, and coping as predictors of depression in congestive heart failure patients. *Psychology and Health, 21*(6), 773–789.

Pedahzur, A., Perliger, A., & Weinberg, L. (2003). Altruism and fatalism: The characteristics of Palestinian suicide terrorists. *Deviant Behavior, 24*(4), 405–423.

Purzycki, B. J., & Sosis, R. (2009). The religious system as adaptive: Cognitive flexibility, public displays, and acceptance. In E. Voland & W. Schiefenhvel (Eds.), *The biological evolution of religious mind and behavior* (pp. 243–256). New York: Springer.

Ross, J. I. (1996). A model of the psychological causes of oppositional political terrorism. *Peace and Conflict, 2*(2), 129–141.

Scholl, B. J., & Tremoulet, P. D. (2000). Perceptual causality and animacy. *Trends in Cognitive Sciences, 4*(8), 299–309.

Stern, J. (2003). *Terror in the name of god: Why religious militants kill*. New York: Harper Collins.

Victoroff, J. (2009). Suicide terrorism and the biology of significance. *Political Psychology, 30*(3), 397–400.

Weinberg, L., Pedahzur, A., & Canetti-Nisim, D. (2003). The social and religious characteristics of suicide bombers and their victims. *Terrorism and Political Violence, 15*(3), 139–153.

White, P. A., & Milne, A. (1999). Impressions of enforced disintegration and bursting in the visual perception of collision events. *Journal of Experimental Psychology: General, 128*(4), 499–516.

Williams, G. C. (1966). *Adaptation and natural selection*. Princeton, NJ: Princeton University Press.

Wilson, D. S. (2002). *Darwin's cathedral: Evolution, religion, and the nature of society*. Chicago, IL: The University of Chicago Press.

Workman, L., & Reader, W. (2008). *Evolutionary psychology: An Introduction*, 2nd ed. New York: Cambridge University Press.

Zuckerman, P. (2008). *Society without god: What the least religious nations can tell us about contentment*. New York: New York University Press.

4

Suicide Terrorism as Social Noise: A Communicative Perspective

Jonathan Matusitz

This chapter analyzes suicide terrorism from a particular perspective of communication: social noise. Coined by Simonson (2001), social noise refers to the ability of being 'attention-grabbing.' It is a method of being incredibly noticeable through noisy, graphic, provocative, or controversial acts. Social noise is a communicative tool with which suicide terrorists send a message. The suicide attack is a medium in and of itself, and it is conveyed not only to the immediate target but also to multiple audiences beyond the direct target. Another key objective of suicide terrorism as social noise is to create change in the audience's attitudes or opinions. Thanks to present-day media, such as mass-mediated images and online videos, the communication of terrorism is limitless, which allows terrorist groups to be more able to make statements, communicate their agenda, or air their grievances to the world at large. The ultimate consequence of suicide terrorism as social noise is that it causes public disorder and spreads to long distances.

This chapter begins with a description of terrorism as a communication process. In order to have a crucial understanding of how social noise operates and creates terrorism for the audience, the author developed a model of the concept as a specific form of communication. What comes subsequently is the heart of this analysis: suicide terrorism as a type of social noise. Also emphasized in this section is martyrdom in Islamist terrorism. In the same train of thought, of particular importance are the effects of suicide terrorism on the audience. In addition to providing a thorough description of what 'audience' means, the author analyzes a specific case study of suicide terrorism: the 1983 Hezbollah suicide bombing against US Marines in Beirut. In this particular instance, eight types of audience were identified.

TERRORISM AS A COMMUNICATION PROCESS

Terrorism is fundamentally a communication process. It is spread through public communication and exposed through mass communication. Terrorism is a communicative 'act' because it targets a much larger audience beyond the immediate targets. The goal of terrorism is to produce fear and signs of fear. In general, terrorist attacks kill fewer people than what was planned, but the attacks leave marks, messages, and images on the audience's mind. They create interferences—that is, internal noises as described in David Berlo's (1960) model of communication. Berlo's model explains how communication is a dynamic process between the sender and receiver, and how they are connected with each other through encoding, decoding, and feedback. The audiences of terrorism are in communication with each other both at the individual and collective levels—and both directly and indirectly. The whole communicative process is included in a larger loop that will, in turn, feed back to the terrorists. On the whole, the interactions between the audiences were already there before the communication loop was created by the terrorist message (Miller, Matusitz, O'Hair, & Eckstein, 2008).

The terrorists have a message to send. The violence is a medium itself, and it is conveyed to the immediate target, usually with destructive effects. From this perspective, terrorism is akin to interpersonal communication because the principle is the same as sending a punch in a person's face or giving a letter to someone. As a type of interpersonal communication, terrorism requires killing or maiming a victim in order to be effective. Nonetheless, the objective of terrorism tends to not just be killing but also cause change, frequently a change in the audience's attitudes or opinions. Therefore, terrorism intends to change the attitudes or opinions of the public (Williams, 1998).

COMMUNICATION OF TERRORISM: SOCIAL NOISE

For Schmid and de Graff (1982), "terrorism can best be understood as a violent communication strategy. There is a sender, the terrorist, a message generator, the victim, and a receiver, the enemy and/or the public" (p. 15). Traditionally, however, terrorism was restrained in its power to propagate its messages in a way that differs greatly from modern methods. Before the advent of television and visual communications, terrorism could not be illustrated by the types of media that were prevalent during those days. As such, terrorist attacks could only be observed by a few individuals. This situation was comparable to Plato's *Republic*, where his ideal civilization was limited to the number of citizens who could be reached through one human voice only. In the Middle-Ages, the zone surrounding an English parish was determined by the range of the church's bell noise, and the early North American settlers built their farms within shouting reach of each other (Schafer, 1994). In all instances, as it was for most terrorist attacks, the reality is easy to explain: communication was limited because the ability to spread messages was limited too.

Terrorists had to develop ways to get their messages sent to larger audiences. The best way was to be 'attention-grabbing,' what Simonson (2001) called 'social noise.' Social noise is a method of being outlandishly noticeable through noisy or controversial acts. When social noise causes public disorder, it propagates to long distances and by causing unpleasant stirs or sensations in the audience, it influences social life sooner or later. Social noise accentuates an important facet of public communication: its power to absorb or terrify the public through both form and content. In this day and age, social noise would be analogous to shock advertising (or shockvertising), a type of advertising that is provocative, distracting, and graphic (Saunders, 1998).

Social noise implies the notion that terrorism is inherently a communicative gesture. Through social noise, terrorists transmit threats and introduce feelings of anxiety, even when the public is far away from the immediate site of the tragedy. To accomplish social noise, terrorists have used various tactics. For example, historically, terrorists have exploited one specific weapon to get their message across: dynamite. Thanks to Alfred Nobel's invention of dynamite in 1866, terrorism spread more easily in the second half of the nineteenth century (Matusitz, 2012). Dynamite was now the ultimate democratic weapon; 'the great equalizer' that enabled revolutionaries to overcome the enormous power of the state. In fact, terrorists called it the 'philosophy of the bomb.' The philosophy was that killing enemies with dynamite was the only feasible social noise and mode of social change (Carlson, 1995).

The terrorists' deeds increased in number, as was seen in the killing of politicians and world leaders. US President William McKinley was shot in 1901. Leon Czolgosz, the man who killed the president, was driven by the advantages of making social noise (Cahm, 2002). If a terrorist group's social noise becomes routine—that is, if the tactics remain the same for the group—such social noise becomes their 'signature method.' In other words, a terrorist group's recurring social noise becomes conspicuously associated with the operational activities of that group. Through the same type of social noise, over time, the terrorist group leaves a mark that speaks to the ideology and intent of the group (Martin, 2010). As this analysis will demonstrate in the case of the 1983 Hezbollah suicide attacks on US Marines in Beirut, suicide terrorism is a type of social noise that speaks to what the group stands for.

SUICIDE TERRORISM AS SOCIAL NOISE

Suicide terrorism is a type of social noise. By definition, suicide terrorism refers to killing oneself (for ideological or political purposes) and other people in the process. For terrorists, suicide terrorism is a useful method because it seems easier and certainly cheaper than most traditional military tactics. Not only does suicide terrorism cost fewer lives, but blowing oneself up seems also more practical than targeting soldiers (Pedahzur, 2004). The terrorist uses his or her body as a weapon, which raises his or her terror quotient above the others. Murray (2006) calls this phenomenon 'biopolitics,' where the terrorist's shattered body parts become damaging shells. Murray (2006) observes that "the attacker's body is literally weaponized. Shards of bone become human shrapnel" (p. 207). This violent act, in turn, is broadcast through television images—an efficient way of creating social noise.

In certain circles of Palestinian society, suicide terrorism has acquired a status symbol, a type of social identification. It has become a visible, external meaning of one's social position and a strong indicator of social status (Cherrington, 1994). The few lucky Palestinians who are designated to be *shaheed*s (i.e., suicide bombers) are lionized as heroes. A whole cultural structure composed of relatives, friends, schools, teachers, religious organizations, media, and political institutions shares and promulgates an intense belief system about martyrdom for the cause (Caracci, 2002). As a type of social noise, suicide terrorism is a ritual act of human sacrifice for the Palestinians: by killing an infidel—like an Israeli—the Palestinian terrorist enacts a type of ritual in which he or she shows him- or herself to be omnipotent over his or her target. Many Palestinian brothers and sisters identify with him or her in this act (Hareven, 1983).

Suicide terrorism has increasingly become normative over the past three decades. The amount of suicide bombings has grown from an average of 3–4 annually in the 1980s to 180 annually between 2000 and 2005, and from 81 in 2001 to 460 in 2005. Suicide terrorism has received much more exposure since the September 11, 2001 terrorist attacks (i.e., 'detonating' oneself through aircrafts crashing into buildings), killing close to 3,000 people, and the suicide bombings in London (on double-decker buses) on July 7, 2005, killing 52 civilians (Atran, 2006). For a certain number of young Muslim radicals, suicide terrorists have become their role models (Sageman, 2008). In fact, during the second Intifada, which started in September 2000, there were so many candidates who applied to be *shaheed*s that recruiters and scouts had an unprecedented pool of applicants. One recruiter even admitted that they were 'flooded' with too many applications (Schweitzer, 2007).

A chief purpose of suicide terrorism is the successful achievement of social noise, as demonstrated in the aphorism, "One man willing to throw away his life is enough to terrorize a thousand." This quote is credited to Wu Ch'I, a Chinese military philosopher, and resembles the statement "kill one man, terrorize a thousand" (which was used by Mao). Suicide terrorists like to emulate a terrorist group's signature method of social noise by directing their attacks toward specific symbolic or economic targets, an approach highly advocated by Osama bin Laden in his recorded speeches. Pape (2005), an expert on suicide bombings, claimed that 95 percent of suicide attacks since the dawn of the twenty-first century have sent the same message to the ummah (the global Islamic community): the armies and powers that occupy a disputed territory *must disengage now*. Suicide bombings, then, aim at creating social noise in order to demoralize various audiences—particularly the immediate targets and the government of the terrorists' enemies.

COMMUNICATING SUICIDE TERRORISM: A MODEL

Upon examining terrorism from a communicative standpoint, Tuman (2003) developed a model of terrorism as a communication process: the terrorist transmits a message to an audience (i.e., the public at large, the government, an organization, etc.) by perpetrating a violent act. It is not the message that constitutes the violence. Rather the violence is encoded within such the terrorist activity itself. Suicide terrorism, too, operates via a communication process and has a rhetorical feature that is detached from the simple force (or intimidation) associated to violence for its own sake. Suicide terrorism may well function to generate discourse among target audiences. The encoding process is dependent on the context: the symbolic tone of the suicide bombing and the ability for exploiting various media to send such a message. In turn, the target audience decodes this message and is also dependent on the context: the means and tools that the audience has for understanding or making sense of the situation—what Tuman (2010) refers to as "constructing its own sense of reality" (p. 19).

Suicide terrorists do not merely commit suicide. They exploit their targets' death (and their own) as a communicative or symbolic gesture. Death becomes an instrument for the transmission of ideas and ideologies. In case there is no clear message, the act is all there is. Short of useful or relevant communication, the event unfolds in its own 'eventness.' It becomes what psychoanalysts refer to as 'acting out.' The message of suicide terrorism is included mostly in the act itself; death is both its method and its significance (Douzinas, 2008). By definition, acting out is a defense mechanism whereby one communicates emotional conflict and feelings through actions, not words (Masterson, 1981). As shown in Figure 4.1, adapted from Tuman's (2003) original terrorism model, a suicide terrorist attack does not operate via a one-way communication process. Instead, the message of suicide terrorism is two-way (interactive) because the first message creates a response, which will then be transmitted to the terrorist either directly (i.e., through government retaliation, public discourse, etc.) or indirectly (i.e., through the interpretation [by the media] of the government's actions, etc.).

At times, suicide terrorists attempt to create fear, panic, and chaos, or draw attention to issues that the media, political establishments,

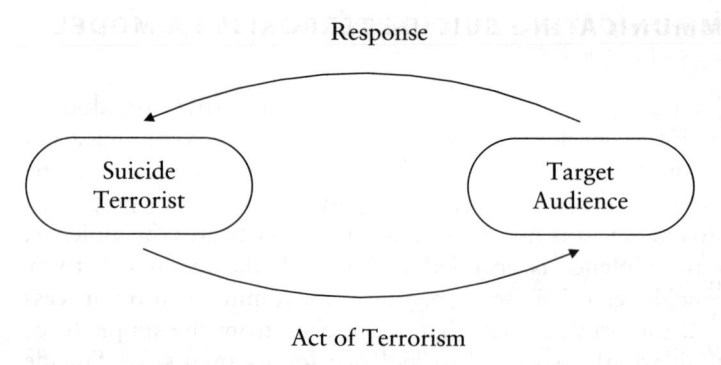

```
            Response
         ←─────────────
    ⏜              ⏜
  ( Suicide )   ( Target   )
  (Terrorist)   (Audience )
    ⏝              ⏝
         ─────────────→
         Act of Terrorism
```

Figure 4.1
Model of suicide terrorism as a communication process
Source: Adapted from Tuman (2003).

or academic conferences have granted little or no treatment. At other times, suicide terrorists attempt to cause the government or institution (which was just hit or driven by an act of violence) to yield to the demands made by specific terrorist groups (Tuman, 2003). Under these circumstances, a chief purpose of suicide terrorism as a communication process is persuasion. As such, the objective is to persuade audiences that chaos and fear will be an inevitable result, to persuade them to take an issue (that has long been ignored) into serious consideration, or to persuade them to make decisions they would not normally take (Tuman, 2010).

MARTYRDOM AS SOCIAL NOISE

A notorious example of suicide terrorism is martyrdom, an immense window of opportunity to draw worldwide attention. Martyrdom implies dying or suffering as a hero. For the West, a suicide martyr is a terrorist, but for terrorist groups (and their sympathizers), he or she is a hero (Pedahzur, 2004). Following the lead of Yusuf Al-Qaradawi, the Hamas terrorist group does not call suicide bombings 'suicides.' Instead, Hamas refers to those who commit those as *shuhada,* or 'martyrs,' and to the suicide bombings as *amaliyat alistishadiya*—'acts of martyrdom' or 'martyrdom operations.' Hamas extols the virtues of its martyrs and recompenses them with the most honorable Muslim burial rites. The terrorist group also provides for the financial needs of the martyrs' families (Saad, 2001).

Many exclusive interviews have been conducted with Palestinian and Afghani martyrs' wives, who are lauding their husbands' decisions to become martyrs. Such type of social noise is a skill in and of itself. A lot of preparation is required and it is usually planned successfully. Following months of training, the martyr-to-be is assigned a target, blows him- or herself up, kills (many) civilians in the process, and attracts massive attention to his or her cause. In addition, to prevent their audiences from being overwhelmed with too much information or routine political and theological rhetoric, Islamic organizers streamline their messages through emotional narratives that build an unforgettable image of the 'heroic martyr' (Hafez, 2007). As such, social noise can be accomplished through online videos, biographies of martyrs, audio recordings, monthly periodicals, and photos posted online. These stories of 'heroes' capitalize on sacred themes of humiliation, spiritual allegiance, and salvation to make their adversaries look bad and motivate their Muslim audiences to commit 'heroic' sacrifices too. The portrayals of martyrs in videos and biographies are highly propagandistic and, usually, do not symbolize the totality of their motivations. Terrorist groups like to attain a high degree of social noise by manipulating stories, not to suggest that such mythologies depict the real motivations of the martyrs (Hafez, 2006, 2007).

The martyrdom video is something to behold. It is a video recording, generally from Islamist militants, that encourages involvement in suicide attacks and dying as a 'hero' during the operation. Such video contains a speech by the martyr-to-be preparing to die honorably for his or her cause. While generally of inferior quality, some videos also incorporate text, music, and sentimental segments. In these videos, the martyr-to-be sits or stands with a black Islamic flag behind. In this respect, social noise becomes a model of visual rhetoric, an art of visual persuasion, graphic communication, and images. It is a situation in which the visual makes a statement to influence an audience (Olson, Finnegan, & Hope, 2008). For propaganda reasons, martyrdom videos are disseminated *en masse* by terrorist groups, especially after the suicide attack itself. The videos are made to keep the audience's memory (of the martyrs) fresh and to rationalize and applaud their actions. The videos are also created to 'lock' the martyrs-to-be by making sure they remain committed soldiers ready to perform their actions to the fullest. The suicide terrorists deliver a public pledge from which they cannot backpedal (Durodi, 2007).

Looking at jihadist martyrdom videos, it is clear that photos, Internet sites, speeches to encourage youths to embrace extreme forms of jihadist ideology, and cinematographic montages like those of the Baghdad Sniper—a so-called Islamist sniper, seen in propaganda videos, who has slain more than 600 US soldiers—all symbolize the high emphasis placed on emotive narratives. Emotive narratives are replete with emotional appeals and frequently mixed with pictures. In this context, in order to intensify resentment within the wider Muslim world, emotive narratives frame Muslims as mistreated or humiliated victims. These emotional appeals are often juxtaposed against still images of Muslims combating US soldiers in Iraq and Afghanistan, or resisting governmental forces in other conflicts such as those in Chechnya and Kashmir. The objective remains the same: to incite emotional responses and transform them into a political agenda (Wright-Neville & Smith, 2009).

The prevailing narratives in martyrdom videos, soundtracks, biographies, etc. revolve around three themes often shown in a sequence (i.e., like a three-act play). In the first act, the narrator describes the abject humiliation and suffering wreaked on Muslims (e.g., in Iraq and other countries). It points toward a conspiracy by the Western 'crusaders' to destroy Muslims and render them responsible for their own predicament. In the second act, the narrator emphasizes the incompetence of present-day Muslim governments and their connivance with the West. This suggests that they endanger the Muslim world by answering to their Western 'masters.' In the third and final act, the narrator promises Muslim victory thanks to martyrs who have trained hard to redress the grief and humiliation of their fellow brothers and sisters. In this process, the narrator stresses the importance of faith in Allah, sacrifice in jihad, and morality in the martyrs' cause. At times, the three narratives are presented separately. At other times, they are staged together to expose a major issue, the root of the problem, and what can be done to solve the problem (Hafez, 2007). By lifting up the martyrs to the status of eternal or extraordinarily moral souls who sacrifice their lives for Allah and the Muslim community, jihadist terrorists generate social noise by (i) averting attention away from their own evil deeds and (ii) ignoring the victims they harm.

EFFECTS OF SUICIDE TERRORISM ON THE AUDIENCE

This section describes the impact of suicide terrorism on the public at large. In addition to providing a comprehensive overview of what 'audience' means, the author deems important to examine that concept even further by looking at a case study: the 1983 Hezbollah suicide bombing against US Marines in Beirut. In this particular instance, eight types of audience were identified.

The Audience: Definition

A key principle of any communication undertaking is to understand the concept of audience. By and large, an audience refers to a group of individuals participating in an event. They do it passively (e.g., by simply being present at an event or attending to a message sent by a sender) or actively (e.g., by intentionally participating in the event or giving feedback to the sender of a message). In any case, the audience represents the interpretive community that reacts or responds to a message (Comer & Kendall, 2007). In previous sections, the argument was made that suicide terrorism is inherently a communicative message. Suicide terrorists communicate by means of the actions they take. The communication that goes on between terrorists and their audiences constitutes a dialogue. This dialogue lays the groundwork for what terrorists want to do or say. Suicide terrorists participate in a dialogue with their audiences beyond their direct targets, both within and outside the group (Gressang, 2001). As the case study on the 1983 Hezbollah suicide bombing will reveal, the terrorists' message tends to change for each audience, even when only one terrorist act has been committed.

Initiating a dialogue with an audience or various audiences is an indication that terrorists, in general, attempt to cause change. For instance, they may try to alter policies, to press for a particular action or series of actions, to delay or inhibit enactment of policy, to galvanize support or compassion, to persuade people to behave in certain ways, or to freeze the audience into inertia. Terrorists communicating with an audience have a positivist attitude as they expect that their message be received, fathomed, and acted upon. To engage in such type of dialogue, terrorists rely on interaction with the audience (Gressang, 2001).

Hence, the audience becomes the public character of terrorism. Suicide terrorism takes on the trait of spectacular public action to influence the psychological and emotional condition of the audience observing the attack. The objective is to trigger, in the audience, a state of anxiety or a feeling of horror. The audience becomes both the second party (direct target of the message) and the third party (target beyond the direct target of the message) of terrorism. Suicide attacks can also be intentionally perpetrated against third parties that have no connections with terrorist groups and their agendas. Again, the terrorist groups' intentions are to coerce governments or other institutions into living up to the terrorist groups' demands (Vasilenko, 2005).

Case Study: Hezbollah Suicide Bombing at the US Barracks in Beirut

On October 23, 1983, during the Lebanese Civil War, two suicide bombers from Hezbollah, a Shi'ite terrorist group based in Lebanon, detonated truck bombs at US Marine barracks located in Beirut, killing 241 US and 58 French servicemen (Jaber, 1997). When such social noise occurs, the recipient can be a large audience—sometimes many large audiences. The suicide bombers secretly attacked Western servicemen to create a frightful state of mind in an audience different than the immediate victims. As this case study will demonstrate, suicide terrorism as social noise constitutes a breathtaking interaction of a social character with multiple meaningful audiences.

The Hezbollah suicide bombing at the US barracks in Beirut generated eight types of audiences. The first audience was the immediate recipient of that fatal suicide attack—those 241 US and 58 French servicemen physically present at the US Marine barracks (Norton, 2009). The second audience was the Lebanese public—that is, the locals who were present at the scene and shocked by the unremitting images of the message delivered to them over TV, on radio, and in print (i.e., newspapers and magazines). The Lebanese public was composed of onlookers—the large public at the site of the terrorist attack. These onlookers witnessed the dynamics of the incident, the general reactions to the tragedy, and political and media assessments of that tragedy (Hammel, 1985). In fact, according to Diaz and Newman (2006), a smoke cloud from the rubble of the bombed barracks could be seen by passengers at the Beirut International Airport (which was miles away from the tragic site).

The third audience consisted of important representatives of the US federal government who felt compelled to react to the Hezbollah suicide attack by sending messages of calmness and equanimity to the American people. The third audience also consisted of various officials, from Secretary of Defense Caspar Weinberger to US President Ronald Reagan (Yoshihara, 2010). The fourth audience was the whole horizon of media corporations. The media's response included coverage and evaluation of the terrorist message, as well as an internal discourse about what narratives on suicide bombing should be broadcast and how they should be reported to the public. Media pundits were the analysts who provided their interpretation of the suicide attack. They were key players because they offered perspectives of the tragedy and displayed labels for what is now the 'Shi'ite enemy.' Even in the context of terrorism, journalists are always in interaction with multiple audiences (Matusitz, 2012). According to Dougherty (1992), the volume of CBS and CNN news reports on the 1983 Hezbollah suicide attack was so high that, for one week, 50 percent of daily night news was devoted to the tragedy.

The fifth audience consisted of allies of the United States (e.g., France and the United Kingdom) or countries that might be neutral to terrorism (e.g., Sweden). After the suicide terrorist act, France launched an airstrike in the Bekaa Valley (east of Lebanon; Motley, 1986). The sixth audience was Hezbollah's own members. The attack boosted the prestige and growth of Hezbollah. Now, the Shi'ite terrorist group was seen by many as the "spearhead of the sacred Muslim struggle against foreign occupation" (Ranstorp, 1997, p. 38).

The seventh audience was an array of rival terrorist organizations. The terrorists' scheming of a multi-audience plot also takes intergroup competition into consideration. Rival terrorist organizations tend to have related goals, compete for funds and support, and try to gain attention, credit, stature, and new members. A significant undertaking like the 1983 Hezbollah suicide bombing would certainly become an efficient terrorist tactic to be emulated by other terrorist groups. Indeed, in the modern Islamist world, Hezbollah was innovative in suicide terrorism. A few years later, Al-Qaeda transferred his members to Hezbollah to receive adequate training. The collaboration between Al-Qaeda and Hezbollah is now a critical point in the diffusion of suicide attacks worldwide (Horowitz, 2010).

The eighth audience was the worldwide Muslim community. Hezbollah viewed the success of its suicide attack as a platform to communicate its global Islamic agenda. By transforming its suicide attack into social noise, Hezbollah effectively sent a message to the 'ummah.' In Arabic, the term 'ummah' refers to the global Muslim community (Brachman, 2008). The message was a call to put an end to Western domination worldwide and, eventually, replace it with a global Caliphate (Poole, 2011). According to Fisk (2002), a major motivation for the suicide attack was the extreme anger expressed by Lebanese Muslims, especially Shi'ites living in the slums of West Beirut and around the airport where the Marines were headquartered. They interpreted the presence of US Marines as an attempt to side with the Maronite Catholics in their domination of Lebanon, and as a violation of Muslims' sacred land.

DISCUSSION

What this analysis has demonstrated is that, through the concept of social noise, it is worthwhile to look at suicide terrorism from a purely communicative perspective. While some articles analyze the communication of suicide terrorism based on rhetoric and symbols, others tend to place emphasis merely on mass-mediated terrorism and framing. This is fine, but it fails to look at the core of communication *per se*. For example, the afore-mentioned case study on the 1983 Hezbollah suicide attacks on US Marines in Beirut has revealed that suicide terrorism for Hezbollah has become an important communicative message. For the past 30 years or so, suicide terrorism as social noise has been their 'signature method.' It is their recognizable *modus operandi*, so much so that they have influenced other groups like Al-Qaeda.

Suicide terrorists communicate through the actions they take. Thanks to the model developed in this analysis, readers now have a better understanding of how suicide terrorists are the senders of a collective message (e.g., 'we have been oppressed by the West') and how both the target audience and multiple subsequent audiences are the collective receivers of the terrorists' message—the audiences, then, construe the incident as a terrorist attack. As we have seen, as a specific type of suicide terrorism, martyrdom epitomizes the concept of social noise. For propaganda purposes, martyrdom videos are distributed in great numbers by terrorist groups like Hamas, especially after the suicide attack itself. Martyrdom is a communicative act intended to cause a response. Two key objectives are to galvanize the Muslim world and send a message of threat or warning to the infidels. Since communication is an interactive process between the sender and the receiver, it follows that the suicide terrorist is the creator of social noise and the target audience is the receiver of what has now become public disorder. Various forms of communication can serve as a conduit for carrying the suicide terrorists' motives. Examples are mass-mediated images, online videos, and so forth.

It is the author's hope that this chapter has enlightened readers on this new perspective of suicide terrorism research. Until we acknowledge and understand the primacy of communication within suicide terrorism, we will not be fully aware of this communicative impact on our very existence.

REFERENCES

Atran, S. (2006). The moral logic and growth of suicide terrorism. *The Washington Quarterly, 29*(2), 127–147.

Berlo, D. K. (1960). *The process of communication: An introduction to theory and practice.* New York: Holt, Rinehart and Winston.

Brachman, J. M. (2008). *Global jihadism: Theory and practice.* New York: Routledge.

Cahm, C. (2002). *Kropotkin: And the rise of revolutionary anarchism, 1872–1886.* Cambridge: Cambridge University Press.

Caracci, G. (2002). Cultural and contextual aspects of terrorism. In C. E. Stout (Ed.), *The psychology of terrorism: Theoretical underpinnings and perspectives* (pp. 57–83). London: Praeger.

Carlson, J. R. (1995). The future terrorists in America. *American Journal of Police, 14*(3), 71–91.

Cherrington, D. J. (1994). *Organizational behavior.* Boston, MA: Allyn and Bacon.

Comer, J. S., & Kendall, P. C. (2007). Terrorism: The psychological impact on youth. *Clinical Psychology: Science and Practice, 14*(3), 179–212.

Diaz, T., & Newman, B. (2006). *Lightning out of Lebanon: Hezbollah terrorists on American soil.* New York: Presidio Press.

Dougherty, B. J. (1992). *Media handling of sensitive military information.* Washington, DC: National Defense University.

Douzinas, C. (2008). July 2, July 7 and metaphysics. In A. Closs Stephens & N. Vaughan-Williams (Eds.), *Terrorism and the politics of response* (pp. 190–210). Abingdon, Oxfordshire: Routledge.

Durodi, B. (2007). Fear and terror in a post-political age. *Government & Opposition, 42*(3), 427–450.

Fisk, R. (2002). *Pity the nation: The abduction of Lebanon.* New York: Nation Books.

Gressang, D. S. (2001). Audience and message: Assessing terrorist WMD potential. *Terrorism and Political Violence, 13*(3), 83–106.

Hafez, M. M. (2006). Suicide terrorism in Iraq: A preliminary assessment of the quantitative data and documentary evidence. *Studies in Conflict and Terrorism, 29*(6), 591–619.

Hafez, M. M. (2007). Martyrdom mythology in Iraq: How jihadists frame suicide terrorism in videos and biographies. *Terrorism and Political Violence, 19*(1), 95–115.

Hammel, E. (1985). *The root: The marines in Beirut, August 1982–February 1984.* New York: Harcourt.

Hareven, A. (1983). Victimization: Some comments by an Israeli. *Political Psychology, 4*(1), 145–155.

Horowitz, M. C. (2010). Nonstate actors and the diffusion of innovations: The case of suicide terrorism. *International Organization, 64*(1), 33–64.

Jaber, H. (1997). *Hezbollah: Born with a vengeance.* New York: Columbia University Press.

Martin, G. (2010). *Understanding terrorism: Challenges, perspectives, and issues.* Thousand Oaks, CA: SAGE.

Masterson, J. F. (1981). *The narcissistic and borderline disorders: An integrated developmental approach.* New York: Routledge.

Matusitz, J. (2012). *Terrorism & communication: A critical introduction.* Thousand Oaks, CA: SAGE.

Miller, C., Matusitz, J., O'Hair, D., & Eckstein, J. (2008). The role of communication and the media in terrorism. In D. O'Hair, R. Heath, K. Ayotte, & G. R. Ledlow (Eds.), *Terrorism: Communication and rhetorical perspectives* (pp. 43–66). Cresskill, NJ: Hampton Press.

Motley, J. B. (1986). International terrorism: A challenge for U.S. intelligence. *International Journal of Intelligence and Counter Intelligence, 1*(1), 83–96.

Murray, S. (2006). Thanatopolitics: On the use of death for mobilizing political life. *Polygraph: An International Journal of Politics and Culture, 18*, 191–215.

Norton, A. R. (2009). *Hezbollah: A short history*. Princeton, NJ: Princeton University Press.
Olson, L. C., Finnegan, C. A., & Hope, D. S. (2008). *Visual rhetoric: A reader in communication and American culture*. Thousand Oaks, CA: SAGE.
Pape, R. A. (2005). *Dying to win*. New York: Random House.
Pedahzur, A. (2004). *Suicide terrorism*. New York: Polity.
Poole, J. J. (2011). *Global warrior: Averting WWIII*. Chevy Chase, MD: Posterity Press.
Ranstorp, M. (1997). *Hizb'allah in Lebanon: The politics of the western hostage crisis*. New York: Palgrave Macmillan.
Saad, R. (2001, December 13). Weapons of the weak. *Al-Ahram Weekly*, Issue No. 564, p. A1. Retrieved from http://www./weekly.ahram.org.eg/2001/564/index.htm
Sageman, M. (2008). A strategy for fighting international Islamist terrorists. *Annals of the American Academy of Political and Social Science, 618*(1), 223–231.
Saunders, D. (1998). *Shock in advertising*. London: B.T. Batsford.
Schafer, R. M. (1994). *The soundscape: Our sonic environment and the tuning of the world*. Rochester, VT: Destiny Books.
Schmid, A. P., & de Graaf, J. (1982). *Violence as communication: Insurgent terrorism and the Western news media*. Beverly Hills: SAGE.
Schweitzer, Y. (2007). Palestinian Istishhadia: A developing instrument. *Studies in Conflict & Terrorism, 30*(8), 683–685.
Simonson, P. (2001). Social noise and segmented rhythms: News, entertainment, and celebrity in the crusade for animal rights. *The Communication Review, 4*(3), 399–420.
Tuman, J. S. (2003). *Communicating terror: The rhetorical dimensions of terrorism*, 1st ed. Thousand Oaks, CA: SAGE.
Tuman, J. S. (2010). *Communicating terror: The rhetorical dimensions of terrorism*, 2nd ed. Thousand Oaks, CA: SAGE.
Vasilenko, V. I. (2005). The concept and typology of terrorism. *Statutes and Decisions, 40*(5), 46–56.
Williams, J. J. (1998). The failure of terrorism as mass communication. *Turkish Journal of Police Studies, 1*(4), 37–52.
Wright-Neville, D., & Smith, D. (2009). Political rage: Terrorism and the politics of emotion. *Global Change, Peace & Security, 21*(1), 85–98.
Yoshihara, S. (2010). *Waging war to make peace: U.S. intervention in global conflicts*. Westport, CT: Praeger.

5

'Mumbai Style': Exploration of a Concept

Mark Dechesne

For some, it has become the image associated with the newest threat posed by jihadis the world over (e.g., Crumley, 2008; Hayden, 2012). For others, it can be more "accurately described by specifying the number of attackers, weapons, tactics, and targets" (NCTC, 2012). But rightfully or wrongly, since Mumbai's days of terror of the last week of November 2008, 'Mumbai Style' has emerged as a prominent concept in the analysis of modern-day terrorism. It has been authoritatively described as:

> *suicidal, in the sense that the boys recruited to carry them out undertake reckless, gun-spraying penetrations of a type that make it very unlikely that they will emerge alive. Also, the assaults usually don't involve getaway plans or tactical exit strategies other than martyrdom. At the same time, these are not "suicide attacks" in the sense that the attackers don't wire themselves up as human bombs. The guerrillas will [...] fight for as long as they can and finally accept their fates at the hands of opposing security forces.* (Coll, 2008)

Given these features, 'Mumbai Style,' otherwise described as *fedayeen* attacks, pose a challenge; a challenge not only for security and intelligence but also for social scientists, trying to grasp the driving forces behind acts of extreme violence, sacrifice, or the combination of both. Clearly, as the words of Steve Coll suggest, it makes perfect sense to both tie *fedayeen* attacks to other forms of suicide terrorism. Yet, it makes equal sense to set them apart, both from tactical and psychological perspectives. This chapter, in the light of the general aim of this volume to come an understanding of suicide terrorism, seeks to do just that: to specify the place of

'Mumbai Style' amidst non suicide and suicide terrorism. In doing so, it seeks to contribute to the sense-making of this horrific terrorist tactic, and to the development of effective countermeasures.

SIXTY HOURS OF TERROR IN MUMBAI[1]

On the evening of the November 21, 2008, a crew of 10 members of the militant organization Lashkar-e-Taiba (LET), leaves the harbor of Karachi. After almost two days on sea, the 10 hijack the Kuber, an Indian trawler, killing four crewmen, and head for Mumbai. On November 26, once close to the Indian coast, the 10 kill the navigator of the trawler, and use inflatable speedboats to make landfall near Cuffe Parade, Mumbai. The militants split up and continue in five groups of two. All groups keep in contact with each other and planners of the attacks in Pakistan.

Somewhat over an hour after landing, a first team reaches Leopold Café by taxi, a bar and well-known hangout place for foreign tourists. The two militants use their AK-47 automatic rifles and hand grenades to attack the unsuspecting bar attendants, killing 11 and seriously wounding 28. They then make their way to the Taj Mahal Hotel, and enter the hotel through the rear entrance. Both before their assault on Leopold Café and after, the duo plant improvised explosive devices (IED) made of Research Department Explosive (RDX). The ones planted after the attack on the café are successfully defused, but an IED planted in the taxi that brought the duo to the café later explodes, killing two passengers and the taxi driver, and wounding 19 bystanders.

At the Taj Mahal Hotel, the duo meets up with a second team that enters through the main entrance of the hotel. The four militants move around in the hotel, and use their AK-47s and hand grenades to kill as many hotel guests as possible. They also use RDX explosives to damage the characteristic central dome of the hotel, and set fire on the 6th floor. The militants kill 36 hotel guests, and leave 28 wounded. The events in the Taj Mahal Hotel become the focal point of worldwide media attention. According to the charge

---

[1] This description is based on the charge sheet filed by the Mumbai Police (2009) and Baweja (2009).

sheet by the Mumbai police on the Mumbai attacks, the terror at the Taj Mahal Hotel lasted for 59 hours, before National Security Guard Commandoes, at the expense of several of its members, could subdue the militants and secure the grounds.

Upon landing, a third team reaches Nariman House by foot. Nariman House has been renamed by its orthodox Jewish owners as Chabad House, and serves as a cultural center for the Jewish community in Mumbai. Before entering the building, the two militants plant two IEDs, one on a main road near Nariman House, and the other at the ground level of the building. Both explode. The militants keep some of the residents as hostage, and force a hostage to speak to the Israeli embassy over phone. The militants also seek to establish contact with the media and allegedly receive live coverage from 'India TV.' While keeping an eye on their hostages, they use their AK-47s and hand grenades to attack people in nearby buildings. Five residents who are taken hostage, all Israeli citizens, die during the attacks, while four Indians, including a National Security Guard Commando, are killed outside the building. Seven people are injured.

A fourth team attacks the Hotel Trident and Oberoi Hotel. In Mumbai, the Hotel Trident and the Oberoi hotel are two separate buildings connected by a passage. The team responsible for the attacks on these buildings arrives by boat near the hotels, and enters the main hall of the Trident Hotel. This happened after an attempt to ignite an IED near the entrance of the hotel failed. The duo kills many guests and hotel personnel upon their entrance in the main hall, and then finds their way to the higher floors of the hotel where they fight for 42 hours with security forces until their death. During the fight, the duo keeps regular contact with planners in Pakistan, while also spreading false information about the militants' intention to the media. Thirty-five are killed, and 24 are wounded in this part of the attack.

A fifth team causes the greatest number of casualties. Upon landfall, the duo, with the only surviving militant Ajmal Kasab among them, move from the landing site to CST railway station by taxi. While in the taxi, they plant an IED under the seat of the driver. Upon arrival at the station, they plant another IED, before entering the main hall of the station. Their AK-47 gunfire and hand grenades kill 52 unsuspecting civilians and police guards, wounding another 108. After the shooting spree at the station, they leave the train station continuing to shoot innocent civilians. The duo enters the Cama Hospital, located nearby the train station, killing seven and injuring ten, among them police officers that sought to protect the hospital. The militants then leave the hospital and engage in a firefight with senior police, killing three and wounding four. This shooting also wounds Ajmal Kasab. The duo then takes hold of the police car and drives through Mumbai center, while shooting indiscriminately, killing another nine and wounding seven. When the car becomes uncontrollable because of two punctures, the duo hijacks a civilian vehicle, a Skoda, and continues its way. Yet, by this time, the police had identified the vehicle and had put up roadblocks to stop it. At one of the roadblocks, at Girgaum Chowpatty, the Skoda is stopped, and after a fight that also caused the death of an Indian policeman, the two militants are wounded and arrested. Only Ajmal Kasab survives his injuries, and can provide a first-hand account of the events. Meanwhile, the IED that was planted under the seat of the taxi had also exploded, killing the driver and a passenger.

WHAT IS BEHIND THE ATTACKS?

The horrific attacks of November 2008 in Mumbai have left 166 citizens dead and another 304 wounded. Within the decade that saw terrorism reach the forefront of public awareness, the Mumbai attacks stand out in terms of their brutality, complexity of operation, and together with others, their lethality, and media and scholarly coverage (cf., e.g., a RAND report by Rabasa et al., 2009). Also, compared to other attacks, quite a number of sources are available to analyze the background of the attacks. First, through the confessions of the surviving militant Ajmal Kasab, we get a sense of the preparations, and motivations, and mindset of the militants involved. Second, through intelligence, most of the conversations between the militants and their planners in Pakistan have been recorded, providing a unique insight in the operation and the mindset of the militants. Third, because the Mumbai attacks happened seven years after the suicide attacks in New York and Washington, DC sparked a worldwide interest in the topic of terrorism; scholarly insights have advanced up to the point that the Mumbai attacks can be put in broader perspective.

The Individual Perpetrator

Through the first-hand interrogations with Ajmal Kasab, we get an understanding of the drivers of the individual perpetrators (e.g., Khetan, 2009). The story of Kasab can be generalized, more or less, to all militants involved in the Mumbai killings.

Born as the middle child among five siblings, Kasab grew up in a small town in the Pakistani province of Punjab. Like others from his village, his parents had a hard time to make ends meet. After leaving school at the age of 13, Kasab first worked in his home village and then left for Lahore to stay with his brother. He briefly returned to his home village and then moved to Lahore again. In this major city, Kasab found a job but failed to make a living. He increasingly got involved in petty crimes. In his confession to the crime branch of the Mumbai police force, he stated that he decided to join the terrorist organization LET in order to get access to weaponry that allowed him to be more effective in his raids. But LET provided more than weapons training. It also taught radical versions of Islam, and provided services and support to its members and their families. Of importance, it has also provided a narrative that legitimizes terror. According to Kasab's recollections, the leader of the organization, Hafiz Sayeed, would lecture the recruits "that Muslims worldwide need to rise in jihad against the infidels' and if [they] would die waging jihad, [their] faces would glow like the moon. [Their] bodies would emanate scent. And [they] would go to paradise" (Khetan, 2009; p. 165; the original text uses we instead of they). But beyond the global jihad, there has also been a more local political agenda. According to Kasab, a jihadi preacher at the training center would proclaim "you are Muslims. You have to get rid of poverty. Look at India. They have raced ahead of us. They kill your people. You have to wage jihad against India."

The Organization

In a remarkable twist of events, the conversations between the militants in Mumbai and their handlers in Pakistan have been recorded. These recordings provide unique insight in the mindset of the killers on the ground (see e.g., Zakaria et al., 2010). Moreover, the recordings provide an indication of the level of sophistication of these attacks. From them, one may infer that the attacks were meticulously organized, planned, and monitored over long distance. There are also other indications to that effect. A forensic report by the New York Police Department (Kelly, 2009), for example, noted that:

> They fired in controlled, disciplined bursts. When our liaisons toured the hotels and railways stations, they saw from bullet holes that shots were fired in groups of three aimed at head level. With less experienced shooters, you'd see bullet holes in the ceiling and floor. This group had extensive practice. And the number of casualties shows it. Ten terrorists managed to kill or injure over 500 people. They were experienced in working together as a unit. For example, they used hand signals to communicate across loud and crowded spaces. And they were sufficiently disciplined to continue their attack over many hours. This had the effect of increasing the public's fear and keeping the incident in the news cycle for a longer period of time.

This observation is also corroborated by Kasab's confession (see Khetan, 2009), in which he alluded to extensive and phased training, starting from religious teachings and basic weapons training to more advanced tactical and operational practice.

The level of sophistication of the attacks and its preparation should not come as a surprise when taking into account they were carried out by LET. Tankel (2011) traces the origins of this organization to 1986 when 'Markaz al-Dawa was-Irshad' (Center for Preaching and Guidance) was founded in Afghanistan by two Pakistani anti-Soviet insurgents, Zaki-ur Rehman Lahkvi and Hafiz Saeed. The two sought to unify a Pakistani Islamist movement called 'Ahl-e-Hadith' (People of the Hadith) through the provision of social services for members and armed struggle in relation to unbelievers. The militant unit of the organization, named LET (Army of the Pure), was officially established in 1990. Although dedicated to the global jihad, the main focus of the organization has been the Kashmir dispute. Throughout the 1990s, LET became an important instrument of the Pakistani Inter-Services Intelligence (ISI) to advance Pakistan's claims on Kashmir. According to Tankel, the LET received substantial support from the ISI to set up its social services in Pakistan (thereby increasing the social support) and to improve their tactical and operational military skills. The support from the ISI also allowed them to use Pakistan as a safe haven from which to operate. These means of support, in addition to the combat experience and training of many of the LET members during the conflict in Afghanistan of the 1980s, made LET into a formidable military organization (see also Coll, 2004).

The Attack Style

Although labeled as 'Mumbai Style,' the complex LET military operation that was carried out in Mumbai had been used before. On the basis of Rana (2004), Tankel (2011) claims it to have emerged as a response to peace talks between India and Pakistan in the wake of the 1999 Kargil conflict (see also Marwah, 2009). Such peace talks posed an existential threat to LET, which owed its existence to the conflict in Kashmir. On July 12, 1999, teams of two to five *fedayeen*s carried out an assault on an Indian Border Security Force camp in Northern Valley of Kashmir, throwing hand grenades and firing automatic machine guns, and fighting until their death. The goal of the assault teams was to maximize damage and instill fear (Tankel, 2011). In a broader strategic context, the goal was to escalate the, at that time, de-escalating violence in Kashmir. With apparent success, the attacks helped the LET to gain support; other groups entered in a competition for the most spectacular and deadly attacks. Most notably, Jaish-e-Mohammed went even further than the LET, introducing suicide attacks to the Kashmir conflict. In the first years of the twenty-first century, LET carried out several high profile *fedayeen* attacks, including an attack on the ground of the Red Fort in New Delhi in December 2000, and in the following months, attacks on the airport and a police station in Srinagar, killing five Indians or more on both occasions. In all these cases, the perpetrators used a coordinated attack with hand grenades and machine guns to inflict maximum casualties.

'Mumbai Style' in Broader Perspective

Although the Mumbai attacks may be characterized as the evolved signature of the LET, some have cautioned against a label suggesting a link between the type of attack and the place or the group. The National Counterterrorism Centre of the US Department of Statement (NCTC, 2012) argues that

> *conventional terrorist attacks can be accurately described by specifying the number of attackers, weapons, tactics, and targets rather than using terms such as 'commando' or 'Mumbai-Style,' and provides a table of 'similar' attacks, including an assault on US military personnel in Frankfurt in 2011, an assault by 'fewer than five attackers' on a hotel in Mogadishu in 2010, and the Beslan middle school assault and hostage taking by 30 attackers in 2004.*

However, from the table, it is not directly obvious what ties these cases together, in terms of weapons used, the targets, or the general description of the attacks.

WHAT, THEN, IS MUMBAI STYLE?

The labeling of the events in Mumbai remains subject to debate. Some have suggested that the attacks can be classified in terms of broader categories, for example, 'armed assault' or given the number of casualties, as 'mass casualty terrorism.' Yet, the Mumbai attacks turn out to be an extreme case on a number of independent dimensions. In fact, 'Mumbai' is an extreme case on so many dimensions, that it is perhaps more accurate to assign a separate label to the attacks, rather than considering it an extreme case of a general category of terrorist acts. How then, can this 'Mumbai Style' be characterized? On the basis of the foregoing analysis, I propose that the combination of four characteristics make the attacks unique. These characteristics can be conveniently characterized by four 'C's': conviction, coordination of attacks, combination of attack methods, and communication.

Conviction

A clear characteristic of the Mumbai attacks has been the willingness of the perpetrators to fight until their death. Given the strength of the perpetrators relative to the defenders of the city, death or capture seem to be the only feasible outcomes. Indeed, the very word *fedayeen* means 'those who sacrifice' in Arabic. An essential element of these attacks, then, is the conviction that one's deeds outweigh the considerable sacrifice. This has also been noted by one of LET's foremost ideologues, Abdur Rahman Makki (2004), who in discussing *fedayeen* attacks observes:

> The Fidayee activity—therefore, constitutes launching a forceful attack on the enemy and throwing a real challenge to it thus displaying firmness of faith-demonstrating both to Allaah وتَ عالٰ ى سبحانه *and His people the courage and valor with which a Believer sacrifices his life for the cause of Islam. This unparalleled sense of sacrifice and love for martyrdom serve as a deterrent of the enemy, forcing him to retreat.*

Coordination of Attacks

A second feature of 'Mumbai' concerns the coordination of the attacks. The attack involved the coordination between duos within an attack team, the coordination between five attack teams, and the coordination between the attack teams and handlers in Pakistan. Coordination between elements has clear tactical advantages. It allows to stay on the offense for a prolonged period of time. Also, in analyses of the Mumbai attack, it is frequently observed that security forces had difficulty deciding where to go as a result of the simultaneous activity of the perpetrators (e.g., Rabasa et al., 2009). Moreover, coordinated attacks convey planning, deliberation and commitment and thereby contribute to the credibility of the organization.

Combination of Attack Methods

A third striking feature of the Mumbai attacks concerns the combination of weapons used. The attacks involved automatic rifles, IEDs, and grenades. Some explosives detonated long after the attackers planted them, while many casualties were caused by direct gunfire. In addition, the attacks involved killings, hijackings, and movement with boats, hijacked cars, as well as prolonged fortification. Indeed, the attacks seem to include the entire repertoire available to terrorists, perhaps with the notable exception of weapons of mass destruction.

Communication

Last here, but certainly not least, communication played a critical role in the Mumbai attacks. In fact, communication played a role in multiple ways. First, communication was critical in the coordination of the attacks, and the follow-up planning by the handlers and attackers on the ground. Second, it allowed the handlers to use reporting on television to give tactical advice and encouragement. Third, the attackers used communication to reach out to diplomatic representatives and the general audience. The hijackers in Chabad House were able to contact representatives from the Israeli diplomatic service and appeared on national television. Fourth, during these communications, disinformation was spread to further confuse security forces and the general public.

'MUMBAI STYLE' RELATIVE TO SUICIDE AND OTHER ASSORTED FORMS OF TERRORISM

Now that 'Mumbai Style' has been defined in terms of four characteristics, we can turn to the issue raised at the outset of this chapter: What is the place of 'Mumbai Style' amidst non suicide and suicide terrorism? I propose that this place can best be determined by focusing on the differences along the dimensions just specified.

At first sight, Mumbai Style appears to have more in common with the *conviction* involved in suicide terrorism than in 'conventional,' non suicide terrorism. To be sure, conviction plays a role in all forms of terrorism. Defined broadly as violence for political or ideological purposes, terrorism virtually always implicates a readiness to hurt others in the service of one's own ideals; something that requires a considerable amount of conviction that one's own interests outweigh others' well-being. Yet, the degree of self-sacrifice in the service of this conviction varies. As already alluded to by LET ideologue Abdur Rahman Makki, Mumbai Style involves 'unparalleled sense of sacrifice and love for martyrdom,' perhaps even more than suicide terrorism whereby death is acute rather than the end of prolonged fighting.

Still, it should be emphasized that Mumbai Style is not the same as suicide terrorism. Abdur Rahman Makki (2004) writes:

a Fidayee action is not suicide it is not killing oneself. It is only a style of fighting.

And then continues:

It is the basic difference between a Muslim Fidayee and a suicidal mind that even under the most critical circumstances, a Fidayee would like to be killed by an infidel or unbeliever.

Thus, the critical difference between a suicide terrorist and the terrorist involved in Mumbai Style is that the former kills him/herself, while the latter avoids death until others impose it on him or her. In terms of contemporary motivational psychology (Higgins, 1998), when it comes to death, the suicide terrorist acts out of a promotion focus, while the Mumbai Style terrorist aims to prevent death.

This discussion ties in with an observation made by the RAND report (Rabasa et al., 2009) on the Mumbai attacks, noting differences in 'framing' of suicide terrorism and Mumbai Style. Whereas in the former, the terrorist act is typically framed as a religious sacrifice performed by a believer, the latter is framed as an act of a soldier acting with firm belief (although ironically the sacrifice made in *fedayeen* attacks have been hailed as more in accordance with Islam, since Islam forbids suicide). Relative to suicide and 'conventional' non suicide terrorism, then, Mumbai Style shares with suicide terrorism an emphasis on unbreakable conviction. Yet, it shares with the non suicidal forms of terrorism an emphasis on a military rather than religious form of heroism.

Although *coordination of attacks* can be considered a defining feature of Mumbai Style, this notion may not be particularly helpful in distinguishing it from the two other forms of terrorism under consideration. Coordinated attacks have become a hallmark characteristic of organized jihadi inspired terrorism, yet they are not exclusive to this category of terrorism. One also finds coordinated attacks among other organized but non jihadi organizations, most notably the Revolutionary Armed Forces of Columbia (FARC) in Columbia and the Shining Path in Peru. As a hypothesis, perhaps coordination is of greater importance to suicide terrorism and Mumbai Style than to other forms of terrorism. Social psychology shows that like-minded others play a critical role in bolstering beliefs (Festinger, 1954; Kruglanski, 2004), and given the considerable sacrifice that suicide terrorism and Mumbai Style entails, sharing the attacks with like-minded others may be a powerful tool to bolster the conviction required to make this sacrifice. The recorded conversations between the attackers in Mumbai and their handlers in Pakistan reveal that psychological support and encouragement are indeed prominent features.

Whereas Mumbai Style may have more in common with suicide attacks than conventional attacks when it comes to coordination, in terms of the *combination of weapons* used, the situation is reversed; it has more in common with conventional attacks. The very nature of the act of suicide terrorism poses considerable restrictions on the weapons of choice, and combining multiple weapons during a suicide operation seems unpractical (and too psychologically demanding). Suicide terrorism, with rare exceptions, involves the use of explosives only. Of interest, it has been noted that the Mumbai attacks could happen because Indian security forces were focused on bombs (Rabasa et al., 2009), partly in response to the Mumbai train bombings of July 2006. With this heightened scrutiny of bomb threats, suicide bombings may have been considered less feasible by the planners of the 2008 attacks. Thus, the combined use of conventional weaponry may have contributed the feasibility of Mumbai Style.

The similarity between Mumbai Style and conventional terrorist attacks and the dissimilarity between Mumbai Style and suicide terrorism are perhaps most pronounced when the role of *communication* is concerned. In suicide terrorism, beside the act itself, there is no communication. In contrast, in conventional terrorism, most notably in the case of hostage taking, communication could play an important role. In Mumbai Style, as outlined before, communication *has* an essential role. In the time span of 60 hours of the Mumbai attack, communication gave the attackers considerable advantages. It provided tactical flexibility and contingency planning through the communication lines between the attackers on the ground and their handlers monitoring the events on television. It also provided the attackers the opportunity to weigh in their perspective while public broadcasting sought to make sense of the events, and to confuse security forces. Finally, in Chabad house, communication with diplomatic representatives created negotiation leeway and hampered the counterattack of the security forces.

In sum, Mumbai Style can be considered closer to suicide terrorism than to conventional terrorism when it comes to conviction, although there are notable differences. Yet, when it comes to the combined use of weapons and communication, Mumbai Style appears to be closer to non suicidal terrorism. In this respect, the present analysis seems to converge with the notion that Mumbai Style is "terrorism with fused insurgency and guerilla warfare" (Crumley, 2008). It combines the psychological ardor associated with (religious) terrorism with the military tactical proficiency associated with insurgency and guerilla warfare.

HOW TO FIGHT MUMBAI STYLE

The present contribution sought to place the style associated with the attacks on Mumbai of 26/11 2008 in perspective relative to suicide terrorism and non-suicide terrorism. The analysis of the events, the perpetrators, the responsible organization, and trends in terrorism research, led to a characterization of 'Mumbai Style' in terms of four characteristics: strong conviction, thoroughly coordinated attacks, extensive combination of used weapons, and multifinal use of communication. It should be apparent that no single tactic will effectively fight this complex set of characteristics. Indeed, the following does not come with aspirations of a complete counterterrorism strategy against Mumbai Style. Yet, in closing, I suggest that the analysis provided in this chapter does point to three issues that might be taken into consideration when developing such strategy.

1. *The importance of attribution:* Since the days of November 2008, warnings for a 'Mumbai Style attack' have frequently popped up in governmental threat assessments and media throughout the world. Yet, in the absence of a clear description of the concept of Mumbai Style, such warnings provide little

guidance on how to counteract on the threat. As a concept, Mumbai Style has been used to describe threats ranging from shooting sprees by lone-wolf attackers to groups that would indiscriminately fire at innocent passers-by (e.g., Hayden, 2012). For such cases, however, attributing the threat as 'Mumbai Style' may be detrimental because several characteristics that make up Mumbai Style are lacking, and the sophistication of Mumbai Style would make it inappropriate to counteract on it with similar measures used to combat lone wolfs or indiscriminately shooting groups. In the case of lone wolfs, for example, communication or coordination, two essential features of Mumbai Style, are lacking. As will be noted below, these features may be critical in dealing with Mumbai Style, and lumping Mumbai Style and shooting sprees by individuals together can only be detrimental to effective counteraction. Thus, it seems critical to come up with a precise attribution when dealing with an emerging terrorist threat. A clearer conceptualization of Mumbai Style is essential in this context. The present chapter can be considered a step to that effect.

2. *Communication: Part of the problem, but possibly part of the cure:* The analysis provided in this chapter has put emphasis on communication. It has been identified as a key characteristic of Mumbai Style. Communication enables coordination between attack teams, tactical information exchange between attackers and handlers, the spreading of disinformation to security forces, and the creation of a narrative to the outside world. Indeed, given the central role of communication in Mumbai Style, one might wonder whether putting an extra effort in disrupting communication could serve as a very effective means to combat it. In this context, one might think of disabling the communication lines between the attackers, and the attackers and their handlers. Also, spreading disinformation could effectively disrupt the coordination in the attack, undermining their offensive advantage. Thus, in countering Mumbai Style, a comprehensive communication strategy may very well be a critical success factor.

3. *Contingency planning:* Unlike suicide terrorism, Mumbai Style involves prolonged fighting, and because of this, strategic contingency planning may be another critical ingredient to

effective counteraction. Indeed, the 'sixty hours' of Mumbai could have been taken as additional characteristic of Mumbai Style. The handlers' access to live coverage of attacks in combination with the communication capabilities of the handlers and attackers, allowed them to adjust the offensive plan as events unfolded. And this makes Mumbai Style different from, and perhaps therefore potentially more damaging than suicide terrorism. Defensive contingency planning can counteract on this threat, although at present, it is unclear how to give shape to such planning. For sure, getting into the minds of the perpetrators will be key asset in this context.

CONCLUSION

This chapter started with the observation that 'Mumbai Style' has emerged as a prominent concept in the analysis of modern-day terrorism. In scientific treaties on suicide terrorism, 'Mumbai Style' is of interest because it shares characteristics of both suicide terrorism and non suicide terrorism. Before addressing the similarities and differences with these two types of terrorism, it was deemed of importance to first consider the characteristics of 'Mumbai Style.' Four Cs were argued to characterize Mumbai Style: conviction, coordination of attacks, combination of attack methods, and communication. A comparison of Mumbai Style with suicide and nonsuicide categories of terrorist attacks led to the conclusion that when it comes to conviction, Mumbai Style is closer to suicide terrorism, yet when it comes to combined use of weapons and communication, Mumbai Style may have more in common with nonsuicide terrorism. The four C's of Mumbai Style also provide some points of attention in developing countermeasures. Attribution is critical to determine whether the notion of Mumbai Style is actually applicable. If it is applicable, a comprehensive communication strategy and contingency planning may very well constitute essential ingredients for an effective response.

REFERENCES

Baweja, H. (2009). *26/11: Mumbai attacked*. New Delhi: Lotus Collection.
Coll, S. (2004). *Ghost wars: The secret history of the Cia, Afghanistan, and Bin Laden, from the soviet invasion to September 10, 2001*. New York: The Penguin Press.
Coll, S. (2008, November 28). Decoding Mumbai. In *The New Yorker*. Retrieved on October 15, from http://www.newyorker.com
Crumley, B. (2008, November 29). The Mumbai attacks: Terror's tactical shift. In *Time*. Retrieved from http://www.time.com/time/printout/0,8816,1862795,00.html
Festinger, L. (1954). A theory of social comparison processes. *Human Relations*, 7(2), 117–140.
Hayden, T. (2012, September 3). Mumbai changed British anti-terror tactics. In *Poliquicks*. Retrieved from http://poliquicks.com/2012/09/03/mumbai-changed-british-anti-terror-tactics
Higgins, E. T. (1998). Promotion and prevention: Regulatory focus as a motivational principle. In M. P. Zanna (Ed.), *Advances in experimental social psychology* (Vol. 30, pp. 1–46). New York, NY: Academic Press.
Kelly, R. (2009). Lessons from the Mumbai. Testimony of police commissioner Raymond W. Kelly for the Senate Committee on Homeland Security & Governmental Affairs. Retrieved on October 15, 2012, from http://www.nyc.gov/html/nypd/html/pr/lessons_from_mumbai_terror_attacks.shtml
Khetan, A. (2009). Inflicting maximum damage and don't be taken alive: Karachi to Mumbai: Terror, step by step. In Harinder Baweja (Ed.), *26/11: Mumbai attacked* (pp. 116–137). New Delhi: Roli Books.
Kruglanski, A. W. (2004). *The psychology of closed mindedness*. New York: Psychology Press.
Makki, A. (2004). *Fedai missions*. Retrieved on October 26, 2012, from http://www.alhonain.com/english_lect/fidai_mission/fidai_missions_iii.htm
Marwah, V. (2009). *India in turmoil: Jammu & Kashmir, the Northeast and left extremism*. New Delhi: Rupa & Co.
Mumbai Police. (2009, February 25). Text of the charge sheet filed by the Mumbai terror attacks cases. In R. Basrar, T. Hoyt, R. Hussain, & S. Mandal (Eds.), *The 2008 Mumbai terrorist attacks: Strategic fallout* (RSIS Monograph No. 17). Retrieved from http://www.rsis.edu.sg/publications/monographs/Monograph17.pdf
NCTC. (2012). *Alternatives to "Mumbai-style" attacks*. Retrieved on October 15, 2012, from http://www.nctc.gov/site/technical/alternatives.html

Rabasa, A., Blackwill, R., Chalk, P., Cragin, K., Fair, C., Jackson, B., et al. (2009). *The lessons of Mumbai* (RAND occasional series paper). Retrieved on October 15, 2012, from http://www.rand.org/pubs/occasional_papers/2009/RAND_OP249.pdf

Rana, M. (2004). *Gateway to terrorism*. New Delhi: Minerva Press India Pvt Ltd.

Tankel, S. (2011). *Storming the world stage: The story of Lashkar-e-Taiba*. New York: Columbia University Press.

Zakaria, F., Matthews, E., Zaidi, H., Ronowicz, S., Appleby, T., Jackson, S., et al. (2010). *Terror in Mumbai* [Television Broadcast]. New York: HBO.

6

Suicide Bombings: Homicidal Killing or a Weapon of War?

Riaz Hassan

The eminent American political theorist Michael Walzer (2004, 2006) describes suicide bombings and terrorism homicidal killing and morally worse than killing in war:

> Terrorists are killers on a rampage, except that rampage is not just expressive of rage or madness: the rage is purposeful and programmatic ... the peculiar evil of terrorism is not only the killing of innocent people but also intrusion of fear into everyday life, the violation of private purposes, the insecurity of public spaces, the endless coerciveness of precaution.

Walzer's writings have been very influential in shaping the debate of the suicide bombings and bombers in the media. Walzer, however, is not alone in labeling suicide bombings as murderous killing (Berko, 2007).

In this chapter, I shall examine whether suicide bombings are homicidal killing, as argued by Walzer, or a weapon of war? This examination would involve exploration of several interrelated questions: Is suicidal bombing a form of suicidal behavior? If not, then should it be viewed as an act of murder or a weapon of war? To establish this, we must also ascertain the nature of war and killing in war, and distinguish war killing from murder. The answers to these questions would help to answering the question, whether suicide bombing is homicidal killing or a weapon of war. These questions are explored in the following discussion.

SUICIDE AND SUICIDE BOMBING

There is an emerging consensus among scholars that suicide attacks are qualitatively different from suicides. After a comprehensive review of relevant literature on the phenomenon of suicide bombing, Grimland, Apter, and Kerkhof (2006) conclude that social processes such as group dynamic, indoctrination, and political factors are decisive in analyzing this problem. They assert that in suicidal bombing, suicide is instrumental in the context of war, not in the context of psychopathology. The act of killing in warfare is more important to understanding suicidal terrorism than the act of suicide.

In another comprehensive review of the topic, Townsend (2007) concludes that suicide terrorism has a range of characteristics which, on close examination, are shown to be different from other suicidal behavior:

> *Suicide terrorists are not truly suicidal and that attempting to find commonalities between suicide terrorists and others who die by suicide is likely to be an unhelpful path for any discipline wishing to further understanding of suicidal behaviour. Equating actions and motivations of suicide terrorists with those of other suicides perhaps does something of a disservice to those individuals who die quietly; alone and with no murderous intent.*

The British–Palestinian psychiatrist Nadia Dabbagh (2005) in her study of suicide in Palestine shows that suicidal behavior in Palestinian society, like suicide in other societies, is caused by the relative degree of social integration, regulation and isolation, as well as social and cultural control and oppression of individuals in society. But suicide bombings by organizations like Hamas and Islamic jihad are targeted acts of resistance and weapons of the weak against an unjust and hated occupier of what the Palestinians regarded as their homeland.

Unlike suicide which evokes feelings of pity and sadness for the victims, suicide attacks evoke emotions of repulsion, fear, anger, and total disbelief that a human being can kill, in such a cold-blooded manner, innocent people who have done no harm to the perpetrator. The main difference between suicide bombing attacks and suicides is that in suicide bombing the primary intention of the act is murder, whereas the primary characteristic of suicide is the absence of murderous intent. In fact, the terrorist's suicide can be viewed as a byproduct of the attack. Typically, suicide attacks involve victims who are unknown to the killer. Moreover, most suicide attacks are carefully planned well in advance with the explicit intention of killing others who have no prior relationship with the suicide bomber (Dabbagh, 2005). Suicide bombing attacks are also different from homicide–suicide because of the temporal spacing of the acts of homicide and suicide. In suicide bombing, the acts are simultaneous (Barraclough & Harris, 2002; Marzuk, Tardiff, & Hirsch, 1992).

WAR AND WAR KILLING

According to ethnographic evidence war, organized lethal violence involving spatially and socially distinct groups is caused by economic factors (land, resources, and plunder), social factors (prestige, honor), revenge (for sufferings), and defense. The order of motives from most inclusive to least inclusive are: political control, economic gain, social status, and defense (Otterbein, 1970; Wright, 1942). The motives for going to war appear to differ according to the nature of the political system. Centralized political systems (states and chiefdoms) go to war for the purposes of achieving political control, conquering, and dominating a territory and its inhabitants to extract economic benefits. In contrast, tribes, bands, and non state groups do not make war to attain political control but for some combination of purposes which include revenge, defense, land, honor, and prestige (Kelly, 2000).

In modern political theory, war is organized violence and an instrument of the state. It is a legal activity when it fulfills certain conditions such as self-defense, fulfilling a treaty obligation toward a state that is being attacked or a humanitarian intervention to safeguard the existence of a political community threatened with either the elimination of the people or the coercive transformation of their way of life. Neither of these actions is morally acceptable. Under these conditions, war is legal and justifiable but only as a method of last resort after all alternatives have been exhausted. Additionally, the conduct of war is always subject to moral criticism and must not directly target civilians and economic infrastructures and must be proportional (Walzer, 2004).

These criteria give legitimacy to certain types of violence and stigmatize other types under the international law. But, as Asad (2007) has argued, the irony of the liberal West's culture of war is: on the one hand, the state's need to legitimize organized violence against a collective enemy (including civilians) and, on the other hand, the humanitarian desire to save human lives. While both war and terrorism are very explicit forms of death dealing, this criterion makes killing in war legitimate and killing by terrorism illegal (Walzer, 2004).

Much of the criticism of terrorism follows from these fundamental precepts of war in political theory. In war and terrorism, innocents are killed but what liberal political theory condemns in war is *excess* and in terrorism its *essence*. But whether state armies kill only those who are legitimately killable is partly what the rules of war address (Asad, 2007). While war, according to Walzer, is the method of last resort, the militants carrying out acts of terrorism against civilians have not been through the necessary steps to justify their actions as being a last resort and are thus not coerced into that action. In his eyes, it is not so easy to reach the last resort. To get there, one must indeed try everything and not just once but repeatedly; politics after all is an art of repetition (Walzer, 2004).

In short, war, an organized violence in which death of the 'other' is encoded in the planning, is the legitimate and legal prerogative of the state under certain conditions. Its legitimacy is grounded in the exclusive power of the state to impose punishments internally and externally. The violence is embedded in the very concept of liberty which is at the heart of liberal doctrine about the foundation of the political community which the state is empowered to defend. The concept presupposes that the morally independent individual's natural right to violent self-defense is yielded to the state and that the state becomes the sole protector of individual liberties denying to any agents other than the states the right to kill at home and abroad (Tuck, 1999). The right to kill is the right to behave in violent ways against citizens who break the original covenant and the uncivilized 'others' who pose a threat to the existence of civilized order and their killing provides security. This is done in the name of self-defense. The justifications of pre-emptive and preventive wars (like the ones in Iraq and Afghanistan) practiced by the modern state are embedded in this doctrine.

The doctrine of moral legitimacy and legality of war also stipulates that the state is coerced into taking this action as the method of last resort after all alternatives have been exhausted. Furthermore, the state armies engaged in war do not target civilian noncombatants. Does this logic of war also apply to terrorists insurgencies involved in suicide bombings? The following two case studies, one from the Palestinian and the other from Sri Lankan terrorist organizations may help us to answer this question.

PALESTINE

In the case of Palestine, terrorist organizations employing suicide bombings claim to be involved in retaliatory violence to defend their *political community* whose very survival is being threatened by Israeli occupation and expansion. If this continues, then it would inevitably lead to the dispossession of the Palestinian homeland amounting to their elimination as people and their way of life. The Palestinian terrorist organizations claim they are engaged in organized violence through suicide bombings only as the last resort and under absolute necessity.

For most Palestinians, violence is the only option to achieve the goal of an independent state. A Palestinian recruiter and trainer of suicide bombers is quoted as saying, "Jihad and resistance begin with the word, then with sword, then with the stone, then with the gun, then with planting bombs, then transforming bodies into human bombs" (Bloom, 2005). The pervasive sense of powerlessness among the Palestinians has made violence an all-powerful symbol of honor. At a profoundly symbolic level, martyrdom is the final and irrefutable statement of the group worth and dignity against, as seen by the Palestinians, an oppressive Israeli occupation. According to the late Hamas leader Dr Abdul Aziz Rantisi, a casualty of Israel's policy of targeted killing of Palestinian terrorist leaders, Hamas and Palestinian society in general believe, "becoming a martyr through suicide bombing is among the highest if not the highest, honour" (Argo, 2003). As regards to civilian death from Palestinian suicide bombings, there appears to be little concern over civilian immunity. For most Palestinians, there is no civilian immunity in Israel due to the universal conscription of men and women. Any civilian is either a current, past, or the future soldier. From this perspective, all Israelis are complicit in the immoral and illegal occupation of the West Bank and Gaza (Bloom, 2005).

Finally, suicide bombing is only one of the weapons used by the three Palestinian organizations engaged in suicide bombings against Israel, Hamas, Palestinian Islamic jihad, and the Al'Aqsa Martyrs Brigades. These organizations have deep rooted mass support in Palestinian society. Their violent confrontations with Israeli occupying forces are well organized and this especially applies to their suicide bombing operations which are well planned before they are executed. From this account, it would appear that Palestinian violence against Israel meets most if not all the attributes of war except one, that it is not carried out on behalf of a state but on behalf of a 'political community' which perceives its very existence and way of life under threat from Israeli occupation. Using Walzer's (2004) terminology, the Palestinian leaders confronted with a potential evil respond by doing evil for the protection of their political community.

Two most common explanations of Palestinian suicide bombings are: (i) they are acts of religiously motivated sacrifice in the form of a martyrdom operation, and (ii) they are acts of secular immortality. They represent opposite ends of the sacred-profane continuum. An eloquent exposition of the first explanation is to be found in the work of Strenski (2003). Drawing on the work of the Durkheimian school, he proposes that the phenomenon of suicide bombings is better understood through religious concepts of sacrifice and gift than through theories seeking to explain it as suicide. Sacrifice is not just a social deed but has a potent religious resonance that transforms it into something holy. In suicide bombing, Strenski argues, sacrifice of oneself is made as a gift to and for the nation or political community that sanctifies it. All Palestinian suicide bombers believe they are giving their lives for the Palestinian nation. Strenski's analysis thus implies that since sacrifice is the essence of religious subjectivity, violence is integral to it.

One can take at least two issues with Strenski's description of suicide bombing. Firstly, his argument is contrary to Durkheim's position. He was the first theorist to identify the social determinants of suicide and he would most certainly have classified suicide bombing within the category of altruistic suicide. Secondly, his description of the motive in terms of sacrifice offers a religious model by means of which suicide bombings can be identified as 'religious terrorism.' That appellation defines the bomber as morally underdeveloped—and therefore pre-modern—when compared with people whose civilized status is partly indicated by their secular politics and their private religion and whose violence is therefore in principle *disciplined, reasonable, and just* (Asad, 2007).

The second explanation describing Palestinian suicide bombings as acts of secular immortality has been offered by Jayyusi (2004) in which she links different types of violent acts as manifestations of different kinds of subjectivities. Jayyusi links Palestinian suicide bombing to a particular type of political subjectivity formed in the context of their relationship to particular power structures. Drawing from Carl Schmitt's idea of 'the state of exception' and Georgio Agamen's Homo Sacer, she concentrates on developing a larger politico-ideological field which includes Israeli policies of occupation and settlements, the Palestinian resistance and international development such as the Iranian Revolution and the Oslo accord.

Jayyusi argues that the Oslo accord was an attempt to institute a local authority over the Palestinians on behalf of the occupying Israeli state. Under the Oslo accord, the entire Palestinian population was held as a hostage to the policing performance of the Palestinian Authority. As the overarching state power Israel was at once beyond the Palestinian zones and yet sovereign over them, the Palestinian Authority under these conditions was caught in an irresolvable contradiction. On the one hand, it was seeking national sovereignty and on the other, conceding it indefinitely to the occupying power by agreeing unconditionally to carry out its policing function. In this power arrangement, something new emerged with the Oslo accord for the Palestinian population; something Jayyusi calls 'an imaginary of freedom' (Jayyusi, 2004).

This 'imaginary of freedom' made the Oslo accord acceptable to the Palestinians in spite of the misgivings of many and resulted in the significant decline in support for militant Islamic movements. In 1999, over 70 percent of Palestinians supported the Palestinian Authority led peace process and the support for suicide bombings declined to 20 percent. By 2003–2004, as it became clear that the inherent contradictions of Oslo would not produce conditions of

Palestinian liberation from Israeli occupation and paradoxically increased their daily humiliation at the Israeli army check points, and did not stop expansion of the Jewish settlements, the attitudes toward the Palestinian Authority shifted dramatically. The Palestinian Authority was seen as unable to stand up to Israeli power and its support among Palestinians plummeted to 22 percent and support for suicide bombings increased to 75 percent (Bloom, 2005).

The consequence was a sense of outrage because Oslo had created the hope that conditions would change but they never did. The Palestinian rage was the consequence of this blocking of the legal, political means of their liberation. As Arendt (1969) has pointed out, when legal political means are blocked, the possibility of acting politically which is part of what makes men individual and therefore human, is also blocked. That rage led to an action which offered them a secular form of immortality. The phenomenon of Palestinian suicide bombing is thus an expression of that secular immortality and not of religious zealotry.

SRI LANKA

The ethnic antagonisms, which arose over the Sri Lankan Tamil minority's agitation for economic, social, and cultural equality gradually gave rise to Sinhalese nationalism and Tamil ethnic chauvinism soon after the independence when the Sinhalese nationalists denied the multiethnic and multireligious character of Sri Lankan society and refused to accept the collective rights of minority groups. The discrimination became institutionalized in the new constitution in 1960s which excluded Tamils from government and other positions of authority, reducing their recruitment in government jobs from 41 percent in 1949 to 7 percent in 1963 while increasing Sinhalese proportions in the same period from 54 to 92. A quota system was imposed on Tamil students entering the universities.

The Tamils responded politically through the Federal Party and through nonviolent protests called Satyagraha but these efforts failed to meet their demands. By the 1970s, Tamils had started to agitate for a separate homeland and their protestations became increasingly violent. In the 1980s, they won some concessions and political rights but discrimination remained palpable. Among the organizations which emerged in this period was a radical group called Tamil National Tigers under the leadership of Vellupillai Prabhakaran, later renamed the Liberation Tigers of Tamil Eelam (LTTE). The main aim of LTTE was the establishment of a Tamil homeland in the northern and eastern provinces of Sri Lanka.

The Sri Lankan government responded to increasing Tamil militancy by promulgating the Prevention of Terrorism Act (PTA) in 1979. Instead of mitigating violence, the PTA escalated Tamil violence in the 1980s. The government responded with additional repressive countermeasures that led to a spiral of increasing brutality and tit for tat violence (Bloom, 2005). In response to the murder of one of their commanders, the LTTE operatives ambushed an army convoy killing 13 Sinhalese soldiers in Jaffna that triggered widespread mob violence killing hundreds of Tamils. New emergency regulations gave wide powers to security forces to kill and bury suspected terrorists without any judicial inquiries. The LTTE called these developments a pogrom against Tamils. After the riots, the government banned the main Tamil political party, pushing Tamils to the LTTE as their main voice.

The Tamil insurgency arose after the failure of other forms of political struggle. The powerful Sri Lankan state dominated by the Sinhalese majority employed the army to oppress the Tamil community. Gradually, the traditional 'homelands' of the Tamil minority became the 'war zones' in which life became increasingly harsh, unbearable, and violent. This gave rise to a widespread perception among the Tamils that their very existence as distinct ethnic and cultural community was being threatened. The LTTE began to employ suicide bombings effectively from 1987 in response to these developments and as a method of last resort. Although the LTTE was finally defeated in early 2009 by the Sri Lankan army, but its defeat has not discredited the ideology which gave rise to the Tamil insurgency.

These case studies demonstrate that the violence of suicide bombings was the method of last resort in both cases. Using indicators of what constitutes war from the above two case studies, we can infer that the LTTE and Palestinian terrorists organizations using suicide bombings in their violent conflicts with the Sri Lankan and Israeli states, respectively, are engaged in organized violence akin to war. The objective in both cases is the protection of a political community and its way of life facing mortal threat from their adversary. In both cases, the violence is organized and planned in which the death of the enemy is encoded. Suicide bombings in these organized violent conflicts are employed as a weapon of war by the militarily challenged and thus the resulting deaths of the combatants and civilians are akin to the casualties of war.

Surprisingly, in the case of war, Walzer (2004) does not apply the same stringent conditions to the state which he imposes on terrorists. Modern states have far greater capacity and capability to kill and destroy human lives than any terrorist organization in the world. For example, the aerial bombing of German civilians by the allied air force during World War II was legitimate but suicide bombing is terrorism. And as terrorism, it is an evil in need not of analysis and understanding but of moral condemnation and firm practical response.

Walzer (2004) believes that suicide bombings in Israel are immoral and evil because they are part of the Palestinian mission to destroy a sovereign political community. The assaults of the Israeli army and air force in the West Bank and Gaza are, therefore, preemptive self-defense and thus legitimate and justifiable. (And by this logic, the Sri Lankan army's attacks on the Tamils are legitimate and justifiable.) The construction of the Israeli–Palestinian conflict in these terms is a typical example of how the liberal intellectuals conceive of the difference between war and terrorism. The century-long history of the conflict, involving expansion on the one side and dispossession on the other, is set aside, and attention is directed instead at present feelings. For all their military strength, Israelis are portrayed as vulnerable and for the Palestinians the years of occupation have been years of disgrace.

This construction also invests the Israeli and Sri Lankan armies with the aura of defenders engaged in a just war against Palestinian and Sri Lankan suicide bombers. The principle that a political community experiencing fatal attacks and facing 'the coercive transformation of their way of life' has the right to defend itself does not appear to apply to the Palestinian and Tamil responses. Their resistance is perceived as engaging in morally unacceptable violence presumably because even after 50 years (and in the case of Palestinians even longer,) of unequal struggle they are not judged to have reached the state of the 'last resort' (Bloom, 2005).

KILLING IN WAR AND TERRORISM

As mentioned earlier, the difference between war killing and suicide bombing is that war is a legally sanctioned act which confers legitimacy on the ensuing killing but the killing perpetrated by unlicensed illegal terrorists is not legitimate. But what about the soldiers who are also taught to hate the enemy they are required to kill? The fact of killing being legally sanctioned is an abstract irrelevance. There are in fact remarkable similarities between war killing and terrorism.

Every war requires making the human killing machine efficient and effective. According to historian Joanne Bourke (1999), basic military training is aimed at making soldiers extremely brutal:

> *The most notorious training regimes were those conducted by the U.S. Marine Corps, but even in the other branches of the armed forces, violence was a common component of military training. In all these training programmes, the fundamental process was the same: individuals had to be broken down to be rebuilt into efficient fighting men. The basic tenets included depersonalization, uniforms, lack of privacy, forced social relationships, tight schedules, lack of sleep, disorientation followed by rites or reorganization according to military codes, arbitrary rules, and strict punishment. These methods of brutalization were similar to those carried out in regimes where men were taught to torture prisoners: the difference resided in the degree of violence involved, not its nature.*

Another account provided by Nordstrom (2004) describes the atrocities inflicted on civilians by the Sri Lankan soldiers in the war with the Tamil Tigers. A Sri Lankan army commander told Nordstrom:

> *It is crazy, it's completely crazy. I can't control my troops. It is awful up there. One of the soldiers (government, largely Sinhalese) is shot by a guerrilla (Tamil), or they run over a land mine, or a bomb explodes, and they go nuts. It's been building up and building up, and they just go wild. The guerrillas have long since melted away, and the soldiers turn their fury on the first available target. Of course, the only people around are*

civilians. They open fire on everyone, they destroy everything in sight, they rape, and torture people they catch on the street or in their homes, they lob bombs into homes and schools, markets and city streets. I've tried to stop them; I try to control the situation. I can't. None of us commanders can—though god knows some don't try. The troops just take off like this and there's no stopping them. We can't discipline them. We can't prosecute them. We can't dismiss them. We'd have no army left if we did. The situation up north is completely out of control, and there isn't a damn thing we can do about it.

One of the purposes of war is to wreck destruction on the enemy. The napalm bombing of Vietnam in the Vietnam War was devastating and the humiliation and torture committed in Abu Graib prison in Iraq were anything but humanitarian acts. The aim of the increasingly sophisticated warfare technology now used by the US and its allies in wars in Iraq and Afghanistan is to identify its targets more accurately to minimize collateral damage and above all to minimize its own casualties. "This humanitarian concern means that soldiers need no longer go to war expecting to die but only to kill" (Asad, 2007).

In short, both war and terrorism kill civilians and combatants. The difference between war killing and terrorism is that under the international law war is legally and morally sanctioned while acts of terrorism are not. Soldiers too are trained to kill and to demonize the enemy through military training and they go to war primarily to kill. War and terrorism are constituted according to different logical criteria, one taking its primary sense from the question of legality and the other from feelings of vulnerability and fear and they are not, therefore, mutually exclusive. It is not true to say that terrorism is singularly evil because it kills civilians and inserts fear in the daily rhythm of life which imposes 'the endless coerciveness of precaution' because war, whether just or unjust, does that too (Asad, 2007).

WAR KILLING AND MURDER

To understand the nature of the act which, as noted earlier, invariably involves deaths of noncombatant civilians, one has to ask whether the resulting deaths are truly homicidal killings or casualties of war. Homicide is the killing of another person, either intentionally or unintentionally. In human societies, the act of homicide is universally regarded as a crime and in many cases accorded capital punishment. The logic behind the capital punishment is to dispose of individuals who have committed the act which is regarded by members of the group to be harmful or threatening to them and to their society. War, on the other hand, is organized lethal violence between spatially different groups in which the deaths of other persons are envisioned in advance. In war, therefore, killing of the members of the other group regarded as the enemy is viewed as a justified or justifiable act of killing and consequently is not regarded as murder deserving capital punishment (Otterbein, 1986).

To determine whether a suicide attack and the resulting deaths of noncombatants are murderous killing or casualties of war requires delineating the boundaries between war and murder. While participants in some forms of altercations and disputes may employ deadly weapons to kill others, war is the only activity which entails lethal violence that is collectively organized and carried out. Another key, and possibly the unique feature of war is "that the deaths of other persons are envisioned in advance and this envisioning is encoded in the purposeful act of taking up lethal weapons" (Bourke, 1999; Kelly, 2000).

As organized violence, war requires advance planning and involves a complex division of labor based on specialization of different types of activities that contribute to warfare. The rational calculations, planning, and organization make war instrumentally different from other related forms of violence such as brawls and riots which derive their nature from their affective spontaneity. War also differs from murder and other related forms of violence in that the use of deadly weapons and force is seen as entirely legitimate by the collectivity that resorts to war (Kelly, 2000; Otterbein, 1986; Walzer, 2004).

The moral appropriateness is integral to the activity of making war. Group members are explicitly recruited to the project of causing deaths of other persons on the grounds that it is legitimate and proper to do so (O'Donovan, 2003; Walzer, 2004). Because war is always collectively sanctioned, participation in war is regarded as an act of national pride and highly laudable. Men and women potential or actual 'killers' who die in war are recognized as national heroes and martyrs. Such characterizations of the fallen in war contrast sharply with murder which is negatively valued by the social collectivity that constitutes the killer's reference group. It is consequently regarded as an illegitimate and criminal act warranting retribution not social recognition. Murder is culturally disapproved, stigmatizing rather than prestigious, and falls somewhere along an evaluative scale that extends from regrettable to heinous.

Killing in war and murder are similar in several ways. Both involve deadly violence and bring grief to the affected parties. The punishment for murder and the punishment enacted on the enemy in war killing are regarded as morally appropriate, justified, and legitimate actions constituting fulfillment of civic duty. But there is one very critical difference between punishment for murder and punishment of the enemy in war. The death penalty, a universal punishment norm for murder, is only applicable to a specific individual, the murderer, whose death expunges the wrong doer from society. War does not excise killers from society but instead targets other individuals who are innocent of direct responsibility for prior killing. In war, the killing of any member of the enemy group is considered legitimate.

War is grounded in the application of the principle of social substitutability and is thus governed by a distinctive logic that is entirely foreign to murder. In war, the killing of an individual is perceived as an injury to his or her group because the logic of war is predicated on group responsibility thus making any member of the killer's collectivity a legitimate target for retaliation. In war, the anger generated by a prior killing or prior action is redirected to an entirely different individual sufficiently peripheral to be unsuspecting. The principle that one group member is substitutable for another in the context of war underwrites the interrelated concepts of injury to the group, group responsibility for the infliction of injury, and group liability with respect to retribution. War is thus cognitively, conceptually, and behaviorally conducted between groups. Murder on the other hand is always conceptualized as deadly violence between individual members of the same collectivity (Kelly, 2000).

The universal consequence for murder is capital punishment (and now life imprisonment in some countries) which is socially sanctioned and morally justified by the participants' community. It is also carried out after a socially sanctioned and organized process of adjudication by especially appointed members of the community. It can be concluded from the above that there are remarkable similarities between killing in war and murder and one crucial difference (Kelly, 2000; Otterbein, 1970). In war, killing is directed against any member of the offending party but in murder the action must be directed only against the actual offender.

Are the casualties from suicide bombing attacks murders or war killing? The preceding discussion and observations would suggest that sociologically, suicide bombing attacks can be classified as a weapon of war and the resulting deaths as war casualties. The groups involved in organizing and sponsoring suicide attacks in the modern world enjoy varying levels of support from their collectivity (Atran, 2003; Hassan, 2001; Oliver & Steinberg, 2005; Pape, 2005). They are engaged in conflict over the occupation of their homeland by a foreign army, as a result of which they feel socially and economically dispossessed and humiliated; the occupation of the homeland is seen as sacrilege and as a mortal threat to their political community and its sacred values and way of life (Atran, 2006; Ginges, Atran, Medin, & Shikaki, 2007). Like war, the suicide bombing attack is planned and its execution envisions in advance the deaths of other persons (Bloom, 2005; Gambetta, 2005; Hafez, 2006; Pape, 2005; Townsend, 2007). Like fallen soldiers in war, suicide bombers are regarded by their groups as martyred heroes who have sacrificed their lives for the nation (Abdel-Khalek, 2004; Hafez, 2007; Hassan, 2001; Oliver and Steinberg, 2005; Roberts, 2005).

GOOD DEATH AND BAD DEATH

According to the liberal doctrine, one of the fundamental conditions for the foundation of political community is the monopolistic control of violence by the state. This presupposes that the morally autonomous individual's natural right to violent self-defense is yielded to the state, making the state sole protector of life and liberty. In other words for a viable society to exist, individuals must be disempowered from killing or murdering others and themselves. The society then empowers certain specific institutions to cause death of others at home and abroad making these institutions death brokers and managers of the trajectories of death and dying in society. As mentioned earlier, the right to kill is the right to behave in violent ways against citizens who break the original covenant and the uncivilized 'others' who pose a threat to the existence of political community and the maintenance of social order and their killing provides security (Elias, 2000; Tuck, 1999). This is the main justification for wars as well as judicial killing in modern societies.

Death brokering refers to the activities of authorities which render death normatively and culturally appropriate. In human societies, medical and religious institutions perform the primary death brokering functions. They control the death and dying process through their expertise by managing how people die and when. Medicine provides curative and therapeutic knowledge and a monopoly over determining the cause of death which legitimizes its authority over how and when death might occur. Religion invokes the authority of the divine covenants pertaining to 'good' (religiously sanctioned) death. These two institutions are central in negotiating meanings and the cultural appropriateness of death and dying between the individual and the society.

Good death invariably involves management of the dying process through symptom alleviation, and attention to the religious, social, and cultural needs of the dying and their loved ones to achieve the normative goal of impending death (Kubler-Ross, 1969; Timmermans, 2005). A good death, in other words, involves 'disempowering' the dying person in respect of all decisions over death and the dying process. The 'bad' death by the same logic is when these characteristics are absent and the individual has control over how and when to die or kill. For example, a death that is negotiated through therapeutic procedures administered by authorized medical personnel is a culturally appropriate death and thus a 'good' death, although the dying person more or less had no power over the dying process. I call this 'disempowered death.' Death that occurs under circumstances in which the dying person has some control over the dying process and the timing of death, a kind of 'empowered death,' is socially and culturally inappropriate death or 'bad' death. Good death is 'normal' and evokes appropriate human emotional responses mostly of grief and sadness. Bad death on the other hand is 'abnormal' and, therefore, stigmatized and evokes a variety of emotional responses ranging from disbelief, anger, and revulsion. The reason why suicidal bombing is stigmatized and evokes the type of emotional responses which lie behind its characterization as homicidal and immoral killing, is that it combines two types of stigmatized (bad) deaths, suicide and murder.

CONCLUDING REMARKS

Is suicide bombing homicidal killing or a weapon of war? In light of the above discussion, we can say that suicide bombing is not suicide. There appears to be a consensus among scholars that suicide bombing is a different order of behavior than suicide. Universally, suicide carries a stigma whereas suicide bombings, like war, carry strong approval of the reference group.

What about the difference between war killing and suicide bombing? In political theory, war is legally sanctioned, organized violence which confers legitimacy on the ensuing killing. But the killing perpetrated by suicide bombers is regarded as illegal because of its peculiar evil of targeting innocent civilians and worse because it inserts fear and insecurity into everyday life, undermining the social order and subjecting society to the 'endless coerciveness of precaution.' It is also regarded as illegal because unlike war, militants carrying out terrorism against civilians are not deemed to have reached the last resort and, therefore, are not coerced into action. I have argued that civilians too die in war. In fact, the state armies are more capable and efficient killing machines than any terrorist organization; that war too injects profound insecurities into the private and public spheres; soldiers too are taught to hate and kill enemy combatants and civilians. The fact of killing being legally sanctioned is an abstract irrelevance. There are in fact remarkable similarities between war killing and terrorism.

The case studies of Palestine and Sri Lanka provide evidence that the strategy of targeted suicide bombings was the method of last resort in both cases. Commenting on the rationality of terrorist organizations, Crenshaw (1990) points out that efficacy is the primary standard by which terrorism is compared with other methods of achieving political goals. Suicide terror is rarely, if ever, the strategy of first choice but tends to follow other strategies deemed less effective through the process of trial and error. "Organizations arrive at collective judgements about the relative effectiveness of different strategies ... on the basis of observation and experience, as much as on the basis of abstract strategic conceptions derived from ideological assumptions—allowing for social learning."

When all legal means of seeking redress are blocked, human beings react with rage and resort to violence. As Arendt (1969) has observed, to resort to violence when confronted with outrageous events or conditions is enormously tempting because of its inherent immediacy and swiftness in order to set the scales of justice right again. What drives suicide bombings are unbearable sufferings and reaching out to immortality for the sake of the political community. As in the case of fallen soldiers, the death constitutes a triumph and a victory. In this respect, the genealogy of the act is profoundly modern and 'this worldly' and not 'other worldly.'

The claim of liberal democracies that they have the right to defend themselves with nuclear weapons which appears to be accepted by the international community is in effect an affirmation that suicidal war can be legitimate. In this way, the suicide bomber belongs to a modern Western tradition of armed conflict for the defense of a free political community. In order to save the nation (or to found its state) by confronting a dangerous enemy, it may be necessary to act without being bound by ordinary moral constraints. Or as Walzer (2004) puts it:

A morally strong leader is someone who understands why it is wrong to kill the innocent and refuses to do so, refuses again and again, until the heavens are about to fall. And then he becomes a moral criminal who knows that he can't do what he has to do—and finally does.

By this reasoning, can the killing of innocents by taking one's own life be the final gesture of a morally strong leader? (Asad, 2007).

As regard to war killing and murder, it is argued that suicide bombing attacks are an act and a weapon of war because of the principle of substitutability which characterizes war killing.

However, under the International Laws of War, the attacks could most likely be classified as 'war crimes.' Article 147 of the Fourth Geneva Convention defines war crimes as:

> *Wilful killing, torture or inhuman treatment, including ... wilfully causing great suffering or serious injuries to body or health, unlawful deportation or transfer or unlawful confinement of a protected person, compelling a protected person to serve in the forces of hostile powers, or wilfully depriving a protected person of the rights of fair and regular trial ... taking of hostages and extensive destruction and appropriation of property, not justified by military necessity and carried out unlawfully and wantonly.*

But this, of course, would apply not only to the groups organizing and sponsoring suicide bombing but also to the actions of the occupying armies and their military and political leaders.

Finally, death is nature's assertion over culture. In nature, death and dying are totally amoral events meaning no more than the physical end of a biological organism. But in human cultures, death is embedded with symbols and meanings and classified as *good* and *bad* largely on the basis of the role of socially sanctioned death brokers in its occurrence. In human society, death occurring from acts such as suicide bombing may well be altruistically driven but paradoxically remains stigmatized because it violates one of the fundamental social imperatives for the existence and survival of human society: that individuals are not empowered to take their or someone else's life. This stigma is a natural check that will restrain the diffusion of suicide bombings. From time to time, certain historical conditions may be instrumental in giving rise to phenomena like suicide bombings and may even confer some form of community support, but like other forms of stigmatized deaths, suicide bombings will remain a rare event. Furthermore, it would always provoke the state's strong retaliation against its perpetrators for violating the imperative norms which also act as a strong check on its occurrence, prevalence, and diffusion.

Suicide bombings, by their very nature, are not only public acts but also acts of public performance in which bodies and ideologies become texts produced between author and audience. Exploration of the meanings of these texts requires critical theoretical, conceptual, and hermeneutical tools which do not distort their meanings. This chapter is a modest contribution toward that goal.

REFERENCES

Abdel-Khalek, A. (2004). Neither altruistic suicide nor terrorism but martyrdom: A Muslim perspective. *Archives of Suicide Research*, 8(1), 99–113.
Argo, N. (2003). The banality of evil: Understanding today's human bombs. Unpublished Policy Paper, Preventive Defence Project, Stanford University.
Arendt, H. (1969). *On violence*. London: Allen Lane.
Asad, T. (2007). *On suicide bombing*. New York: Columbia University Press.
Atran, S. (2003). Genesis of suicide terrorism. *Science*, 299(5612), 1534–1539.
Atran, S. (2006). The moral logic and growth of suicide terrorism. *The Washington Quarterly*, 29(2), 127–147.
Barraclough, B., & Harris, C. (2002). Suicide preceded by murder: The epidemiology homicide-suicide in England and Wales. *Psychological Medicine*, 32(4), 577–584.
Berko, A. (2007). *The path to paradise: The inner world of suicide bombers and their dispatchers*. Westport: Praeger Security International.
Bloom, M. (2005). *Dying to kill: The allure of suicide terror*. New York: Columbia University Press.
Bourke, J. (1999). *An intimate history of killing: Face to face killing in twentieth century warfare*. New York: Basic Books.
Crenshaw, M. (1990). The logic of terrorism: Terrorist behaviour as product of strategic choice. In Walter Reich (Ed.), *Origins of terrorism: Psychologies, ideologies, theologies, states of mind*. New York: Cambridge University Press.
Dabbagh, T. S. (2005). *Suicide in Palestine: Narrative of despair*. Northhampton, MA: Olive Branch Press.
Elias, N. (2000). *The civilizing process: Sociogenetic and psychogenetic investigations*. Oxford: Blackwell.
Gambetta, D. (2005). *Making sense of suicide missions*. Oxford: Oxford University Press.
Ginges, J., Atran, S., Medin, S., & Shikaki, K. (2007). Sacred bounds on rational resolution of violent political conflict. *Proceedings of the National Academy of Science of the USA*, 104(18), 7357–7360.
Grimland, M., Apter, A., & Kerkhof, A. (2006). The phenomenon of suicide bombing: A review of psychological and non-psychological

factors. *Crisis: The Journal of Crisis Intervention and Suicide Prevention,* 27(3), 107–118.

Hassan, N. (2001). An arsenal of believers: Talking to 'human bombs'. *New Yorker.* Retrieved from http://www.newyorker.com/archive/2001/11/19/011119fa_FACT1

Hafez, M. (2006). *Manufacturing human bombs: The making of Palestinian suicide bombers.* Washington, DC: United States Institute of Peace.

Hafez, M. (2007). *Suicide bombers in Iraq: The strategy and ideology of martyrdom.* Washington, DC: United States Institute of Peace.

Jayyusi, M. (2004). *Subjectivity and public witness: An analysis of Islamic militancy in Palestine.* Unpublished paper for the SSRC Beirut Conference on Public Sphere in the Middle East.

Kelly, R. C. (2000). *Warless societies and the origin of war.* Ann Arbor: The University of Michigan Press.

Kubler-Ross, E. (1969). *On death and dying.* New York: Macmillan.

Marzuk, P. M., Tarddiff, K., & Hirsch, C. S. (1992). The epidemiology of murder-suicide. *JAMA,* 267(23), 3179–3183.

Nordstrom, C. (2004). *Shadows of war: Violence, power, and international profiteering in the twenty-first century.* Berkeley: University of California Press.

O'Donovan, Oliver. (2003). *The just war revisited.* Cambridge: Cambridge University Press.

Otterbein, K. F. (1970). *The evolution of war: A cross cultural study.* New Haven: HRAF Press.

Otterbein, K. F. (1986). *The ultimate coercive sanction.* New Haven: HRAF Press.

Oliver, A. M., & Steinberg, P. (2005). *The road to martyrs square: A journey into world of the suicide bomber.* Oxford: Oxford University Press.

Pape, R. (2005). *Dying to win: The strategic logic of suicide terrorism.* New York: Random House.

Roberts, M. (2005). Savaite symbols, sacrifice and Tamil tigers. *Social Analysis,* 49(1), 67–93.

Strenski, I. (2003). Sacrifice, gift, and the social logic of Muslim 'human bombers'. *Terrorism and Political Violence,* 15(3), 1–34.

Timmermans, S. (2005). Death brokering: Constructing culturally appropriate deaths. *Sociology of Health and Illness,* 27(7), 993–1013.

Townsend, E. (2007). Suicide terrorists: Are they suicidal? *Suicide and Life-Threatening Behaviour,* 37(1), 47.

Tuck, R. (1999). *The rights of war and peace: Political thought and international order from Grotius to Kant.* Oxford: Oxford University Press.

Walzer, M. (2004). *Arguing about war.* New Haven: Yale University Press.

Walzer, M. (2006). The ethics of battle: War fair. *The New Republic*, 15(2).
Wright, Q. (1942). *A study of war*. Chicago, IL: University of Chicago Press.

Section II

Suicide Terrorism: A Process

7

The Psychology of Suicide Terrorism[*]

Jerrold M. Post, Farhana Ali, Schuyler W. Henderson, Stephen Shanfield, Jeff Victoroff, and Stevan Weine

The events of September 11, raised terrifying questions for the public about the nature of the adversary what President Bush declared to be the "war on terrorism." What kind of people serve as human guided missiles, as the mate "smart bombs," sacrificing their lives kill thousands of civilians? And what the teenage boy wearing a suicide bomb and exploding himself in a pizza parlor, killing and wounding more than twenty teenagers, or the young mother who detonates herself, killing scores in a shopping mall, or the daily occurrence in Iraq and the increasing frequency in Afghanistan of suicide bombings? The lay assumption is that surely the suicidal hijackers and the suicide bombers must be crazed fanatics.

This inevitably led to questions addressed to the psychiatric profession. After all, expertise in the psychopathology of suicide, of what drives people to take their own lives, is one of the hallmarks of our profession, and we ought to be able to explain this terrifying phenomenon.

The purpose of the paper is to review current understandings of the psychology of suicide terrorism for psychiatrists and other mental health professionals to help them better understand this terrifying phenomenon. At the outset, it is necessary to dismiss descriptions of suicide bombers as insane. What seems incomprehensible in another person has often been described as "mad" or "insane." It should be understood that such characterizations of suicide bombers

---

[*] First published originally in 2009 in *Psychiatry, 72*(1), 13–31. © Guilford Publications, Inc. Reprinted with permission from Guilford Publications, Inc.

have no psychiatric support. Indeed, terrorist groups attempt to screen out mentally disturbed recruits—after all, they represent a security risk (Horgan, 2005; Laqueur & Alexander, 1987; Silke, 2003). Martha Crenshaw, a prominent international terrorism expert, has observed that "the outstanding common characteristic of terrorists is their normality" (Crenshaw, 1981). McCauley and Segal, in a major review of the social psychology of terrorist groups, found that "the best documented generalization is negative; terrorists do not show any striking psychopathology" (McCauley & Segal, 1987). The purpose of looking into the roles of individual, group, and social psychology is not to deny agency or legitimacy or to disavow a broad range of contributing factors to the development of suicide bombers, but to understand as fully as possible an increasingly common and deadly human behavior.

While it may be tempting to assume that all of those who kill themselves share some underlying psychobiological characteristics, such as acting out of psychic despair, there are other entirely different frameworks, such as Durkheim's distinction between altruistic suicide, intended to benefit society, and fatalistic suicide, arising out of personal despair (Durkheim, 1951). Pedazhur and colleagues have raised the question of whether "suicide terrorism" better fits into this sociological framework and exists independent from any psychological traits (Pedazhur, 2005).

This paper examines various psychological models that may contribute to the explanation of suicide bombing, and then looks at various areas where psychiatry may be able to contribute to the interdisciplinary understanding of this act.

DEFINITIONS AND KEY CONCEPTS

"Terrorism" and "terrorist" are contested terms (Poole, 2006; United Nations, 2004). As Bruce Hoffman observes, the definitions often reflect the perspectives of the defining agency (Hoffman, 1998, p. 38). So, definitions by the Department of State will emphasize the political nature of the act; those of the Department of Justice and the FBI will reflect the illegal, criminal nature of the act (United States Department of Justice, 2001); while those of the Department of Defense will define terrorism as part of the spectrum of low intensity conflict; and the USA Patriot Act, 2001, focuses on the nature of the target population, that is, civilians versus military targets. It is important to distinguish terrorism from guerilla warfare and insurgency. A key differentiating factor for many experts is that terrorism is symbolic and seeks to undermine the authority of the dominant power, but lacks the military strength to overthrow the government. The goal of an insurgency is usually the overthrow of a political system, and an insurgency occupies territory which it seeks to expand. Of note, armed resistance is another term used by terrorists to legitimate their violent acts, considered illegitimate by the target population. What is important to remember is that these terms are employed for their rhetorical power and as propaganda by both sides.

Alex Schmid, in his classic Political Terrorism (Schmid, 1983) reviewed some 109 definitions of terrorism and identified elements in common among these definitions. One of the important distinctions he makes is between the target of violence (i.e., the innocent victim or non-combatant) and the targets of attention, of which he identifies three: 1) the target of terror, referring to the members of the same class as the target of violence; 2) the target of coercion, whom the terrorists threaten with, for example, "unless you the government give in to our demands, we will kill these hostages"; and 3) the target of influence, which is usually the West or the establishment. Many of the definitions he reviewed also called attention to the "extranormality" of the act, that it purposefully violated the rules of "just war," by targeting civilians, using means such as beheading designed to horrify, and the randomness of the act in terms of time and place, all of which are purposefully designed to terrorize.

Terrorism then is generally, but by no means universally, recognized as violence or the threat of violence against noncombatant populations in order to obtain a political, religious, or ideological goal through fear and intimidation. It is a criminal act that is often symbolic in intent. The target of violence differs from the targets of attention.

The term suicide itself is also disputed. In an interview project with incarcerated Palestinian terrorists, a question to a suicide bomber dispatcher as to how, given that the Koran proscribes suicide, they could justify suicide terrorism as being in the name of Allah, evoked anger: "This is not suicide. Suicide is weak, it is selfish, it is mentally disturbed. This is istishhad [martyrdom or self-sacrifice in the service of Allah.]" (Post, Sprinzak, & Denny, 2003). Thus extremists have reframed the acts as "martyrdom operations." In contrast to the Buddhist monks in Vietnam who immolated themselves in protest against the Vietnam War, acts in which no one else was killed or injured, contemporary "suicide bombers" kill themselves in order to kill others, leading some commentators in the United States and Israel to employ terms that focus on the larger effects of the attacks and the resultant murder of other people, labeling them "homicide bombers." Raphael Israeli's graphically entitled Islamikaze: Manifestations of Islamic Martyrology (Israeli, 2003), in likening the suicide bombers to the Japanese kamikaze bombers at the end of World War II, emphasizes the violent mass casualty goal of the suicide bombers. The term "murdercide" was introduced by Michael Shermer, again emphasizing that the suicide element is instrumental to the act of homicide (Shermer, 2006).

In addition to the suicide terrorists associated with militant Islam, which we will consider in some detail, it is important to observe that not all of suicide terrorism is inspired by conventional religion, and does not all represent killing in the name of God. In particular, there are three non-religious groups associated with suicide terrorism: the Tamil Tigers (LTTE) of Sri Lanka, the Kurdistan Workers Party (PKK) of Turkey, and the Chechen separatists. For the PKK, LTTE, and Chechen separatist groups, the cause of establishing their separate nation (Kurdistan for the PKK, Tamil Eelam for the LTTE, and an independent Chechnya) has come to be a matter of faith for which the "true believers" will give their lives. This in turn reflects the powerful impact of their destructive charismatic leaders, Abdullah Ocalan of the PKK and Vellupillai Prabhakaran of the Tamil Tigers, upon their followers, for whom they have god-like stature (Post, 2007, p. 67).

Suicide terrorism associated with Islamic groups is prominent in Western and European discourse, signifying also that the actions of some terrorist groups such as al-Qaeda are having their intended effect, and spreading fear through larger Western populations. Furthermore, the practice of suicide terrorism by these groups is a major security threat that confounds U.S. and coalition military operations in Iraq and Afghanistan and is a continuing destabilizing issue in the Israeli-Palestinian conflict.

SUICIDE TERRORISM IN THE ISLAMIC CONTEXT[1]

It is therefore important at the outset to provide a précis of suicide terrorism in an Islamic context. As Mohammad Hafez emphasizes in his excellent study of Islamic suicide terrorism, *Manufacturing Human Bombs*, there are three proscriptions in the Koran related to the topic of suicide terrorisms: the prohibitions against suicide, against killing innocents, and against killing Muslims (Hafez, 2006). We will discuss several concepts where these proscriptions against suicide terrorism have been reframed: jihad, the return of the Caliphate and Salafism.

Jihad

Suicide terrorism is often conflated with the notion of jihad, which is also often considered synonymous with "holy war" and "radicalism." However, Imam Muhammad Magid of ADAMS, a mosque and community center in Sterling, Virginia, argues, "Nowhere in the Qur'an will you find holy war attributed to jihad" (Magid, 2006).

Jihad is an act of Islamic worship and is derived from the Arabic verb, jahada, which means "effort and striving" (Abualrub, 2002, pp. 78–79). While there are many forms of jihad, all of which are defined by a set of rules, jihad is frequently interpreted as a self-defense: defense against temptation, defense against Satan, defense against the unjust. Four important jihads are the jihad of the heart, which commands Muslims to have a heart that is pure and free of evil; the jihad of the tongue, which commands Muslims to give voice to the words of the prophet; the jihad of the deed, which commands Muslims to do good works for the ummah, the community of observant Muslims; and finally, the jihad of the sword, which commands Muslims to take up the sword

---

[1] Note: This section of the paper explaining the struggle within Islam and the manner in which the extremist refraining of jihad has been used to justify suicide terrorism is drawn from a major essay on Islam in the contemporary world prepared by Farhana Ali, a senior analyst at the RAND Corporation, who served as a consultant to the Group for the Advancement of Psychiatry committee.

against those who take up the sword against Muslims. The jihad of the sword is a defensive jihad, and it is this jihad that is often mistranslated as holy war.

Some Muslim clergy have justified the use of violence against civilian and military targets by issuing fatwas (pronouncements) granting permission to fight outside the original parameters of Islamic jurisprudence. These scholars argue that warfare today is asymmetrical, which necessitates new rules of warfare, with new strategies and approaches to defeating the perceived enemies of Islam. Hence, some scholars permit the use of suicide bombings, for both Muslim men and women.

As with "terrorist" and "suicide," words like "jihad" are put to political use. Leading U.S. based Muslim jurist and scholar, Khaled Abou El Fadl, maintains that "not all social and political frustrations lead to the use of violence," but the rhetoric of belligerence that developed in countries like Egypt, Saudi Arabia, and Pakistan were able to "exploit an already radicalized discourse with the expectation of resonating with the social and political frustrations of a people" (Abou El Fadl, 2005).

The Return to the Caliphate

In their attempt to re-appropriate Islam as a total way of life, several major figures emerged to cultivate a new Islamic polity that romanticized the vision of the Khalifah[2]. This refers to the period following the death of Muhammed, when his followers, the caliphs, were intended to carry on Muhammed's traditions and legacy. Powerful Muslim rulers, including the period of the Ottoman Empire, governed the Islamic world until the founder of the modern state of Turkey, President Mustafa Kemal Ataturk, abolished the caliphate in 1924. This was the ideological foundation for the Islamie revolution in Iran in 1979 led by Ayatollah Ruholla Khomeini. Osama bin Laden borrowed the caliphate ideal as the solution for Muslims living under Western governments and legal codes; he used this term to appeal to a disenfranchised Muslim population, searching to reestablish their historic identity

---

[2] The golden era of the Caliphate refers to the rule of a democratically chosen Caliph until the fall of the Ottomans in 1924.

within the modern sociopolitical context in the nineteenth and twentieth centuries. In his speeches, bin Laden frequently uses the phrase "eighty years ago," referring to the period when the Ottoman Empire last held sway, before the transformational act of Ataturk. For example, immediately after 9/11 in taped remarks bin Laden stated:

> What America is tasting now is something insignificant compared to what we have tasted for scores of years. Our nation [the Islamic world] has been tasting this humiliation and degradation for more than eighty years. Its sons are killed, its blood is shed, its sanctuaries are attacked, and no one hears and no one heeds. (AlJazeeraTV, 2001)

Salafism

Insurgents, extremist networks, and their supporters increasingly reflect the teachings of Salafi-Jihadis, who derive their core beliefs from Salafism[3], a doctrine calling for the return to the glorious days of Islam in which Muslims lived according to the principles of the righteous predecessors (Ali, 2000, p. 11). By taking back the faith to the early days of Islam, Salafis offer a worldview that promises to establish a united Muslim community, with "Islam and knowledge [as] the property of all Muslims[4]." Recognizing this is critical for two reasons: 1) Salafis are challenging the present-day sociopolitical environment by calling Muslims to

---

[3] Mainstream Salafis, however, do not believe in violent action, or at least, do not participate in mass killings, beheadings, and wage war against the perceived infidels. Today, Salafis are as diverse as Islam. Hence, no two Salafisms are alike, just as no two Muslim countries practice Islam in the same way. All Salafis agree that the Qur'an and the Sunnah is the path towards peace, justice, and equality, and most Salafis share a common goal, which is to preserve their Islamic heritage and identity by reestablishing the Khalifa. But how Salafis intend to recreate the Caliphate in contemporary Muslim society, and in Western countries with large Muslim minorities, remains unclear. To understand the Salafi doctrine, see Abdul-Khaliq (2004) and Ali (2000).
[4] The righteous or 'pious predecessors' is a reference to the Companions of the Prophet Muhammad and the first three generations of Muslims.

accept the "true" teachings of its predecessors[5]; and 2) the Salafi-Jihadi ideology, the violent offshoot of Salafi doctrine, will likely overtake the post al-Qaeda movement.

The Salafi-Jihadis form a small, but powerful, group of extremists who support al-Qaeda's goal of establishing an Islamic caliphate to replace Western-imposed democratic rule and autocratic or apostate Muslim regimes. Though a minority in the Muslim world, Salafi-Jihadis maintain a vast transnational support network that has challenged non-violent Muslim activists for accepting the status quo and/or choosing to join the political process to voice their concerns, rather than participating in jihad to replace jahiliyya (barbaric or man-made) for a hakimiyya (righteous or God-conscious) government[6]. Salafi-Jihadis therefore contend that man-made rules, developed by secular or national governments, contradict the rule of God. In his book, Knights Under the Prophet's Banner, Ayman al-Zawahiri, bin Laden's second in command and designated successor, reaffirms this right to establish the Muslim state in the heart of the Islamic world[7], an objective shared by other Salafi-Jihadists who agree that jihad is the instrument that will protect Muslim interests and achieve results. In a July 2005 interview (Al Hayat, 2005) in Al Hayat, Jordanian theoretician Abu Muhammad al-Maqdisi supports jihad as one of the duties dictated by our faith . . . [and] through our previous

---

[5] The way of the Salaf has been described in the Qur'an and Sunnah, also called hadith, the recorded teachings and sayings of Prophet Muhammed by Muslim scholars. The two most well-known scholars of hadith are Sahih Bukhari and Sahih Muslim. According to Bukhari, the Prophet said to his daughter Fatima "Indeed, I am for you a blessed Salaf." (no. 2652). In the Qur'an, the salaf is described as the "rightly guided." (Verse 2:137)

[6] These terms are explicitly described in the work of Egyptian revolutionary, Sayyid Qutb. In his book, The Shadow of the Qur'an, Qutb wrote, "Man is at the crossroads and that is the choice: Islam or jahiliyya. Modern-style jahiliyya in the industrialized societies of Europe and America is essentially similar to the old-time jahiliyya in pagan and nomadic Arabia. For in both systems, man is under the dominion of man rather than of Allah [Arabic word for God]."

[7] Translation provided by Venzke, & Ibrahim (2003). For Zawahiri, the meaning of jihad means "removing the current government [Sadat] through resisting it and changing the current regime to establish an Islamic government instead," from The Road to Al Qaeda (Zayat, 2004, pp. 42–43).

experience of jihad action in Afghanistan, Chechnya and Bosnia, we found out that the blessings of jihad include reviving the youths of these countries and creating a blessed awakening there.

By communicating a narrative focused on an Islamic renaissance, Salafi-Jihadis provide "powerful answers to modern questions and anxieties" (Haykel, 2005). They offer an alternative form of resistance[8], relying on violent action to achieve their strategic and tactical goals. As the opportunistic vanguards of Islam, their narrative is rooted in saving the Muslim Ummah from moral corruption and Western interference. It is but a short step from this requirement for violence in pursuit of justice for the Muslim people to radical Islamic clerics, such as Ayatollah Fadlallah, the spiritual mentor of Hezbollah, invoking the extremity of the suffering Muslim people as justifying acts, such as suicide, that in normal times would be prohibited by the Koran. It was Fadlallah that sanctioned the suicide truck bombings of the U.S. embassy and the Marine barracks in Lebanon in 1983. Hezbollah has since abandoned the tactic of suicide terrorism in favor of guerilla warfare.

THE PSYCHOLOGY OF TERRORISM

Understanding the psychology of suicide terrorism must necessarily be rooted in an understanding of the psychology of terrorism. In preparation for the International Summit on Democracy, Terrorism, and Security, held in Madrid, Spain, in March, 2005, on the first anniversary of the Madrid train station bombing by Islamist militants, a number of committees were formed to explore the roots of terrorism. The Committee on the Psychological

---

[8] The persuasive architects of Islamic thought produced the necessary language for resistance. Cognizant of the Muslim sentiment during the period of colonization and the influences of Western-supported independence movements, they crafted a treatise for action, capitalizing on the frustrations within Muslim society at that time. The struggle for independence in a pre and post-colonial world "generated a variety of local and regional 'nationalisms' in which ... the persistence of Islam and the constant, though varied, role it maintains" in the Muslim world.

Roots of Terrorism[9] prepared a summary consensus document emphasizing that:

> explanations at the level of individual psychology are insufficient. It is not going too far to assert that terrorists are psychologically "normal" in the sense of not being clinically psychotic. They are neither depressed, severely emotionally disturbed, nor are they crazed fanatics. (Post, 2005b, pp. 7–12)

The committee report went on to single out the crucial role of group and organizational psychology, emphasizing the importance of "collective identity":

> A clear consensus exists that it is not individual psychology but group, organizational and social psychology that provides the greatest analytic power in understanding this complex phenomenon. Terrorists have subordinated their individual identity to the collective identity, so that what serves the group, organization or network is of primary importance. For some groups, especially national-separatist terrorist groups, this collective identity is established extremely early: hatred is "bred in the bone." This in turn emphasizes the socio-cultural context, which determines the balance between collective and individual identity. (Post, 2005c)

Accepting that no single model can explain suicide terrorism, our goal now is to review psychological contributions to understanding suicide terrorism, which is a multifactorial phenomenon that must be considered from an interdisciplinary perspective.

EXPLANATORY GROUP MODELS OF SUICIDE TERRORISM

Collective identities are shaped within the social and cultural milieus in which they develop. Jessica Stern, who has enriched

---

[9] Note: Three members of the GAP Committee on Terrorism and Political Violence, Jerrold Post, Jeff Victoroff, and Stevan Weine served on the Committee on the Psychological Roots of Terrorism, which was chaired by Jerrold Post.

terrorism scholarship with her revealing interviews, observed that "Hopelessness, deprivation, envy, and humiliation make death, and paradise, seem more appealing." She quoted an elderly resident of Jenin who told a visiting reporter: "Look how we live here. Then maybe you'll understand why there are always volunteers for martyrdom. Every good Muslim understands that it's better to die fighting than to live without hope" (Jacobson, 2001, p.38). Thus through the act of martyrdom, despair is transformed into hope - a widespread belief in the Palestinian community. Collective identity and the group and social processes that consolidate that collective identity play a crucial role both in leading Muslim youth onto the path of terrorism and in reframing suicide as martyrdom.

Entrance onto the Path of Terrorism

Jihad and the resistance begin with the word, then with the sword, then with the stone, then with the gun, then with planting bombs, and then transforming bodies into human bombs.—Munir alMakdah, suicide bomb trainer (Bloom, 2005, p. 27).

People join terrorist groups at different stages of life. However, the entrance onto the path of terrorism often occurs long before actually becoming a member of the group. For some, it starts very early indeed, as exemplified by the empirical data concerning Palestinian suicide terrorists and their dispatchers. In the Palestinian territories, acceptance and celebration of suicide bombing is apparent from childhood on, as evidenced by photographs of infants and children with toy suicide bomb-belts. Children have listened to their parents' stories of humiliation, indignation, and loss. In interviews with incarcerated Palestinian terrorists, almost all indicated that it was in the mosque that they first heard of the manner in which their parents' property had been taken, when they were set on the path of terrorism and martyrdom (Post et al., 2003). (Emphasis is given here to Palestinian groups because of the richness of the available data; these observations do not necessarily apply to other groups.)

A child's life extends beyond the family, and particularly to schools. The signs on the walls of the Hamas-run kindergartens read: "The children of the kindergarten are the shaheeds of tomorrow" (Kelley, 2001). At an Islamic school in Gaza City run by Hamas, an 11-year-old student states:

I will make my body a bomb that will blast the flesh of Zionists, the sons of pigs and monkeys . . . I will tear their bodies into little pieces and cause them more pain than they will ever know.

According to the article which reported the episode, his classmates responded Allah Akbar (God is great). The teacher, demonstrating that the entire system is deeply involved, yelled, "May the virgins give you pleasure," referring to one of the rewards awaiting martyrs in paradise, while the principal smiled and nodded his approval. The value of martyrdom continues to be emphasized throughout the student's education, continuing into university. Signs in the classroom at Al-Najah University in the West Bank and at Gaza's Islamic University state, "Israel has nuclear bombs. We have human bombs" (Kelley, 2001).

Similarly, the final exercise of the summer camp sponsored by the Palestinian Authority has young campers with ski masks or keffiyas wrapped around their faces, storming a mock Israeli Defense Force outpost, and the campers who were able to "kill" the simulated Israeli soldier won the award for their bunk. They were being trained, not to be terrorists, but to be soldiers joining the revolution.

Mohammed Rezaq, Exemplar of Generational Transmission

For Mohammad Rezaq, an Abu Nidal terrorist tried in federal court in Washington, D.C., for skyjacking in 1997, the generational transmission of bitterness and hatred started before he was born (Post, 2000). His mother was eight years old in 1948 at the time of the War of Independence, which Palestinians call "the catastrophe," when her family was forced to leave Jaffa, a predominantly Muslim suburb of Tel Aviv, and went to her grandfather's farm on the West Bank. In the 1967 war, when young Rezaq was eight years old, his family was forced to leave and ended up in a refugee camp in Jordan. Expressing her hatred for the Israelis, his mother remarked bitterly, "This is the second time this is happening to me."

In school in the refugee camp, with UNESCO support, Rezaq was taught by a member of the PLO who told him and his fellow students, "The only way to become a man is to join the revolution and take back the land stolen from your parents and grandparents." When he carried out his terrorist act, he was fulfilling his destiny. At last he was doing something to advance the cause of the Palestinian people to regain their homeland. Rezaq is an exemplar of the manner in which historical forces, family history, and being socialized to become a soldier for the revolution interacted to impel frustrated, alienated, and despairing youth on the path to terrorism.

One interesting sidebar that emerged from the detailed history of Rezaq and his entrance and participation in the Abu Nidal terrorist group concerns his encounter with a Palestinian psychiatrist. After Rezaq narrowly escaped death in an explosion at a cafeteria he had just vacated in Lebanon during the "war of the bombs," Rezaq transiently experienced some PTSD symptoms. Confirming the consensus by the Committee on the Psychological Roots of Terrorism that terrorist groups screen out emotionally disturbed individuals, Rezaq was sent for an evaluation to a Palestinian psychiatrist who certified that he was emotionally stable and fit to return to duty.

ADOLESCENT PSYCHOLOGY AND SUICIDE TERRORISM

Suicide bombers have typically been late adolescents or young men. An early (conducted after the first intifada, 1993–1994) Israeli post-mortem study of 93 suicide bombers—that is, reconstruction of the lives of suicides—revealed a group of 17–22 year-old uneducated, unmarried, unemployed, and unformed youth. More recently, while the age range has expanded, and women have joined the ranks of suicide bombers, the core group remains late adolescent males (Merari, 2005).

Adolescence and youth is a period of experimentation, of identity formation, of a struggle for autonomy, and a time of dealing with issues of intimacy (see Keniston, 1972; Smetana, Campione-Barr, & Metzger, 2006; Steinberg & Sheffield Morris, 2001). As bonds with parents are being loosened, the peer culture is particularly influential. Anat Berko's study of failed Palestinian suicide bombers revealed the importance of the peer culture (Berko, 2007). Moreover, in this developmental epoch, alternate sources of authority are sought. Thus Muslim adolescents seeking to consolidate their identity are especially vulnerable to the siren song of hate-mongering leaders, including radical imams, who identify external causes for the misery of the lives of the youth. "It's not us, it's them. They are responsible for our problems." So framed, it is not only not immoral to strike out against them, but becomes a moral imperative, especially when it is cast as a sacred obligation, as is the case for the youthful members of Hamas, Hezbollah, al-Qaeda, and affiliated groups and like-minded individuals.

Before entering the final pathway of suicide terrorism, the youth enter a path of radicalization, what Ariel Merari has characterized as the suicide bomber "assembly line." Subjects interviewed reported how empowered they felt after a life of insignificance. One incarcerated member of the Fatah movement, asked about the meaning of striking out against the enemy, responded:

> *I regarded armed actions to be essential, it is the very basis of my organization and I am sure that was the case in the other Palestinian organizations. The aim was to cause as much carnage as possible. The main thing was the amount of blood. An armed action proclaims that I am here, I exist, I am strong, I am in control, I am in the field, I am on the map. An armed action against soldiers was the most admired ... the armed actions and their results were a major tool for penetrating the public consciousness.* (Post et al., 2003, p. 18)

So it is power for the powerless, significance for the insignificant. This is exemplified by interviews conducted by Nicole Argo, as cited by Hafez (Hafez, 2006, p. 50). According to one would-be bomber, emphasizing the altruistic nature of the expressed motivations, "I did this because of the suffering of the Palestinian people. The falling of shuhada [those martyred by Israeli forces] ... and the destruction everywhere in Palestine ... I did this for God and the Palestinian people." Another said, "I believe the operation would hurt the enemy.... Also [a] successful mission greatly influences society. It raises the morale of the people; they are happy, they feel strong." In this context, the messages that adolescents receive, extolling a Utopian and transcendent immortality for the suicide bomber, may be particularly attractive. In the context of multiple social and economic stressors, the promise of martyrdom and a hero's death, freedom from conflict and an idyllic life hereafter in paradise are themes that would be attractive to many adolescents.[10]

A research program utilizing semistructured interviews with 35 incarcerated terrorists from the Middle East, both secular nationalists from Fatah and the Palestinian Front for the Liberation of Palestine, and radical religious extremists, from Hezbollah, Hamas and the Palestinian Islamic Jihad, found that the major influence on the decision to join an organization was the social environment. As one terrorist remarked, "Everyone was joining" (Post et al., 2003). The peer group was of much greater influence, and in many cases it was a friend or acquaintance in the group who recruited the subject. The family was often surprised by the decision to enter the path of terrorism, reinforcing Berko's observation that the family of a suicide terrorist was often the last to know that their child was on the path to suicide.

Over 80% of the secular group members reported growing up in communities that were radically involved, and most reported first having their political consciousness aroused by sermons they heard as children in the mosque. A Fatah subject reported

I belong to the generation of occupation. My family are refugees from the 1967 war. The war and my refugee status were

---

[10] Note: Among Palestinians, there is a high rate of unemployment. Young Palestinians are not able to use their education or make a living in a larger world. Recent interviews with young Palestinians on the West Bank reveal considerable despair. Similarly, in Egypt, and across the Middle East, marriage, the gateway to independence, is being deferred because of unemployment, the government's inability to provide adequate schooling, and an economy without jobs. In Egypt, the average age at which men now marry is 31. In Iran, 38 percent of the 25–29 year-old men are not married. The unemployment and inability to marry has been associated with widespread situational despair, which is associated with a turn towards religion. Their dreams stifled, Egypt's young have turned to Islamic fervor. In 1986, there was one mosque for every 6,031 people; today the figure, with a population nearly doubled, is one mosque for every 745 people (M. Slackman "Dreams Stifled, Egypt's Yong Turn to Islamic Fervor." *Washington Post*, February 17, 2008, pp. Al, 12, 13). But economic hardships do not seem to distinguish suicide terrorists from the larger body of youth. Indeed Berko found that the failed suicide bombers she interviewed came from rather comfortable economic circumstances, and their acts were described in altruistic terms, as being for the Palestinian people.

the seminal events that formed my political consciousness and provided the incentive for doing all I could to regain our legitimate rights in our occupied country.

Suicide bombers are promised absolution for parental sins which suggests a sense of failure and guilt on the part of the adolescent suicide bomber (Keniston, 1972). Opinion polls of young Palestinians reveal a generation more supportive of armed struggle and terrorism than their parents, although it may be that in later adulthood, some will reject the fiery beliefs they held as youth (Erlanger, 2007).

CONTRAST BETWEEN PALESTINIAN SUICIDE BOMBERS AND 9/11 SUICIDAL HIJACKERS

Heretofore the discussion has been particularly concerned with Palestinian suicide terrorism. The Palestinian suicide bombers were unformed youth—unmarried, uneducated, unemployed. Once they entered the safe house, they were always accompanied lest they backslide, and were physically escorted to the operation.

In contrast, the 9/11 suicidal al-Qaeda hijackers were older, 28–33—Atta, the ringleader was 33—from comfortable middle class homes, and many had higher education. Atta and two of his colleagues were in Master's Degree programs in the Technological University in Hamburg. And they had been on their own in the west, in some cases for upwards of seven years, simulating blending in, while carrying within them like a laser beam their mission to give of their lives while taking thousands of casualties. We see them as fully formed adults who had subordinated their individuality to the group cause of radical Islam as articulated by the destructive charismatic leader Osama bin laden.

Mark Sageman, in a study of 400 al-Qaeda members, found that three quarters of the members come from comfortable middle class and upper class homes, with 63% having attended college (Sageman, 2004). As he observed, these were "the best and the brightest." Three quarters were professionals or semi-professionals, mainly from scientific disciplines. The recent "doctors" plot in Great Britain further highlights this characterization. An interesting finding that contrasts with the lay assumption is that few had backgrounds in religion. And his demographic analysis stands in sharp contrast to the Palestinian suicide bombers, with 73% married, most of whom had children.

AL QAEDA VERSION 2.0

A new direction has occurred in the last decade, accelerated by the war in Afghanistan post 9/11, which basically destroyed al-Qaeda version 1.0 with its centralized command and control, financial resources, training, and operational planning. Al-Qaeda version 1.0 has morphed into al-Qaeda version 2.0 which is decentralized, a semi-autonomous network operating out of hubs and nodes, so that al-Qaeda provides a loose umbrella, providing support and ideological coherence, but not direct operational control.

Of great concern to Western security forces are the new recruits to the global salafi jihad coming from second and third generation émigré/diaspora populations who emigrated to Europe originally from South Asia and North Africa, and who failed to be integrated culturally and were secondarily radicalized within these nations, often at radical mosques. The March 2004 Madrid train station bombing was committed by members of the Algerian diaspora; the London transit bombings of 7/7/2005 was carried out by British citizens of South Asian (Pakistani) backgrounds, as was the foiled coordinated airline hijacking plan of August, 2006. In the latter case, these were not "home grown" terrorists but were in close touch with their Pakistani roots and group leaders had reportedly received training in explosives and operations from al-Qaeda in Pakistan.

As was noted in the Terrorism Summit consensus statement, "Although most Muslim immigrants and refugees are not "stateless," many suffer from an existential sense of loss, deprivation, and alienation from the countries in which they live. They are often exposed to extreme ideologies that radicalize them and can facilitate entrance into the path of terrorism" (Post, 2005b, p. 9). The distress of the diaspora community has been confirmed by the Pew Global Attitude Survey (June 22, 2006). The issue of émigré/diaspora psychology has emerged as a major source of terrorist extremism.

While the purpose of this paper is not to provide a comprehensive review of the literature on terrorist psychology and the psychology of suicide terrorism, but rather to expand on the consensus view of experts on the psychology of terrorism summarized above, with special reference to suicide terrorism, we will comment on several social psychological and social process theories which in our judgment usefully contribute to understanding the phenomenon[11].

SOCIAL PSYCHOLOGICAL AND SOCIAL PROCESS THEORIES

Social Process Models

Active energy takes people through a series of difficult moral choices. Once a choice has been made, it is difficult to go back. Ariel Merari, a noted Israeli terrorism researcher, has addressed the "suicide bomber assembly line." He describes the manner in which an individual progresses from being recruited, to being publicly identified as a "walking martyr, the living dead," and then, to a final testament being videotaped while holding a Kalashnikov and Koran just before the act of martyrdom. It is extremely difficult to reverse oneself at the last minute after moving through this sequence; the shame and humiliation would be too great. In The Staircase to Terrorism, Fathali Moghaddam addresses the progress to terrorism as a series of steps on a narrowing staircase, with each step making it increasingly difficult to turn, further limiting the range of options ahead, until the individual feels choiceless and joins the group (Moghaddam, 2005). By implication, in a still narrowing staircase, there is a series of steps from terrorist to suicide terrorist, another way of conceptualizing Merari's "suicide bomber assembly line."

Hafez has emphasized three requirements for a campaign of suicide terrorism: a culture of martyrdom, a strategic decision by the group to use this tactic, and a willing supply of volunteers (Hafez, 2006). A number of scholars have emphasized the importance of

---

[11] Note: For a comprehensive review of psychological research on terrorism, see Jeff Victoroff "The Mind of the Terrorist: Review and Critique of Psychological Approaches," Journal of Conflict Resolution, 49, 3-42, 2005.

socialization and of the social context in which socialization occurs. Merari emphasizes that becoming a terrorist is "normal" within the Palestinian cultural context.

Mechanism of Moral Disengagement

Albert Bandura has applied theories of moral disengagement that he pioneered to the special population of terrorists (Bandura, 1990). Not unlike the socialization of soldiers, the demonization and dehumanization of the enemy facilitates transforming an act that violates their moral precepts into one which has societal value. Consider, for example, the following characterization of Israelis by an incarcerated Palestinian terrorist who, despite never having met an Israeli, other than at a checkpoint, is totally certain of their evil nature:

> *You Israelis are Nazis in your souls and in your conduct. In your occupation you never distinguish between men and women, or between old people and children. You adopted methods of collective punishment, you uprooted people from their homeland and from their homes and chased them into exile. You fired live ammunition at women and children. You smashed the skulls of defenseless civilians. You set up detention camps for thousands of people in sub-human conditions. You destroyed homes and turned children into orphans. You prevented people from making a living, you stole their property, you trampled on their honor. Given that kind of conduct, there is no choice but to strike at you without mercy in every possible way.* (Post et al., 2003, p. 12)

It should be stressed that similar sentiments concerning the Palestinians as evil are made by Israelis. The belief that members of "the other" in a conflict are evil is an example of the fundamental attribution error. The term refers to the tendency to overestimate the importance of dispositional or personality factors as causes of observed behavior by other people. In contrast, the actor-observer discrepancy refers to the tendency of the victim to justify his acts as required by "the other[12]." Thus the Palestinian quoted above feels

---
[12] See Ross & Nisbett (1991). Irving Janis incorporates this distinction in his concept of "group think," presented in Janis (1972).

justified in his acts, just as some Israeli counterterrorist officials feel justified in theirs. Each side feels like a victim, whose acts are compelled by the behavior of the other.

Intergroup Relations Theory, In-Group vs. Out-Group Enmity

Vamik Volkan in The Need for Enemies and Allies emphasizes the psychological "value" of enemies in constructing social identity. Through family and significant adults, such as teachers, we are socialized concerning those to feel comfortable with, those to treat as feared strangers (Volkan, 1988). The crystallization of the shared comfort of the familiar is the psychological foundation of nationalism. The fear of the stranger is the psychological foundation of the concept of the enemy.

The Psychology of Charismatic Leader–Follower Relationships

Post has characterized the powerful relationship between charismatic leaders and their followers (Post, 1986; Post, 2004). As we have come to understand the willingness of the suicide bombers to give their lives for an identified cause, for many religious terrorists, the subordination of individual identity to collective identity, as defined by the destructive charismatic leader, is crucial. This is true not only for the followers of charismatic religious leaders, such as Osama bin Laden and the former Hamas leader Sheikh Ahmad Yassin, but also for the "true believers" in the secular cause of Kurdish nationalism, who were devoted to Abdullah Ocalan, as well as the Tamil Tigers seeking Tamil independence who were devoted to Vellupillai Prabhakaran.

Deindividuation

This concept is closely related to the power of destructive charismatic movements. A number of scholars have addressed the social psychology of individuals in a collective, and the manner in which group norms can come to dominate individual morality. Deindividuation theories propose a subjective deindividuated state that causes a transgression of general social norms. Zimbardo, who pioneered the use of the term deindividuation has contrasted individuation, reason, and order versus deindividuation, impulse, and chaos (Zimbardo, 1969). Diener emphasized the lack of self-awareness when an individual is embedded in a group (Diener, 1980). As to how the influence of collective psychology can contribute to anti-social behavior, Postines and Spears have made a valuable contribution (Postmes & Spears, 1998). Their meta-analysis of deindividuation theory as an explanation of collective and anti-normative behavior found that groups and individuals conform more to situation-specific norms when they are "deindividuated," supporting a social identity model of deindividuation effects. This emphasis on the importance of social identity is consistent with the consensus finding of the Psychological Roots of Terrorism committee consensus statement, cited earlier (Post, 2005b, pp. 7–12).

EXPLANATORY INDIVIDUAL MODELS OF SUICIDE TERRORISM

There was a clear consensus among experts on terrorist psychology at the International Summit on Democracy, Terrorism, and Security that the most important explanatory factors for terrorism were to be found at the collective level, that there were no identifiable individual factors explaining becoming a terrorist, and that there was no unique terrorist mindset. Nevertheless, we are left with the disquieting question of why among large numbers of people exposed to a common environment, only a few become suicide terrorists. It is important to emphasize that as clinicians, the members of the committee were predisposed to find individual psychopathological explanations, but in this major review we simply did not identify discriminating individual psychopathological factors. That there was significant situational depressive and traumatic background in the populations from which the suicide bombers emerged is clear, but we were not able to identify factors which discriminated between the broader population and the much smaller number of suicide bombers.

A suicide bomber dispatcher interviewed by Berko asked recruiters for "sad guys" (Berko, 2007, p. 7). At first reading, this suggests that depressed individuals were being sought. But as Berko pursued this matter, the interview revealed that what he meant by "sad guys" was not depressed individuals, but "those who were social nonentities and had no status but who might get recognition by dying, those with low self-esteem . . . , men and women who have trouble finding themselves . . . bitter . . . at their marginality . . . who are willing to try anything to feel they have worth and to win the approval of society and their families"—in effect, "losers". The issue of underlying low self-esteem and the redemptive consequences of becoming a suicide terrorist has been emphasized by Raphael Israeli, who concluded that the act gave them "the opportunity to expand their own ego, and the newly acquired comradeship sustains their self-esteem and selfimportance" (Israeli, 2003). This concept of the "expanded ego" relates of course to the collective psychology of charismatic leader–follower relationships addressed above. No longer an isolated failing individual, now he is identified with the collective esteem of the shaheeds, the martyrs. Merari has reported that about one-third of intercepted shaheeds, examined during incarceration in Israel, exhibit depression, but they may have been depressed because of incarceration or their failure to carry out their martyrdom operation. Speckhard and colleagues have reported that virtually all Chechen suicide bombers have suffered severe traumatic experiences, and that their life course turned toward suicide bombing only after those experiences, but the base rate of trauma is so high among Chechens that its frequency might be as high among non-suicide bombers. Victoroff and colleagues found that depression was significantly associated with support for terrorism among teenaged refugee boys in Gaza, but as Victoroff acknowledges, there is a major gap between support for terrorism and becoming a terrorist suicide bomber. Moreover, it is manifestly impossible to conduct rigorous controlled research studies comparing those who do carry out suicide terrorist operations with the broader population who support the cause but do not carry out "martyrdom operations" (Victoroff, 2005).

There is anecdotal reporting that the trigger for many suicide terrorists, moving them from being supporters of the cause to taking action for the cause, was the death of a friend or sibling in a terrorist action. Sageman found that nearly all suicide terrorists have had at least one relative or close friend killed, maimed, or abused by their enemies (Sageman, 2004). Berko reports that suicide terrorists for the most part do not have economic problems nor do they have severe emotional disturbances, although many had fantasies of their families and society regarding them as "shaheed heroes" (Sageman, 2004, p. 9).

One interesting finding by Berko is that "potential suicide bombers describe the sensation of being 'uplifted,' a kind of elation when they reach the decision of istishhad, that is, to become shaheeds" (Sageman, 2004, p. 10). Experienced clinicians will recognize in this statement something that seems to resemble the peace and joy manifested by seriously depressed individuals when they commit themselves to the decision to suicide, often mistaken as reflecting clinical improvement. Yet Berko, in discussions pursued by the lead author, was adamant that her explorations with the families and friends of suicide bombers indicated that there were no changes in mood, no apparent depression, and that their child/sibling/friend seemed normal before the act, by which they were shocked and surprised.

KEY QUESTIONS AND CONCLUDING REMARKS

This review of the social and psychological factors pertinent to suicide terrorism leaves us grappling with difficult questions. For example, one of the current dilemmas is that for every terrorist killed or captured, there are ten more waiting in line to volunteer. Nasra Hassan, a Pakistani Muslim journalist with the United Nations, who has conducted extensive interviews with terrorist officials and with the "human bombs" and their families, reported that a Hamas leader told her: "Our biggest problem is the hordes of young men who beat on our doors, clamoring to be sent. It is difficult to select only a few. Those whom we turn away return again and again, pestering us, pleading to be accepted" (Hassan, 2001). What can be done to decrease recruitment? How can we counter the mobilization and radicalization of potential members?

If it is true that children enter the path of terrorism and martyrdom early, by the time they are late adolescents they have been exposed to the bitter gruel of hatred and the requirement for revenge, extolling the value of martyrdom for, in some cases, upwards of fifteen years. Attitudes change very slowly, and absolutist attitudes are notoriously impervious to change, indicating that interventions must occur before those absolutist attitudes are consolidated. How can parents be mobilized to inhibit the entrance of their children onto this deadly pathway?

Grief and despair are not always psychopathological, but psychiatrists have a long history of working with people who are experiencing these emotions. What are the effects on the prevalence of suicide bombings of the prohibitions against public expressions of grief after such bombings? What are the effects of celebrating these deaths? What happens when there is a suppression of the public expression of a sense of painful loss? Nasra Hassan's interview with a mother grieving the loss of her son in a martyrdom operation stated that if she had known, she would have cut open her heart with a cleaver, stuffed her son inside, and sewn it up to protect him, suggesting a major gap between the public requirement for celebration and private grief (Hassan, 2001, p. 41).

As we have noted, there are at least three prohibitions against suicide terrorism in the Koran. And yet, the extremist refraining of suicide terrorism as "martyrdom operations" has not been countered. What can be done to have moderate Muslim theologians, educators, and political leaders counter this extremist reframing? What steps can be taken to help some of the states particularly at threat from extremism to moderate their educational systems, to open up their societies?

The underlying question is, can we prevent suicide terrorism? Not in an absolute sense, but efforts towards reducing this phenomenon are obviously of the highest importance, and these efforts must derive from understanding the phenomenon. There are encouraging reports of the positive effects of using former terrorists to deradicalize militants (Kurlantzick, 2008). Indonesia, in particular, has reported striking success in winning militants' "hearts and minds," sending former members of Jemaah Islamiyah, the principal Indonesian militant Islamist terrorist organization, into Indonesian prisons to wean radicals away from terrorism. In 2004, Saudi Arabia instituted a deradicalization program, offering reduced prison sentences to jailed militants who undergo intensive classroom sessions. Egypt, Singapore, Malaysia, and Jordan have instituted similar programs. Great Britain's Muslim contact program is working with domestic Muslim groups to help deradicalize potential Muslim militants.

If we consider that suicide terrorism is the result of a complex psychosocial paythway, it is imperative to institute programs to inhibit individuals from entering that path in the first place and to facilitate exit from that pathway. Elements of such a program, which are informed by the social psychological/group emphases described above, ought to include: 1) inhibit potential terrorists from joining the group in the first place; 2) produce dissension in the group; 3) facilitate exit from the group; and 4) reduce support for the group and delegitimate its leaders[13].

Further work is called for, and nearly all parties would agree that this work must be multi-disciplinary. There are important social, political, and human rights issues to which psychiatrists can add their voice. Clearly, these call for major policy initiatives well beyond the boundaries of traditional psychiatry, but our understandings of the processes that lead youth into this deadly path can contribute to focused interventions. One contribution that psychiatrists can make in communities under stress is through improved access to psychological services, such as those provided by the Gaza Community Health Program. This may reduce the net level of psychic distress, increase the prevalence of hope, and conceivably reduce the allure of self-destruction in the name of a militant ideology.

One way to reframe terrorism, drawing upon these diverse perspectives, is to see it as a totalizing response that emerges out of numerous conflicts, decisions, and choices. The terrorists may ultimately say that they are confronted with one simple imperative (for example, a desire to damage and seek revenge against what they see as an occupying power), but arriving at this point requires the negotiation of various roles and social obligations, as well as a multitude of possible interpretations of these roles and obligations, some of which may be conflicting (such as whether a good son will abandon his parents by dying, or whether a good son is obliged to avenge the insult to his parents, etc.). Prior to engaging in terrorism, the terrorist must navigate a hierarchy of values in tension. These may include a sense of individuality versus a sense of belonging to a community; the perceived power and veracity of their religion versus the perceived humiliation of that religion by others, and, for that matter, conflicts within that religion; ways of judging right and

---

[13] For an expansion of these elements of an information operations program see Post (2005a).

wrong, and ascribing innocence and guilt; social and politically determined notions of us versus them; a personal sense of pride versus humiliation; and, desires for the worldly versus the heavenly. An individual makes a series of choices based on all these factors, which centrally includes questions of identity and belonging, ultimately resulting in whether or not to engage in suicide terrorism. These acts of suicide terrorism are then re-narrativized as a total resolution (an attack on Western values, on freedom, policies, etc.), both by perpetrators and by those who respond to such attacks.

Embedded in the development of a suicide terrorist is a process of balancing, negotiating, or rejecting these tensions and values. The reason why this is important is that it acknowledges that at every stage in the development of a suicide bomber, there are cultural, social, and political dimensions to the choice, as well as individual psychological choices. The extent to which one will sacrifice oneself for one's community, for example, is determined by sociopolitical, historical, and individual relations to that community, as well as the sociopolitical and historical construction of that community. Thus, it is simplistic to say that a terrorist easily rejects individual identity for the sake of a community, or merely reads or misreads Islamic scripture. Instead, if one is to understand how someone becomes a suicide terrorist, one is compelled to examine these different routes, rather than only accepting the final, devastating action as explanatory.

The immediate consequence of this framework is that efforts to prevent suicide terrorism must be directed at all the necessary but insufficient factors that result in suicide terrorism. A political framework may not explain why one individual is willing to sacrifice for the community while another is not. A sociocultural framework may not account for why one person will resist what another could not imagine doing; a psychological framework may not be able to account for economic and historical grievances. Understanding how these choices are made (the way they are narrativized and understood locally) is as essential as an understanding of why these choices are made (local loyalties, conceptions of choice, the way logic is used, the role of teachers and authority figures, etc.). Thus, while anthropological, psychological, political, and moral models may all have something to add, none can work independently; cross-disciplinary collaboration appears warranted, indeed is required.

Considering the growing number of vulnerable individuals in émigré and diaspora communities, interventions that respect cultural differences while concomitantly helping to integrate the refugees with the host society will be important. Community-based interventions aimed at promoting community and individual level changes that would support greater incorporation and integration of refugees and diaspora youth into the political culture of Western liberal democracies could significantly reduce the flow of alienated Muslim émigrés into the globa salafi jihad.

REFERENCES

Abdul-Khaliq, & Abdur-Rahman, S. (2004). *The Scientific Basis of the Salafi Da'wah*. New Delhi, India: Millat Book Center.

Abou El Fadl, K. (2005). Islam and the theology of power. *Islam For Today*. Retrieved on September 10, 2005, from Islam for Today Web site: www.islamfortoday.com/elfadl01.htm.

Abualrub, J. (2002). *Holy wars, crusades, jihad*. Columbia, MD: Madinah Publishers.

Al-Jazeera TV. (2001). In Osama bin Laden's own words: October 17, 2001. Retrieved December 2007 from September 11 News Web site: http://www.septemberllnews.com/OsamaSpeeches.htm

Ali, M. M. (translator) (2000). *A statement and clarification of al-Salafiyyah: Concepts and principles*, by Shaykh 'Abd al-'Aziz ibn 'Abd Allah ibn Baz. Suffolk: UK: Jam'iat Ihyaa' Minhaaj al-Sunnah.

Bandura, A. (1990). Mechanisms of Moral Disengagement. In W. Reich (Ed.), *Origins of terrorism: Psychologies, ideologies, theologies, states of mind* (pp. 161–191). New York: Cambridge University Press.

Berko, A. (2007). *The path to paradise: The inner world of suicide bombers and their dispatchers*. London: Praeger.

Bloom, M. (2005). *Dying to kill: The allure of suicide terror*. New York: Columbia University Press.

Crenshaw, M. (1981). The causes of terrorism. *Comparative Politics*, 13(4), 379–399.

Diener, E. (1980). Deindividuation: The absence of self-awareness and self-regulation in group members. In P. B. Paulus (Ed.), *The psychology of group influence* (pp. 209–242). Hillsdale, NJ: Lawrence Erlbaum.

Durkheim, E. (1951). *Suicide: A study in sociology*. Glencoe, 111: The Free Press. Translation by J. Spaulding & G. Simpson.

Erlanger, E. (2007, March 12). Years of strife and lost hope scar young Palestinians. *New York Times*, http://www.nytimes.com/2007/03/12/world/middleeast/12intifada.html

Hafez, M. (2006). *Manufacturing human bombs: The making of Palestinian suicide bombers*. Washington, DC: United States Institute of Peace.
Hassan, N. (2001). An arsenal of believers: Talking to the 'human bombs'. *The New Yorker, 77*(36), 36–41.
Haykel, B. (2005). Salafi Thought and Contemporary Islamic Politics. A paper presented to a United States Government conference.
Hoffman, B. (1998). *Inside terrorism*. New York: Columbia University Press.
Horgan, J. (2005). *The psychology of terrorism*. London: Cass Publications.
Israeli, R. (2003). *Islamikaze: Manifestations of Islamic martryotogy*. Portland, OR: Frank Kass Publishers.
Jacobson, P. (2001, August 19). Home-Grown Martyrs of the West Bank Reap Deadly Harvest. Sunday Telegraph, 20, as cited in Stern, J. (2003). *Terror in the name of God: Why religious militants kill*. New York: HarperCollins.
Janis, I. (1972). *Victims of group think: A psychological study of foreign-policy decisions and fiascos*. Boston: Houghton-Mifflin. "Jordan jihad theoretician Al-Maqdisi views disagreement with Al-Zarqawi," Al Hay at website, London, in Arabic, July 10, 2005.
Kelley, J. (2001). The secret world of suicide bombers. Devotion, desire drive youths to 'martyrdom' Palestinians in pursuit of paradise turn their own bodies into weapons. *USA Today*, June 26, 2001, A01.
Keniston, K. (1972). *Youth and dissent: The rise of a new opposition* (pp. 3–69). New York: Harcourt.
Kurlantzick, J. (2008, January 6). *Fighting terrorism with terrorists*. Los Angeles Times, http://articles.latimes.com/2008/jan/06/opinion/op-kurlantzick6
Laqueur, W., & Alexander, Y. (1987). *The terrorism reader: The essential source book on political violence both past and present*. New York: Meridian.
Magid, I. M. (2006). *Personal communication to Farhana Ali*, Spring 2006.
McCauley, C., & Segal, M. (1987). Social Psychology of Terrorist Groups. In C. Hendrick (Ed.), *Group processes and intergroup relations, Vol. 9 of Annual review of social and personality psychology*. Beverly Hills, CA: SAGE.
Merari, A. (2005). Social, organizational and psychological factors in suicide terrorism. In T. Bjorgo (Ed.), *Root causes of terrorism: myths, reality and ways forward* (pp. 70–86). New York: Routledge.
Moghaddam, F. (2005). Psychological processes and "the staircase to terrorism." *American Psychologist, 60*(9), 1039–1041.
Pedazhur, A. (2005). *Root causes of suicide terrorism: The globalization of martyrdom*. New York: Routledge.

Post, J. (1986). Narcissism and the charismatic leader-follower relationship. *Political Psychology, 7*(4), 675– 688.
Post, J. (2000). Murder in a political context: Profile of an Abu Nidal Terrorist. *Bulletin of the Academy of Psychiatry and the Law* (Spring, 2000).
Post, J. (2004). *Leaders and their followers in a dangerous world: The psychology of political behavior.* Ithaca, NY: Cornell University Press.
Post, J. (2005a). Psychological operations and counter-terrorism. *Joint Force Quarterly, 37,* 105–110.
Post, J. (2005b). *Psychological roots of terrorism. Addressing the Causes of Terrorism, Vol. 1, The Club de Madrid Series on Democracy and Terrorism.* Madrid, Spain: Club de Madrid.
Post, J. (2005c, August). When hatred is bred in the bone: The psychocultural foundations of contemporary terrorism. *Political Psychology, 26*(4), 615–636.
Poole, S. (2006). *Unspeak: How words become weapons, how weapons become a message, and how that message becomes reality.* London: Little Brown.
Post, J. (2007). *The mind of the terrorist: The psychology of terrorism from the IRA to alQaeda.* New York: Palgrave MacMillan.
Post, J., Sprinzak, E., & Denny, L. (2003). The terrorists in their own words: Interviews with 35 incarcerated Middle Eastern terrorists. *Terrorism and Political Violence, 15*(1), 171–184.
Postmes, T., & Spears, R. (1998). Deindividuation and anti-normative behavior: A meta-analysis. *Psychological Bulletin, 123*(3), 238–259.
Ross, L., & Nisbett, R. (1991). *The person and the situation: Factors of social psychology.* New York: McGraw Hill.
Sageman, M. (2004). *Understanding terror networks.* Philadelphia, PA: University of Pennsylvanian Press.
Schmid, A. (1983). *Political terrorism: A research guide to concepts, theories, data bases and literature.* New Brunswick, NJ: Transaction Books.
Shermer, M. (2006, January). Murdercide: Science unravels the myth of suicide bombers. *Scientific American,* p. 33.
Silke, A. (2003). *Terrorists, victims and society: Psychological perspectives on terrorism and its consequences.* West Sussex, England: Wiley Blackwell.
Smetana, J., Campione-Barr, N., & Metzger, A. (2006). Adolescent development in interpersonal and societal contexts. *Annual Review of Psychology, 57,* 255–284.
Steinberg, L., & Sheffield Morris, A. (2001). Adolescent development. *Annual Review of Psychology, 52,* 83–110.
United Nations. (2004). *A more secure world: Our shared responsibility.* Report of the Highlevel Panel on Threats, Challenges and Change.

Retrieved January 2008, from United Nations: Official Site Web site: http://www.un.org/secureworloVreport2.pdf
United States Department of Justice. (2001). *Terrorism 2000/2001.* Retrieved January 2008, from Federal Bureau of Investigation: Official Site. http://www.fbi.gov/publications/terror/terror2000_2001.htm
Venzke, B., & Ibrahim, A. (2003). *The al-Qaeda threat: An analytical guide to al-Qaeda's tactics and targets.* Alexandria, VA: Tempest Publishers.
Victoroff, J. (2005). The "mind of the terrorist": a review and critique of psychological approaches. *Journal of Conflict Resolution, 49*(1), 3–42.
Volkan, V. (1988). *The need to have enemies and allies: From clinical practice to international relationships.* London: Jason Aronson.
Zayat, M. (2004). *The road to Al Qaeda: The story of bin Laden's right-hand man.* London: Pluto Press.
Zimbardo, P. (1969). The human choice: Individuation, reason, and order vs. deindividuation, impulse and chaos. In W. J. Arnold and D. Levine (Eds.), *Nebraska Symposium on Motivation* (pp. 237–307). Lincoln, NE: University of Nebraska Press.

8

The Militant Jihadi Ideology of Martyrdom as Short-lived Psychological First Aid for Trauma and Loss

Anne Speckhard

Terrorism—that is political violence aimed at civilians—is a phenomenon that relies on the interaction of four things: (i) a group with a political agenda purporting to represent the political goals of some segment of society; (ii) an ideology the group uses to justify its use of violence against civilians; (iii) vulnerable individuals who resonate to the group and its ideology enough to join and agree to carry out acts of terrorism; and (iv) some level of social support existing for the group, its ideology, its violent acts, and its members (Speckhard, 2012). The militant jihadi ideology—that is used by Al-Qaeda and its many affiliate groups—is an ideology that promotes violent acts carried out by individuals and terrorist groups made up of Muslim members against their proclaimed enemies—'crusader' Western governments and their citizenry as well as the citizens of their own countries who are perceived as supported by Western governments.

While some are convinced of and indoctrinated into the militant jihadi ideology by religious argument and faulty logic alone (in which false religious statements are accepted as first premises and the logic for terrorist attacks against civilians built from there), most of them who join the militant jihad do so for reasons other than pure logic—many of them are emotionally based. For those who actually join terrorist groups and enact suicide terrorism in particular, individual vulnerabilities generally form the basis by which this ideology finds a foothold in their minds and souls, ultimately convincing the individual to be willing to sacrifice his own life to take the lives of others. This chapter explains how in conflict zones particularly, but in non conflict zones as well, where deep psychological vulnerabilities exist among Muslims and converts to Islam, the militant jihadi ideology is able to offer short-term psychological first aid—temporarily attending to the psychological needs of the person following it. If offers only a short-term remedy however, because it often ends in death of the person adopting it.

THE MILITANT JIHADI IDEOLOGY

Militant jihadi ideologues claim to represent the one true Islam and in doing so they hijack mainstream Islamic beliefs by incorporating many sacred scriptures, beliefs, and traditions into its weave. Indeed today we see that many young Muslims, especially those growing up in conflict zones, or affected by them, are raised with a subset of beliefs shared with militant jihadis, beliefs instilled during early childhood socialization. One of the most serious theorist writing on behalf of the militant jihadi ideology is a Syrian, Al-Suri who wrote that Al-Qaeda should work hard to widely spread its ideology to gain a diffuse and large group of followers in the coming generation who could ultimately rise up and might even self-organize into decentralized cells if necessary to carry out attacks on their own (Lia, 2008; Paz, 2005a). His hope in some ways has partially come to pass as there has been gradually over the years an increased acceptance of many of the militant jihad's tenets among mainstream Islamic believers. For instance, suicide bombing which was at first abhorred by most Muslims, is now often accepted as a legitimate defense for those living under occupation—Palestinians in particular—and glorified by many who would not otherwise endorse terrorism as Islamic 'martyrdom.' Likewise, female involvement in the militant jihad is also now much more widely accepted, although in some circles it is still resisted, and the use of weapon of mass destruction (WMD) which was at first rejected by militant jihadis has increasingly come to be accepted (Paz, 2005b).

The process whereby individuals come to accept the militant jihadi ideology and go on to enact terrorism—that is, move along the terrorist trajectory—is as multifaceted and contextual as there are persons in the world. However, one can see that the motivational states for taking part in terrorism differ according to those who live in conflict and non conflict zones (Speckhard, 2012).

INSIDE CONFLICT ZONES

From my research interviewing militants and terrorists inside conflict zones, I have learned that those who join militant jihadi terrorist groups and adopt the 'martyrdom' ideology to go on to take part in a suicide terrorist attack, do so largely out of motivations of deriving from traumatic loss and bereavement, loss of resources and territory, anger, desire for revenge, a desire to express individual and communal outrage, and frustrated aspirations. Indeed those who are exposed to violent conflict, especially young persons, often develop symptoms of posttraumatic stress disorder (PTSD) and dissociative phenomena (Speckhard, 2005, 2006, 2012; Speckhard & Akhmedova, 2005b, 2006).

POSTTRAUMATIC STRESS DISORDER (PTSD)

Individuals suffering from PTSD generally experience frequent intrusive thoughts or flashbacks of the traumatic experiences they have undergone and this incessant re-experiencing of acutely painful posttraumatic memories causes the body to go into a state of hyper-vigilance so that individuals with PTSD often suffer sleep disturbances, inability to concentrate, rapidly accelerating heart rate, sensations of panic, along with many other symptoms severely impeding normal psychosocial functioning.

Generally, individuals with PTSD attempt to avoid the triggers that cause flashbacks trying to shut down the constant re-experiencing and gain time to cope and hopefully regain normalcy as they put their traumatic experience into some kind of perspective. But in a conflict zone, avoidance of traumatic triggers is rarely possible and posttraumatic re-experiencing can be unremitting. And when a posttraumatic reminder triggers them into flashbacks, they may again feel the terror as though it is present in the here and now. In that case, the individual may feel so caught up in re-experiencing the pain of the past that they cannot decode accurately between the past and present-day experience—it becomes so mixed up in the traumatic flashback. That confusion can cause the individual to be thrust into a dissociative fog where they cannot think clearly and feels overwhelmed. Also one may only find relief from the posttraumatic recall when entering into dissociative states in which the individual deadens himself—that is, becomes emotionally numb and detached.

TRAUMATIC DISSOCIATION

Dissociation is a disconnection between a person's thoughts, memories, feelings, actions, or sense of identity. In healthy functioning people, normal dissociation occurs along a spectrum and may include experiences such as daydreaming and losing awareness of time while driving (as in 'highway hypnosis'), getting lost in work or heavily absorbed in a book or movie, all of which involve losing touch with awareness of one's immediate surroundings for a short period of time.

Pre-traumatic dissociation is also a normal phenomenon occurring in healthy people during or surrounding the time period of a traumatic event. In these cases, during and shortly after the trauma, one may become disconnected from one's emotions, thoughts, or other cognitive functions. This is quite common in response to traumatic exposure and is resolved for most people over a short period of time. For example, during a car accident, a personal assault or a natural disaster, many people may report a sense of time slowing down and then re-experience a series of flashbacks of what occurred until they can piece together the fragmented pieces of memory into a narrative recall of what actually occurred under terrifying circumstances. The occurrence of pre-traumatic dissociation may be a predictor of the onset of PTSD.

Persons who experience repeated terror states long after a traumatic episode may not have been able to fully integrate their terrifying experience into consciousness and the memories remain dissociated from continuous normal conscious awareness—except when they are triggered by reminders of it. For example, a person who has witnessed a violent death who cannot integrate the horrific experience into normal consciousness may continue well beyond the traumatic episode to undergo a cycle of flashbacks, avoidance, and hyper-arousal, or panicked bodily responses to triggers and reminders of the original trauma. He may then become caught up in a dysfunctional cycle in which he avoids traumatic triggers and flashbacks along with highly aroused mind/body states so much so that his normal functioning becomes impaired. This is the essence of PTSD.

Dissociation and PTSD, I found in my interviews, are quite active ingredients in the terrorist mix in terms of determining individual vulnerability to responding to the appeal of the militant jihadi ideology to potential recruits living inside conflict zones. And an overwhelming amount of psychological pain, in combination with the ability to dissociate from one's emotions—to narrow one's focus to the mission at hand and to go emotionally numb, appear to be prerequisites to suicide in general and to the ability of individuals to act as suicide bombers—as will be explained more in further sections (Speckhard, 2005, 2006, 2012; Speckhard & Akhmedova, 2005a, 2006).

Moh, a Palestinian from Gaza who suffered countless societal and familial traumas expressed his PTSD and psychic numbing this way, "I feel like I have no feelings, like my heart really wants to scream, shout, fight and cry but somehow my body keeps stopping it, but not on purpose." In this state, Moh was desperate for deliverance from his psychic pain and ripe for anyone who could offer a viable escape—perhaps even if it involved suicide, although he finally escaped Gaza (Speckhard, 2012). Killing and injury of one's loved ones, torture, and imprisonment are all traumatic stressors that occur in conflict zones and that can act to impel an individual to seek out a militant jihadi terrorist group to 'treat' psychological suffering.

PSYCHACHE, TRAUMA, DISSOCIATION, AND SUICIDE BOMBING

Edwin Shneidman (1993), one of the world's premier suicidologists, demonstrated that he could predict suicidal behavior based on a concept called psychache—defined as unbearable psychological pain, hurt, or anguish. Those bearing the heavy burden of psychache were the most likely to suicide. Shneidman (1995) saw suicide as a way of stopping one's consciousness and shutting down this unbearable psychological pain.

Bruce Bonger (2004) who studied normal suicide found in his research that many people audio, or videotape their suicide and that he could learn a lot about their mental state at the time of their final act by reviewing these recordings of normal suicides that were carried to completion. In nearly every case he found, the suicidal person generally became emotionally detached, strangely calm and went 'dissociative' or emotionally numb, as he came closer to carrying out the act.

When one reflects on overwhelming psychic pain it makes sense that at some point when it becomes too much it may require a 'shut down' response and if no other way to shut it down other than suicide exists—at least in the individual's perception—the dissociative defense may need to be engaged in order to carry out the suicide. Indeed, one might ask—without the ability to numb emotions how else could someone overcome the normal survival instinct in order to kick the chair, pull the trigger, or in the case of a suicide bomber, pull the strap that will detonate himself along with all his victims? Without dissociation, actually taking one's life may be too horrible of an idea to contemplate, much less to enact.

And it appears that not only is the dissociative defense active, but that for some, there is also a sense of euphoria or empowerment that kicks in when contemplating suicide. One warning sign that a normally suicidal person is serious and may imminently take his own life is if his depression suddenly lifts and he appears to be lighthearted and no longer burdened with overwhelming psychological pain. Indeed when he is totally prepared and committed to exit life, he may in the interim feel ecstatic. This sense of euphoria may also be a somewhat automatic neural defense—probably an opioid response to the horror of contemplating and even active planning suicide—especially if doing so in a violent manner. In my interviews and research about real and potential suicide bombers, I found these same markers of suicidal behavior also present in suicide terrorists (Speckhard, 2005, 2006, 2012; Speckhard & Akhmedova, 2005a, 2005b).

DISSOCIATION, SENSE OF EMPOWERMENT, AND EUPHORIA IN HYPOTHETICAL SUICIDE BOMBERS

Starting with the hypothetical, I (with three of my students) carried out a carefully executed 'thought experiment' with normal students of different nationalities at a European university who were asked to imagine themselves in the place of a failed Palestinian suicide bomber who had worn a bomb to his target but been arrested before detonating. Once established into the role-play these students were asked, among other things to 'recall' putting on the suicide vest and how they felt wearing it and going to their target. Amazingly, the students who imagined in a role-play putting on a suicide vest exhibited markers of suicide including signs of dissociation, euphoria, and lightness of being. For instance, one young female student while 'in role' stated:

> I had no fear—[I experienced] more of a tranquility.... The journey wearing the belt—it was like a dream, I floated along. I interacted with people but my mind was not there. I was not totally unconscious, but it was a muted scene, my senses were dulled. It felt euphoric, everything at ease.

When asked what it was like being arrested the student answered, "Like being woken up from a dream" (Speckhard, Jacuch, & Vanrompay, 2012).

More than half of the subjects during their role-plays went 'dissociative' at the point of being asked to 'recall' what it was like to strap on a bomb. They described how the bomb made them feel invincible, and how they felt like were floating, or outside of their own body, once it was strapped on. Some described euphoria. Others described emotional numbing (Speckhard et al., 2012).

It was astonishing to find ordinary students with no knowledge of suicide bombing—some did not even know where Israel is—who, after in imagination strapping on bombs, described experiencing the same dissociative effects as real bombers, floating outside of their bodies, feeling emotionally numb, euphoric or all powerful. It underlines that if this response shows up even in a role-play with normal students, we, as humans, must have some internal mechanism to detach from ourselves and our emotions to be able to kill ourselves. Dissociation in suicide must be innate (Speckhard et al., 2012).

DISSOCIATION AND EUPHORIA IN ATTEMPTED/ FAILED SUICIDE BOMBERS

The testimony of failed bombers bears this effect out as well. Omaia Damaj who I interviewed (with Yoram Schweitzer) in Israeli prison recalled how euphoric she felt waiting for 55 days before being activated on her suicide mission: "I felt myself above the ground." Her face took on a look of elation as she told me, "I felt myself as a soul, as if I was playing. I felt happiness. I felt like there was something running in front of me—my destiny." And as she continued to recall and re-enter this psychobiological state she had previously experienced waiting to go on her mission she became giggly and giddy—almost as though she was drunk. When asked if she wavered at all at that time, Omaia recalled, "No I never wavered. I never wanted to change my mind." Indeed as Omaia went deeper into her recall of that time and re-experienced the euphoria she felt then, she admitted it felt like being 'high' although she had claimed that she had used no substances to induce such a mental state at the time (Speckhard, 2012).

DISSOCIATION AND EUPHORIA IN ACCOMPLISHED SUICIDE BOMBERS

The same findings bore out in interviews with real terrorists. For instance, in the case of suicide bomber Darinaabu Aisha whose family members I interviewed, I learned from my colleague Yoram Schweitzer that Nasser, her sender while interviewed in prison, told Schweitzer that Darine was very calm and happy even as she was being equipped for her mission suggesting Darine had psychologically entered a dissociative state, seemingly emotionally detached from the horror she was about to enact and that she was possibly even euphoric (Y. Schweitzer, personal communication, November 02, 2007).

In Gaza, the widow of Tayseeral-Ajrami, who had bombed himself in an act of terrorism, when asked how her husband acted the night before he went on his mission recalled: "At about nine p.m., at night, he started looking at people, looking at their faces—his children, his mother, me," she stated.

And his cousin also recalled his psychological detachment: "You feel like he is next to you, but his mind is not with you."

It also seems that Tayseer entered the ecstatic state that suicide bombers often claim having felt before going to enact their missions. His wife told me:

One day before, he came home from work and he played an Islamic tape and started to dance with the children. On the day he went, his father said 'Wow you seem to be very happy!' Tayseer told his brother, 'I have my wife and children.' Then he added, 'There is only one thing missing. I want to blow myself up.' Only I paid attention to this.

Tayseer's cousin also recalled that on his 'martyr' video, "he is very happy, like before marriage or going on a vacation. He said, 'My dear wife, I just want you to be happy. Please don't be sad for me'" (Speckhard, 2012).

DISSOCIATION IN VOLUNTEERS FOR SUICIDE MISSIONS

When I interviewed Palestinian leader of the Al Aksa Martyrs Brigade, Zakaria Zuebedi in Jenin in 2005, during the second Intifada, about the many bombers he had dispatched on suicide missions he made some insightful comments about traumatic dissociation among this population as well, remarking: "They are completely different than us [fighters]. They have only one decision. We have many options. [For the fighter] the thought of running away is always available. [The fighter's] thoughts are always offensive. We go and shoot." But he explained, unlike the fight/flight response seen in fighters, those who have decided to become 'martyrs' are already in many ways dead in their minds. Zubeidi explained, "For the martyr all the cells in his mind are dead except for one." When I asked if the people who volunteer for suicide missions have seen a lot of death, been traumatized or have PTSD, Zubeidi answered, "They have flashbacks all the time and for them death is a mercy" (Speckhard, 2012).

LIVING DEATH AND A SENSE OF A FORESHORTENED FUTURE AMONG POTENTIAL 'MARTYRS'

Indeed I heard distressed comments about 'living death' from many Palestinians who during the second Intifada were exhausted from conflict, grief, and daily states of hyper-arousal and posttraumatic stress. PTSD also often involves a sense of a foreshortened future so much so that the sufferer does not expect to live a long life or carry out normal functions of life such as finishing school, getting married, or having children. This was something I found in interviews of traumatized individuals from Chechnya, Iraq, Kashmir, Palestine, and other conflict zones—they were steeped in overwhelming psychic pain or psychache and did not see much of a future. They felt emotionally dead and were actively using dissociation as a defense (Speckhard, 2012).

To those who already feel dead and who do not see a good future in front of them, the militant jihadi ideology offers suicide in a glorified form—Islamic martyrdom. And the offer of leaving their posttraumatic painful and dissociated state of being—where one does not feel really alive, is contrasted by the terror group, to a life in paradise with all the rewards of martyrdom. These rewards include a life of pleasure, implied sexual gratification, peace, and also that one need not feel guilty about leaving the family behind because they too will be granted entry into paradise by virtue of their relative's act of martyrdom. In the case of suicide terrorism, all it takes is donning a suicide vest, pushing a button, and stepping from this reality into the next (Speckhard, 2012).

So, we see the power of the militant jihadi ideology. It can move someone from a state of 'living death,' deep emotional pain, constant flashbacks, posttraumatic arousal, terrifying nightmares, inability to concentrate, survivor guilt, and a sense of an already foreshortened future by offering them a fantasized future in the afterlife—the passage to that they can be in at least partially in charge of rather than being the helpless pawn of fate that many feel who live in a conflict zone. And grasping toward this future imparts a deep sense of calm, possibly euphoria up to the minute they push the button or pull the cord if they believe that they are exiting this misery to gain eternity and in doing so also expressing the collective outrage. And, if there exists enough social support for taking this action to become a 'martyr,' then they can also expect to be glorified, celebrated, and remembered by one's family and society (Speckhard, 2006, 2012).

DISSOCIATION IN A TERRORIST SENDER OF SUICIDE BOMBERS

Zubeidi, the Palestinian sender of suicide terrorists mentioned earlier, also recalled in his interview with me, personally experiencing a deeply dissociative and suicidal state at one particular crisis moment when he had decided to die rather than be re-arrested and returned to Israeli prison. Zubeidi had engaged in many gunfights with the Israelis, but once found himself cornered by Israeli soldiers and thought he was seemingly overcome. He recalled that at first he decided to exit his hideout shooting and trying to take out as many enemies as possible knowing he would die doing so. He said that deciding to 'martyr' himself in this way he entered a deeply dissociative trance that enabled him to open the door and walk toward his certain death, but then in stepping out of the door he suddenly realized that he could possibly fight and escape. "You can say this [dissociative episode] happened in two stages," Zubeidi explained, his black eyes flashing:

> *It's a point you reach. The first stage was when I was inside the room. I took a look from the window. I decided I want to die. But when I got my weapon ready and jumped up, I decided not to die. I felt like the feeling of being a martyr when I jumped up, but it changed just when I opened the door. In one flash my feelings changed from asking to be martyred to cursing.* (Speckhard, 2012)

COUNTERING DISSOCIATIVE STATES WITH ANGER

It is interesting to me that Zubeidi, like so many others, I interviewed countered his dissociative state with anger. He also differentiated his own dissociative response which was temporary and quickly moved from the frozen dissociative trance of the traumatized individual to the fight and flight response of a still functioning mind from that of the suicide bombers who he described as constantly in a state of dissociated 'psychic death' and who thus volunteer for their self-enacted exits from this world (Speckhard, 2012).

Another young woman I interviewed in Palestine, the daughter of a frequently incarcerated terrorist leader explained that she often experiences dissociative states in which she loses her mental functions. She explained its occurrence: "When I lose someone, when someone is arrested, shot or killed. I reach a point when I cannot concentrate on anything. I feel I am lost, too." When asked how she recovers herself, she stated that she countered this hyper-aroused and dissociative state common to trauma victims—the loss of concentration and loss of self—with anger, saying, "Anger pushes me further. It gives me hope" (Speckhard, 2012).

DISSOCIATION IN A TERRORIST ASSASSIN

When I asked Hamdi Quran, the Palestinian assassin of the Israeli Tourism Minister Rehavam Zeevi to tell me about the time period leading up to his mission he recalled: "I knew for two months that I will do it." Hamdi's eyes became unfocused as he returned in memory to that time period recalling, "I rehearsed it. Everything was ready. I went twice to the hotel. I slept there and got familiar with it" (Speckhard, 2012).

When I asked him his feelings during that time he recalled, "The feeling of getting revenge. It made me not feel anything. I was really focused on success, no way to fail." His remarks reminded me of the Belgian thought experiment—he sounded to me like they described imagining themselves on a suicide mission—their focus narrowed in on the mission and revenge—all other emotions dissociated from consciousness. Hamdi it turned out also had his own traumatic past having witnessed too much violence and having lost loved ones to the conflicts in the two Palestinian Intifadas (Speckhard, 2012).

So whether sending an operative to outright explode himself or to fight and kill in a potentially suicidal mission, it seems that terrorist groups learn to identify those whose anger can no longer keep them present and for whom psychache is overwhelming, and life has become a burden of 'living death.' Those persons are ready to suicide but would probably never enact a normal suicide—forbidden as it is in their culture and religion. However, when the idea of 'martyrdom' is sold to them as a short-lived type of psychological first aid, the groups find willing recruits—willing to trade in their foreshortened, painful lives and take the chance that blowing themselves up along with their intended victims will successfully cross them over into the long awaited bliss of paradise. And for some—weapons are supplied to fight and risk death as a 'martyr.'

PTSD, TRAUMATIC BEREAVEMENT, AND THE WISH TO REUNITE WITH A LOVED ONE

Traumatic bereavement is also a grave marker of vulnerability to being recruited into the militant jihad for a 'martyrdom' mission. Normal grief involves a state of denial, bargaining, and hopelessness in which work of grieving demands that the individual eventually let go of the past and make new attachments to replace those formerly filled by the deceased. In the short term, however, it is completely normal for a bereaved individual to express a desire to die—in order to rejoin his deceased loved one.

In the traumatically bereaved, the grief process is often highly complicated and blocked by the presence of PTSD. What should be normal grieving gets caught up in a cycle of overwhelming psychological pain and bodily hyper-arousal as the death is traumatically re-experienced in flashbacks, nightmares, intrusive thoughts, etc. and the concomitant cycle of trying to shut it all down in attempts to avoid. And sometimes, there is even posttraumatic amnesia for parts of the death event. These all impede the normal grief process and make letting go and forming new attachments difficult.

Arin Ahmed, a failed Palestinian suicide bomber and Elza Gazuyeva, a successful Chechen suicide bomber each volunteered for and went on their missions shortly after the violent death of their significant other (at the hands of the Israelis in Arin's case[1] and the Russian Federal Forces in Elza's case). In both cases, the two women quickly changed as a result of traumatic bereavement, adopting the dress and attitudes of the fanatic groups, and they each went to the extremists begging to be equipped for a suicide mission to revenge on those who had killed their loved one (Speckhard, 2012).

---

[1] There is some dispute over whether Arin's boyfriend was indeed killed by an Israeli missile or blew himself up when working on an explosive in his car, but Arin attributed his death to Israeli missile fire.

In the case of Elza Guzuyeva, her husband and brother had been dragged by Russian Federal Forces from the home, beaten in front of her eyes and later found dead with marks of torture on their bodies. In three-month time, Elza equipped with a suicide bomb went to the military man in charge of taking her loved ones and blew herself up killing him as well. In Arin's case, she also suddenly became extremist in her dress and beliefs and went to a terrorist group begging for a bomb in response to her boyfriend's death. The terror group welcomed her inner state of traumatic bereavement and she was sent on her mission in only two weeks' time.

If Elza had only been traumatized—but never exposed to an ideology and group that glorified taking one's own life in order to kill others, and stood ready and willing to equip her, she would never have been able to carry out her suicide act. Instead, she would have mourned and struggled her way through the posttraumatic stress and traumatic bereavement of her husband's and brother's deaths and possibly become a psychologically damaged person. But eventually, it is likely she would have made a livable adjustment to her grief—as most war and murder survivors do—without becoming violent. Arin Ahmed also would never have nearly carried out a suicide attack[2] had there not been a ready terrorist group with an ideology that fit her grief and trainers to equip her who were willing to capitalize on her state of traumatic bereavement (Speckhard, 2012). So, we see that all the elements must be present for the militant jihadi 'first aid' to work—there must be a group to equip the vulnerable individual, the ideology that fits his or her pain, and some degree of social support for accepting the ideology and the group's violent means and goals.

PTSD, PRISON, AND TORTURE

In conflict zones, especially when terrorism abounds, the opposing side often resorts to rounding up security detainees and imprisoning large numbers of potential and real plotters. And if imminent attacks are suspected, some of these detainees may even be tortured. While in the short term this may thwart terrorism, it also provides fertile

---

[2] Arin Ahmed wearing a bomb turned back from her mission at the last moment.

ground for the militant jihadi ideology to take root. Not only are prisons often recruiting and indoctrination centers for terrorist groups—having been imprisoned and mistreated or tortured, is itself a type of traumatic stress that may then contribute to individuals' increased vulnerability to the militant jihad (Speckhard, 2012).

For instance, when Palestinian terrorist leader Zubeidi told me that he would rather be killed—and 'martyr' himself by shooting as many Israelis as possible before being shot dead, then go back to prison, he was remarking on the horror he had experienced as a caged animal. He described it thus: "going back to prison is like going to a piece of hell. Prison, even if only a cage, with no torture—it takes all your achievements. In one moment it all disappears. You always keep remembering—the outside, the outside.... You start to hallucinate." And he recalls that when he was cornered by the Israelis he wanted to die rather than be rearrested as he got a flashback of the horrors of being imprisoned: "[At that moment] I got the whole tape rewound, the whole prison, flashbacks of the prison" (Speckhard, 2012).

After many interviews with Palestinians who had been jailed in their youth, or even later in their twenties, and also interviews with Chechens about tortured and detained loved ones, I have come to understand how arrest and imprisonment is a clear traumatic stressor for many. The complete powerlessness, helplessness, and stress of imprisonment, especially if torture was involved leave these traumatized individuals with many serious symptoms of posttraumatic stress. They are in need of help to calm them from the psychological trauma upon their release, but there is often no one who can help. Even parents often cannot protect their minor children in situations such as this, and often times, the parents are also traumatized by their child's sudden arrest and have no access to psychological help and stigma even if they were to seek it. This leaves those who have been imprisoned at the mercy of terrorist groups who can offer them the 'martyrdom' ideology to enter into a state of calm euphoria as the group equips them for revenge (Speckhard, 2012).

A Palestinian, Hamid spoke to me about being a prisoner in Israel under administrative detention, what he called an 'open check' prisoner with no conviction or sentence. His terms in prison stretched before him with no clear end in sight and when he was released he lived in constant fear of being re-arrested—a state he told me, felt like no life at all. Clearly traumatized by his time in prison, I feared that it would be easy for a group to take advantage of his constant fear of being imprisoned again and feeling that his life is already a type of 'living death'—that pushed a bit further, he could easily be manipulated by terrorists into giving up his life for the cause as a 'martyr' (Speckhard, 2012).

The Palestinian parents of Nidalabu Shaduf, a suicide bomber, told me that their son volunteered for a suicide mission after many of his friends had been 'martyred'—violent imprints that made him desperate enough to want to take his own life. They also described the experiences of Ismael, Nidal's brother, who was imprisoned afterward showing how and what happens in prison can cause PTSD:

> With Ishmael [Nidal's brother while in prison], the Israelis brought pieces of his corpse in order to put him under pressure to confess, as well as threats of destroying his house! . . . In fact, they destroyed the house of his father. Their torture can be on high levels. They press on the prisoner with psychological methods. For instance, they take pictures of you first in prison and another one when in miserable shape one month after the torture and show it to you. It's some kind of psychological torture. They want the prisoners [under interrogation] to see only the detective and to listen to loud music so you feel you are all alone in this world. And of course they bring you fake news of your parents. 'Your father has died.' 'Your brother died.'[3]

Of course a son who returns from these types of prison experiences is unlikely to be psychologically calm and may find comfort in promises of a better life after passing from this one—even if the passing is violent and aimed at hurting others (Speckhard, 2012).

PTSD, HYPER-AROUSAL, AND THE MARTYRDOM IDEOLOGY

With PTSD, the sufferer generally has recurrent thoughts, feelings, entire memory states that can feel very much like full sensory movies

---
[3] Unpublished research interviews in Palestine, 2005.

replaying of the traumatic event, and the associated bodily states of fear, inability to concentrate, nervousness, sweating, racing heartbeat, shallow breathing, etc. This latter is called hyper-arousal. Fugitive terrorist, Zubeidi described his state of hyper-arousal at night when he believed the armed Stealth was flying overhead searching for him in attempts to target an assassination saying, "A person at night goes insane, he is annoyed, and feels aware," Zubeidi recounted, adding, "It happens to me daily" (Speckhard, 2012).

Some trauma survivors find the anxiety suffered in states of hyper-arousal so physiologically painful that they seek death 'as a mercy' as Zubeidi referenced it, and they volunteer for 'martyrdom' missions (Speckhard, 2012). And while simple suicide is forbidden, according to the militant jihadis, 'martyrdom' is not. A group that can arm one to strike the enemy, carry out revenge, and bring a glorious end to one's personal pain while expressing outrage and causing suffering to the other side with the promise to immediately cross over into paradise is powerful indeed. It provides a short-lived but powerful anecdote to the psychache of PTSD and posttraumatic hyper-arousal (Speckhard, 2012; Speckhard & Akhmedova, 2005a).

PTSD AND INCREASED FANATICISM AND IDENTIFICATION WITH THE AGGRESSOR

In Chechnya, my research associate Khapta Akhmedova found that among those she studied the more severe their traumatization from conflict was, the more likely they were to become fanatical and extremist in their beliefs. I found a similar response among many that I interviewed, and we found the same in our joint work in Chechnya (Akhmedova, 2003; Speckhard, 2012; Speckhard & Akhmedova, 2005a, 2005b, 2006).

It is normal for individuals who are facing life-threatening circumstances to turn to religion for answers and when things are chaotic to possibly gravitate to more fundamentalist views that offer structure and surety. Thus, when threat is high as in conflict zones, the militant jihad finds a perfect foothold.

A young Palestinian girl described to me her response when her life was threatened of turning away from modern culture and finding comfort in turning to the fundamentals of her religion:

> *Since the (second) Intifada, I know I can be killed anytime. Before it started, when I was in high school I wanted to be a Spice Girl. All my friends decided which one we were, and I was Baby Spice. I wanted to be modern and wore my veil only after school. Then when the Intifada started, I was in a minibus with a group of girls when gunshots fired in our direction. If the bus was not moving so fast, one of us would have been shot dead. At that moment, I became so afraid of dying!*[4]

She goes on to explain that after this experience she could not stand to think of dying without her veil (hidjab) on, fearing that failing to follow the traditions of her faith at the moment of her death might compromise her eternal soul (Speckhard, 2012).

Victims in conflict zones often cannot stand to face their own powerlessness in the face of random and chaotic violence—especially if their victimization occurred in childhood—and may copy by identifying with the power of the aggressor, preferring to remember what hate and power feel like versus powerlessness and pain. This identification can result in re-enacting the aggressor's actions when memories of pain and powerlessness are triggered. Avoiding re-experience of overwhelming emotional pain, the victim chooses to put himself in the opposite position and aggresses on other, new victims. This phenomena explains why child abuse survivors can grow up to be abusers, why violence gets repeated over and over again, often being carried out by victims who should have empathy, but who cannot stand to recall their own powerlessness and why victims of violence in conflict zones may choose to become violent themselves.

We found this in one of our Chechen interviews with a woman named Laila, who recounted: "I will never go to kill civilians who are not guilty in anything, but after the death of my brother, I have thoughts about blowing myself up in some checkpoint with military men." This in itself would be revenge-seeking behavior but as she goes on to explain a recent event it was clear that she could no longer stand the feelings of victimization and powerlessness she was experiencing (Speckhard, 2012).

Laila found herself on the bus from Grozny into neighboring Ingushetia where she had to get out at all of the numerous

---
[4] Unpublished research interviews in Palestine, 2005.

checkpoints and in doing so she was unable to deaden her feelings of rage against the Russian soldiers. Deeply traumatized over the loss of her brother and the societal wide conflict, she was finding it increasingly difficult to carry on in the face of daily humiliations and dangers and remain passive.

"At the last checkpoint, our bus was stopped by Russian service men," the woman recalls of the scene, her voice laced with anger. "They ordered all of us to leave the bus and to show our passports. We got off and the servicemen with their dogs began to check the bus" (Speckhard, 2012).

This checkpoint is particularly well known and feared by Chechens because at the time it had a 'pit' into which Chechens were sometimes thrown for many days, their stories usually ending badly.

Her anger bubbling inside, as all the riders were taken off of the bus, coupled with the terror of knowing any one of them could be hauled off to the pit—to be tortured and perhaps eventually killed—lit the fuse of a bomb ticking inside her. Like anyone faced with overwhelming threat to life Laila had three instinctual choices: to fight, take flight, or freeze. Without even thinking it over, her brain identified with the aggressors and chose to fight (Speckhard, 2012).

"After checking my passport I moved a little to the side and waited for the check to end," she recalled. "I saw nearby two soldiers drinking beer, and their automatics lay near them. I don't know how I did it, or what for—during that moment there were not any thoughts in my head," she recalls. "I approached them and snatched up an automatic and pointed it at these two soldiers and told them, 'Hands up!'" (Speckhard, 2012).

What this subject is describing is a severe dissociative moment in which her posttraumatic rage took over. Common in extreme trauma survivors, it occurs when overwhelming fear, anger, or other strong emotions are triggered by reminders of pasttrauma(s), severely altering their normal state of consciousness and battling helpless terror they move to cold anger in order to be able to cope. In these moments of rage, the individual may feel nothing, stop thinking rationally, feel outside of their own bodies, or fail to record memories. This subject describes having no thoughts that drove her actions—that she acted automatically—choosing senseless aggression as the involuntary defense to her consuming feelings of fear and powerlessness (Speckhard, 2012).

"They turned pale, absolutely white—such fear was in their eyes!" she recalls of her short moment of power. "I don't remember how long I held them under the barrel" (Speckhard, 2012).

> *Some women from our bus ran up to me and took the gun away and put it back in its place, and put me into the bus quickly. Then all the people in the bus screamed at me, that I am not a normal person and so on. They were very frightened—but I didn't feel anything.* (Speckhard, 2012)

In this case, we see a severely traumatized person under so much threat that her normal cognitive functions dropped out and her brain judged for itself in its altered state how to save her—in this case choosing aggression. It took some time to return to her normal self (Speckhard, 2012).

Although this subject prayed to Allah to stop her from taking violent actions, when her PTSD was severely triggered, she, in a trance-like state, succumbed to re-enacting what had been done to her many times—this time with her in the empowered position. Interestingly, her reaction appears both non volitional and irresistible. Given her posttraumatic grief and rage coupled with her posttraumatic dissociative tendencies, she could also have fallen prey to the militant jihadi ideology enacting terrorism as a means of restoring her sense of self-empowerment under threat. They would have told her that her prayers to Allah to restrain her posttraumatic rage are unnecessary and that Allah wants her to take up arms, kill her enemies and if need be 'martyr' herself in doing so. They would have taught her that to suicide is a sin, but to 'martyr' oneself is to honor God and family and that 'martyrdom' will take her out of her overwhelming emotional pain and bring her to a good end—but in reality the militant jihadi ideology is just short-term psychological first aid for the traumatized that in the long-term ends in the death of the one who applies it (Speckhard, 2012).

This woman recalled of her non volitional behavior, "Now I understand that I could have been arrested or killed in that place, but I don't know how I did it" (Speckhard, 2012).

DEFICITS OF PSYCHOLOGICAL ASSISTANCE FOR TRAUMA, LOSS, AND DISSOCIATION IN CONFLICT ZONES

Individuals can and do heal from PTSD but often professional help is necessary. In conflict zones such help is rarely available and even when it is it may not be culturally acceptable to pursue it. In 2005, during the height of the second Intifada, I spoke with Palestinian young men in the West Bank who were happily surprised to learn that I am a psychologist. They told me, "You know there is no place to go to get help here, no psychological services. My friends and I discuss this often." On my side, I was surprised that young men would be discussing the non availability of psychological services. They were part of a highly traumatized population with no psychological assistance (Speckhard, 2012).

While some will turn to alcohol, drugs, sexual acting out, or any remedy that deadens the pain, some despairing victims in conflict zones where militant jihadis and the 'martyrdom' ideology is active will also turn to ideologies and actions that promise what seems to be an honorable exit from life—taking their own lives while killing their enemies.

Elza Guzuyeva and Arin Ahmed, both traumatically bereaved and living in a conflict zone where no psychological assistance was readily available turned to terrorist groups to help them deal with their overwhelming grief and anger and they were offered psychological 'fixes' although short-lived ones. If there had been no exposure to a terrorist group or ideology and little social support for taking such a turn, neither would likely have become a suicide bomber. It took a terrorist group and an extreme ideology to take advantage of them in their most vulnerable moments of posttraumatic grief, to turn each into a bomber who was willing to kill and be killed. Deep and often repeated psychological traumatization coupled with exposure to a terrorist group and ideology is necessary ingredients to make an ordinary person into a terrorist. And the more social support there is, the easier the decision becomes. And Laila who picked up arms against the Russians, turning herself from victim to aggressor could also likely have had her psychological vulnerability manipulated by a group that tells her that to suicide is a sin, but to 'martyr' oneself is to honor God and family.

If she fell into the hands of the militant jihadis, they would tell her that 'martyrdom' can take her out of her overwhelming emotional pain and bring her to a good end—but in reality, the militant jihadi ideology is just short-term psychological first aid for the traumatized that in the long-term ends in the death of the one who applies it (Speckhard, 2012).

Non-conflict Zones

How the militant jihad takes advantage of vulnerable individuals inside conflict zones is relatively simple to understand from a trauma psychology perspective, but how does the militant jihad operate in non-conflict zones? What vulnerabilities and hooks inside the individual does the ideology rest upon in order to draw willing recruits to these groups and to enact terrorism?

Despite many counterterrorism experts arguing that poverty is not a contributor to terrorism I found in the slums of Morocco that along with frustrated aspirations, extreme poverty was a great vulnerability among those recruited to become the Casa Blanca suicide bombers. When I went to interview their close friends in the Sidi Moumen slum in 2007, experiencing the slum myself and hearing the pain and desperation of their stunted lives—caught in poverty and unemployment—while seeing a completely other life on satellite TVs and over the Internet—and even by walking just outside of the slums—seeing that with a job and money there is another life to be had, I began to understand. By no fault of their own—other than place of birth—they are sentenced to dull lives where they have few good choices. The would-be bombers of Casa Blanca were facing lives that were completely blocked with frustrated aspirations on all fronts. Even though education is, as their friends told me, provided by the state, it will not lead to jobs as long as they are slum dwellers, and without jobs they have no chance of normal sex lives or marriage and only a bleak endless future of nothingness. And all lack any positive means of escape from overwhelming despair and psychic pain. Instead, each found his own negative means of escape: drugs, prostitutes, and hopes of clandestine illegal migration while the bombers found theirs in 'martyrdom.' So they can be petty criminals, drug addicts, frequenters of prostitutes, stowaways, or other negative identities that all end badly and have few, to no good paths in life (Speckhard, 2012).

Of course, for the Casa Blanca bombers it was not only poverty and desperation that turned them into terrorists. It also took a terrorist recruiter and an attractive ideology to convince the boys who 'martyred' themselves that this was an instant gateway to paradise. But for young men caught up in hopeless despair, poverty, a life with no future and drug addicted, the lethal cocktail of terrorism worked. And in this case, the lethal cocktail consisted of the same four elements as usual with the contextual elements of a slum in Morocco: (i) young men filled with overwhelming individual vulnerabilities, (ii) a recruiter to introduce and seduce them into a virulent ideology (using Islam as his starting point) that in the short-term answers their psychological needs (cleaning them up from drugs and restoring their sense of dignity and purpose), (iii) a group to equip them, and (iv) social support in the immediate milieu and worldwide to glorify their decision to carry out their acts of terrorist violence (Speckhard, 2012).

But it is not only poverty that creates vulnerability in non conflict zones. Traumas occur in non conflict zones as well and all the same elements apply in these cases. For instance, the downfall of Muriel Deguaque, the first white European female suicide bomber, followed after she suffered a deep trauma along with exposure to a terrorist group and ideology.

In Muriel's case, she had been deeply traumatized by the death of her brother in an accident and was deeply troubled with post-traumatic stress, survivor guilt, and complicated mourning. Her first response to her trauma had been turning to drugs and failing to function but when she was exposed to people ready to take advantage of her vulnerabilities, she was led into the militant jihadi interpretation of Islam. In her quest for a new and redeemed identity, Muriel first renamed herself with the Islamic name Myriam, cleaned up from her drug habits and began on the Salafi path before stepping into Takfiri beliefs and embracing the Al-Qaeda ideology. A guilt-ridden woman would certainly resonate with the promise of being absolved of her drug using past and deep self-condemnation over surviving when her brother did not and gaining instant access to paradise upon completing her suicide act. There she found a way to cleanse herself of her survivor guilt by becoming strictly fundamentalist and a group who helped her retain that feeling of being okay with the world—as long as she kept deepening her commitment to their cause and ultimately gave her life to it. That is the fundamental problem with the psychological first aid that the 'martyrdom' ideology offers—one always needs to trade in one's life for that sense of peace. Looking at Muriel Deguaque's psychosocial history shows the same lethal cocktail of suicide terrorism as exists inside conflict zones: (i) a vulnerable individual; (ii) hooked up to a group that is willing and able to equip her for violence; (iii) convinced of an ideology that meets her psychological needs—cleansing her of her survivor guilt, offering her instant admission to paradise, where she hoped to reunite with her brother, and that gave her the courage to carry out her act; and (iv) social support for doing so (Speckhard, 2012).

Another vulnerability that is active in non conflict zones includes deep guilt over some forbidden behaviors—sexual acting out, homosexuality, drug use, etc. Muslims are never assured their sins will not block them from paradise, except in the case of martyrdom, so when a recruiter finds an individual heavily burdened with guilt he can more easily sell the idea. Similarly, for those Muslim immigrants of first- or second-generation descent living in Europe, social marginalization, discrimination, frustrated aspirations can all combine to make the militant jihad appeal to a desire for meaning, belonging, self-esteem, and even to a sense of the heroic and adventure. Likewise when there is a missing father, the bonds of brotherhood extended by the militant jihadi group can be strong indeed. Lastly, militant jihadi ideologues and recruiters working in non conflict zones also have become adept at bringing images of the conflict zones to their potential recruits and this can create secondary traumatization. For instance, the Casa Blanca slum dwellers told me that their friends—the actual bombers—had watched film after film of human rights violations and sufferings of Palestinians, Chechens, Iraqis, etc. Such propaganda materials are used to traumatize and inflame outrage and motivate recruits to want to sacrifice themselves for the cause (Speckhard, 2012).

SUMMARY

Militant jihadi terrorist groups are adept at using their ideology and the bonds of brotherhood to psychologically vulnerable individuals offering them psychological 'first aid' to motivate them to take part in 'martyrdom missions,' basically exchanging their troubled lives for the 'short-term' fix offered for the trauma, loss, and dissociation that is ubiquitous in conflict zones and other psychological vulnerabilities that exist in non-conflict zones.

REFERENCES

Akhmedova, K. (2003). Fanatism and revenge idea of civilians who had PTSD. *Social and Clinical Psychiatry, 12*(3), 24–32.
Bonger, B. (2004). *Suicide terrorism.* Paper presented for Suicide Terrorism: Strategic Importance and Counterstrategies, NATO Advanced Research Workshop, Lisbon, June 10–14.
Lia, B. (2008). *Architect of global jihad: The life of al-Qaida strategist Abu Mus'ab al-Suri.* New York: Columbia University Press.
Paz, R. (2005a). *Al-Qaeda's search for new fronts: Instructions for jihadi activity in Egypt and Sinai.* PRISM Occasional Papers, 3(7).
Paz, R. (2005b). Global jihad and WMD: Between martyrdom and mass destruction. *Current Trends in Islamist Ideology, 2,* 74–86.
Shneidman, E. S. (1993). Suicide as psychache. *Journal of Nervous Mental Disorders, 181*(3), 145–147.
Shneidman, E. S. (1995). *The suicidal as psychache: A clinical approach to self-destructive behavior.* Lanham, Maryland: Jason Aronson, Inc.
Speckhard, A. (2005). Understanding suicide terrorism: Countering human bombs and their senders. In J. S. Purcell & J. D. Weintraub (Eds.), *Topics in terrorism: Toward a transatlantic consensus on the nature of the threat.* Washington, DC: Atlantic Council.
Speckhard, A. (2006). Sacred terror: Insights into the psychology of religiously motivated terrorism. In C. Timmerman, D. Hutsebaut, S. Mells, W. Nonneman, & W. V. Herck (Eds.), *Faith-based radicalism: Christianity, Islam and Judaism between constructive activism and destructive fanaticism.* Antwerp: UCSIA.
Speckhard, A. (2012). *Talking to terrorists: Understanding the psychosocial motivations of militant jihadi terrorists, mass hostage takers, suicide bombers and "martyrs".* McLean, VA: Advances Press.
Speckhard, A., & Akhmedova, K. (2005a). Talking to terrorists. *Journal of Psychohistory, 33*(2), 125–156.
Speckhard, A., & Akhmedova, K. (2005b). Mechanisms of generating suicide terrorism: Trauma and bereavement as psychological vulnerabilities in human security – The Chechen case. In J. Donnelly, Anna Kovacova, Joy Osofsky, Howard Osofsky, Caroline Paskell, & J. Salem-Pickartz (Eds.), *Developing strategies to deal with trauma in*

children—A means of ensuring conflict prevention, security and social stability. Case Study: 12–15-Year-Olds in Serbia (Vol. 1, pp. 59–64). Brussels: NATO Security Through Science Series E Human and Societal Dynamics, IOS Press.

Speckhard, A., & Akhmedova, K. (2006). The making of a martyr: Chechen suicide terrorism. *Journal of Studies in Conflict and Terrorism, 29*(5), 429–492.

Speckhard, A., Jacuch, B., & Vanrompay, V. (2012). Taking on the persona of a suicide bomber: A thought experiment. *Perspectives on Terrorism, 6*(2), 51–73.

9

Are Suicide Terrorists Suicidal?

Bruce Bongar, Uri Kugel, and Victoria Kendrick

For many people, suicide attacks are the symbol of terrorism than any other terrorist tactic, these attacks demonstrate terrorists' determination and devotion—to the extent of killing themselves for their cause—alongside their ruthless willingness to kill others indiscriminately. (Merari, 2010, p. 3)

Suicide terrorism is a deadly act of violence that has been on the rise around the world in the last few decades. A suicide attack has been defined as "an assault, intended to achieve a political objective, performed outside the context of a conventional war, in which the assailant intentionally kills himself for the purpose of killing others" (Merari, Diamant, Bibi, Broshi, & Zakin, 2009).

Suicide attacks still remain a deadly weapon in recent years despite a sharp decline in the number of attacks since 2007, that is, 520 attacks in 2007 compared to 279 in 2011 (The National Counterterrorism Center [NCTC], 2011). In 2011, there were over 10,000 terrorist attacks which affected nearly 45,000 victims in 70 countries and resulted in over 12,500 deaths (NCTC, 2011). It was also found that armed attacks and bombing constituted nearly 80 percent of all terrorist attacks in 2011 while suicide attacks only accounted for 2.7 percent. Although suicide attacks accounted for less than 3 percent of all attacks, they lead to more than 21 percent of all terrorism-related fatalities. It is important to note that although most instances of suicide terrorism and martyrdom in the past few decades have been related to extreme Islamism, there are cases where suicide attacks have been executed by organizations that are not related to Islam entirely or partly. Such examples include the Tamil Tigers in Sri Lanka, and part of the Chechnyian movement (Burnham, 2011; Kumar, Mukherjee, & Prakash, 2012).

In addition to death fatalities, suicide attacks also injure a great number of people. In Iraq, from 2003 to 2010 for every civilian death (12,284 in total), there were approximately three injured (30,644 in total; Hicks, 2011). Several studies have shown that injuries resulted from suicide bombers are commonly more severe compared to injuries sustained with non suicide bombing-related injuries (Aharonson, Klein, & Peleg, 2006; Hicks, 2011). Thus, the consequences of such attacks on the health, mental, and financial aspects of a population and country are rather large. The high fatality rate and severity of injury related to suicide attacks emphasize the importance in understanding the individuals who plan and carry out the attacks.

Research has highlighted numerous facets of the general phenomenon of suicide including socioeconomic factors, age, gender, and marital status. These facets focus on the personality characteristics of people who take their own life as well as life experiences that lead up to or increase the likelihood of committing suicide. Research of suicide terrorism and what drives certain people to partake in suicide attacks have been topics of interest for many years, but little consensus has been made on the profile and common characteristics of suicide bombers. Terrorism is not an area that can be easily studied psychologically due to the simple fact that most suicide terrorists die. Thus, raw data are rather scarce as several authors mentioned previously (Crenshaw, 2007; Lankford, 2010; Townsend, 2007). As a result of the difficulty to conduct direct interviews with suicide terrorists, a significant portion of the research to date is based on public records including news reports, demographics, video recordings, psychological post-mortem analysis, as well as testimonials from family members of suicide attackers. These indirect observations are important resources of information but they are insufficient in providing strong data on the phenomenon of suicide terrorism. Thus, any conclusion made about the question whether suicide terrorists are indeed suicidal should be taken with caution.

What Is Suicide?

To best answer the question whether suicide terrorists are in fact suicidal, one should compare suicide terrorism to other acts of suicide. Roy (1988) outlined three main categories of suicide based on the previous work of the French sociologist Emile Durkheim. These categories include: the egoistic suicide (emphasized by a lack of social and family support), the anomic suicide (emphasized by a damaged relationship between the individual and society), and the altruistic suicide (which is characterized by excessive integration with sociocultural constructs, e.g., hara-kiri, suicide-bomber). Most widely understood is the act of egoistic suicide in which a person takes his or her own life intentionally and voluntarily (Roy, 1988). This type of suicide is most commonly associated with depressive symptoms, loss of hope, mental pain (Bongar, 2002b) and was responsible for approximately 38,000 deaths in 2010 in the United States (Centers for Disease Control and Prevention, 2010).

Durkheim (1951) distinguished three forms of altruistic suicide: obligatory, optional, and acute. Obligatory altruistic suicide is where social norms direct suicide in distinct situations. One example includes the suicide of wives after the death of their husbands. Optional altruistic suicide is defined as resulting when suicide is considered a merit, but is not obligatory as in Seppuku (Hara-Kiri), which is a form of Japanese ritual suicide by disembowelment and beheading. Finally, acute altruistic suicide is the desire to die in order to combine with a deity as the conclusive expression of a religious belief (Merari, 2010). Along with egoistic, anatomic, and altruistic suicide, there is another category that includes martyrdom and suicide terrorism that focuses on suicide related to religious and/or political beliefs. Martyrdom is the suffering of death on account of adherence to one's religious faith (e.g., participating in combat and getting killed in action) while suicide terrorism is the intentional killing of oneself in the hope of killing others for a politically driven objective (Kruglanski, Gelfand, & Gunaratna, 2012). The ways in which the different types of suicide are related or not related have been a recent point of debate.

Current Debate

In the interest of establishing a profile of a suicidal terrorist, a question was raised whether suicide terrorists are in fact suicidal and if the psychological process leading up to a suicide attack is any different than that which leads up to egoistic suicide, altruistic suicide, or martyrdom. The current debate is not only surrounding the similarities and differences found between these acts of suicides but also around the characteristics and profiles of people involved in these acts (Hirvikoski & Jokinen, 2012). Currently, the literature on suicide terrorism shows little consensus on a specific personality type or risk factors that could assist in establishing profiles of potential suicide attackers (Townsend, 2007). This is largely due to the fact that suicide attack and the process leading up to it are multidimensional and multidetermined (Townsend, 2007). Some of these dimensions include psychological, social, spiritual, and ethical aspects and these, as found in the current debate, have similarities and differences depending on the type of suicide.

Another debate focuses on the difference between martyrdom and suicide terrorism. Martyrdom, as defined by Kruglanski, Gelfand, and Ganaratna (2012), involves death for one's own convictions or imparting a grand sense of personal significance, while suicide terrorism is directed at taking one's own life in hopes of killing others for political gains (Merari, 2010). Some believe that putting themselves in a combat situation without the prospect of survival in order to offer their life for their convictions, such as in suicide terrorism, is still martyrdom (Schirrmacher, 2012). There is little agreement to where the line is drawn between suicide terrorism and martyrdom. Leenaars, Ben Park, Collins, Wenckstern, and Leenaars (2010) found when comparing martyr letters to egoistic suicide notes that the state of mind of martyrs is more extreme and the pain martyrs feel is reported to be more unbearable.

SCOPE OF THIS CHAPTER

While studying the topic of suicide terrorism, it is important to keep in mind other instances of murder–suicides such as domestic violence, shooting-rampages, and school shooting. Lankford and Hakim (2011) suggested that there might be several similarities between suicide terrorists and individuals involved in murder–suicides. However, most cases of murder–suicides involved males killing their (estranged) intimate female partner and then committing suicide (Liem, Barber, Markwalder, Killias, & Nieuwbeerta, 2011). Therefore, and due to the fact that most suicide terrorists are sent by organizations to commit the act, this chapter addresses suicide terrorism as attacks conducted by terrorist organizations and will not go into discussing incidents such as domestic violence, school shootings, and shooting rampage that have sometimes been referred to as suicidal attacks, or incidents of homicide–suicides (Preti, 2008).

SIMILARITIES BETWEEN SUICIDE TERRORISM AND OTHER ACTS OF SUICIDE

There have been some suggestions that suicide terrorism is similar to the act of altruistic suicide or egoistic suicide (Townsend, 2007). Lankford (2010) proposed that suicide terrorists might actually be suicidal as he reviewed findings which support the claim that some suicide terrorists exhibit several key characteristics of egoistic suicide: (i) the desire to escape the world; (ii) the desire to escape moral responsibility for their actions; (iii) the inability to cope with a perceived crisis; and (iv) a sense of low self-worth. Lankford (2010) thus urged researchers to promote work in the field of suicide terrorism and to not conclude just yet that suicide terrorists are not suicidal.

Probably, the biggest similarity between egoistic suicide and suicide terrorism is the development of tunnel vision close to the final stage of execution. It is sometimes the case that tunnel vision develops in egoistic suicide (Bongar, 2002b). Similarly, the act of a suicide attack often involves several dissociative processes, such as tunnel vision, altered states of attention, detachment from feelings and the body, semi-hypnotic ecstasy, and spiritual awakening (Orbach, 2004).

DIFFERENCES BETWEEN SUICIDE TERRORISTS AND OTHER ACTS OF SUICIDE

There are some significant differences between suicide terrorism and other acts of suicide. As such, some authors suggest that suicide terrorism is actually a unique phenomenon (Merari, 2010; Townsend, 2007). These differences can be divided into several groups including: differences regarding the act, differences in motivations, and differences in the profile of the perpetuator.

Differences Regarding the Act

Additionally, there are some significant differences between the act of suicide terrorism and egoistic suicide: (i) self-destruction by suicide terrorism is commonly aimed at causing fear and terror among the target population, whereas self-mutilation and self-destruction in egoistic suicide are aimed at eliciting sympathy and understanding from a target audience. Further, egoistic suicide is mostly aimed at one's self and not at others. Thus, clearly suicide terrorism is aimed at killing and not at dying; (ii) there are notions that suicide terrorism is not perceived as an act of suicide by the agent or the supporting factors. Rather that it is an act of martyrdom, based on the Islamic principles of jihad (holy war), and thus, is considered a legal behavior (Abdel-Khalek, 2004); (iii) while an act of egoistic suicide chooses death as an escape or a plausible end to a difficult period of life, suicide terrorists view themselves as immortal (Hassan, 2001; Orbach, 2004). Thus, they see a continuation to life in their action and not a definitive end; and (iv) the act of suicide attack is planned and prepared by an organization rather than by the individual. As such, it is used as a tactical and strategic weapon (Hassan, 2010). Thus, as an organizational act it differs greatly from an individual act of egoistic suicide, which is motivated by self-destruction or a wish to escape pain. Suicide terrorism also differs from acts of altruistic suicide as it is initiated, promoted, assisted, and executed by an organization. Most acts of altruistic suicide are initiated by personal motives to help others or to demonstrate for a certain cause (e.g., jumping on a grenade to save brothers in arms; burn oneself in protest).

The act of suicide sometimes requires planning and careful execution (Bongar, 2002b). However, when compared to acts of egoistic suicide, the preparation, careful planning, and precise execution involved in suicide terrorism far exceeds those of the first. Such preparation includes several steps (Hassan, 2010; Orbach, 2004):

1. Recruitment for the act (whether it is a bottom-up recruitment or a top-down recruitment).
2. Initiation to the organization and to the act of martyrdom. Once the individual has been recruited, they will be initiated as a living martyr by a high-ranking operator and commonly by a spiritual authority.

3. Seclusion and training which includes direct religious and political indoctrination, training in the use of explosives or weapons involved in the attack, and preparation for facing death.
4. The final days before the attack is a highly structured period in which the behavior and mindset of the suicide are shaped to form a dissociative tunnel vision and focus on their coming act. This is achieved by contemplating the importance and consequences of their action, purification and religious practices, praying, chanting, and fasting.

DIFFERENCE BETWEEN KAMIKAZE PILOTS AND SUICIDE BOMBERS

A good comparison example to demonstrate the difference between the act of suicide terrorism and other acts of suicide is the case of Japanese Kamikaze pilots during World War II (WW-II). There has been previous references to suicide terrorists as Islamikaze (Israeli, 2003), that is the similarity between Japanese Kamikaze pilots who crashed their airplanes intentionally as a tactic against the US Navy in WW-II and modern-day suicide terrorists who are mostly, but not all, Muslim. However, kamikaze attacks in WW-II and terrorist suicide bombings have one essential difference. The Japanese Kamikazes directed their attacks at military targets, whereas terrorists largely target civilians as a means to terrorize the population and institutions of a country.

Wallace (2004) conducted interviews with Japanese pilots who survived performing Kamikaze strikes against US Navy forces in WW-II. The interviewees distinguished themselves from suicide bombers on three main points: (i) Kamikaze pilots were ready to die out of love for their country, whereas suicide bombers are driven by hatred and revenge; (ii) The Shinto religion offers no reward of life after death, whereas Islamic suicide bombers are promised a place in an afterlife; (iii) Kamikaze pilots volunteered for the task and were motivated solely by patriotism, whereas suicide bombers are often recruited, indoctrinated, and sometimes promised financial help to their family following completion of their mission.

Martinez (2007) studied the last letters of 661 killed-in-action Kamikaze pilots sent to their families and friends. Out of 661 Kamikaze pilots, the strongest motivation was committing the act for parents and family. None of the pilots showed religious belief to be a motivation for committing the act. Additionally, the analysis concluded that: (i) Kamikaze pilots did not act under coercion; (ii) Kamikaze pilots were not largely motivated by Japanese cultural attitudes toward suicide; (iii) Kamikaze pilots were not motivated by religious concerns; (iv) Kamikaze pilots were not largely motivated by concern for the future welfare of their families; (v) pilots were motivated by being aware that their deaths might help Japan achieve some significant military successes; and (vi) pilots felt that their death was a honorable and beautiful contribution. These findings stand in contrast with findings that attribute suicide bombers' motivation as: (i) desire for revenge (Hassan 2010; Rosenberger, 2003) both on a collective level (Araj, 2012) and on a personal level (Fields, Elbedour, & Hein 2002; Kushner, 1996; Moghadam, 2003); (ii) religious inspiration (Araj, 2012); and (iii) desire for liberation of the homeland (Araj, 2012).

SUICIDE TERRORISM AS A GROUP PHENOMENON RATHER THAN AN INDIVIDUAL PHENOMENON

Hassan (2010) suggests that suicide terrorism should be considered an organizational phenomenon rather than an individual phenomenon. It is used due to its cost effectiveness, flexibility, lethality, and tactical efficiency in reaching high-value targets. The act symbolizes the high resolve and dedication of the individuals to the group and by such deters the enemy. In addition, Hassan (2010) points to the fact that suicide terrorism is a political act and not just a manifestation of religious extremism. For the individual, it is a mean larger than just dying and killing others which includes:

> *community approval, political success, liberation of the homeland; personal redemption and mark of honour, achieving an exalted status of martyr for the survival of the community; signaling unwillingness to accept subjugation, revenge for personal and collective humiliation, a symbol of religious or nationalistic convictions guilt, shame, material and religious rewards, escape from intolerable everyday degradations of life under occupation, boredom, anxiety and defiance.* (Hassan, 2010, pp. 42–43)

Furthermore, the decision whether, how, and when to execute a suicide bombing attack is mostly done at the organizational level and not at the individual level (Hassan, 2010; Hasso 2005). This decision is mostly based on the tactical and strategic needs of the organization. In contrast, the timing and execution of other forms of suicide are largely dependent on the individual's decision that will determine the *if*, *how*, and *when*.

An additional corroboration for the notion that suicide terrorism is a group-oriented process and not an individual one can be seen in the lack of female suicide bombers in Afghanistan. In general, the use of women as suicide bombers is considered to be an advanced terrorist weapon due to the moral impact of their action and their capacity to evade security procedures that might stop male suicide bombers (Dearing, 2010). Between 2001 and 2010, there have been 414 suicide bombings in Afghanistan, out of which 99 percent were conducted by men. This low figure stands in contrast with other countries and terrorist groups. In Iraq between 2003 and 2010, about 4 percent of the attacks were conducted by women. In Sri Lanka, 21 percent of suicide attacks were conducted by women. Chechen militants used women in 40 percent of their attacks. The Kurdistan Worker's Party used women almost two-thirds of the time (Dearing, 2010). The low rate of use for women as suicide bombers in Afghanistan is attributed to several factors. These factors include cultural characteristics unique to the Taliban and Pashtuns, which decrease their willingness to use females as suicide bombers. Additionally, terrorist groups in Afghanistan enjoy a relative freedom of movement. Thus, this trend indicates that the decision to commit suicide terrorism is not determined by the individual, but rather that these organizations have a lesser need for female suicide bomber and they shape their tactical and strategic use of suicide bombers to include men only (Dearing, 2010).

MOTIVATIONAL DIFFERENCES

Whereas in egoistic suicide the main motivation of the suicide is to end suffering and bring to the cessation of mental pain (Bongar, 2002b), the real goal of suicide terrorism is to create terror (Pape, 2005). It seems that a great deal of suicide bombers' motivation has been nurtured and indoctrinated for years in the media, mosques and in the cultural atmosphere since childhood or early adulthood (Merari, 2010; Orbach, 2004).

Orbach (2004) described the following motivation for suicide attacks in the case of Palestinian suicide bombers: (i) determination and enthusiasm strengthened from success of previous attacks; (ii) hate and ideological rage against different religious, cultural, and ethnical groups; (iii) glorification of the suicide bomber (Shahid); (iv) heavenly rewards; and (v) recognition and materialistic benefits for the family of the bomber.

Hassan (2010) emphasizes the role that humiliation plays in the background of the life of many suicidal terrorists. Humiliation sometimes affects the individual suicide directly and often is directed at the culture of the individual, thus promoting a collective sense of humiliation. Such humiliation brings about anger, rage, and often seeking revenge against the humiliation agent. Seeking revenge and acting against humiliation is often not the case with other types of suicide with the exception of homicide–suicide.

Pittel and Rübbelke (2012) suggest three main categories of motivations for individuals to execute suicide attacks. Those are: (i) posthumous effects: rise in the social and monetary status of the attacker's family; 'immortality' of the attacker; accomplishment of political, religious, and social goals; (ii) announcement effects: admiration and rise in status of the attacker before the attack; and (iii) defection effects: negative consequences arising in case the attacker does not carry out the attack.

In summary, the difference in motivation between egoistic suicide and suicide terrorism is quite clear. In the first, the wish of the individual focuses on cessation of life and suffering, whereas in the latter the focus is on various achievements that include personal, group, familial, political, material, and emotional gains. It is noteworthy to mention that Lankford (2010) sustains the opinion that some suicide terrorists actually do hold the desire to escape the world and/or improve their situation in the afterlife.

DIFFERENCES REGARDING THE PROFILE OF THE SUICIDE

Bongar (2002b) describes several basic elements of completed suicide: (i) mental pain and suffering; (ii) self-hate, shame, guilt, and self-blame; (iii) development of tunnel vision which prevents the individual's capacity to consider other alternatives to the current situation; (iv) the idea of the end of suffering; and (v) acute hopelessness. Considering these elements, it seems that in most cases, tunnel vision is the only element that manifests among suicide terrorists as they approach the execution of their action. However, it is important to mention that some suicide bombers, especially in the case of Palestinian suicide bombers, have suffered personal loss and experienced various degrees of material, mental, emotional, and cultural sufferings (Abdel-Khalek, 2004; Araj 2012). Additionally, Lankford (2010) suggests that suicide terrorists might actually be suicidal. He reviews some findings which support the claim that some suicide terrorists exhibit several key characteristics of egoistic suicide: (i) the desire to escape the world; (ii) the desire to escape moral responsibility for their actions; (iii) the inability to cope with a perceived crisis; and (iv) a sense of low self-worth.

Bongar (2002a) lists the following as risk factors in most cases of suicide: male, age 60 or older, widowed or divorced, living alone, unemployed or having financial problems, recent adverse events, such as job loss or death of someone close, clinical depression, schizophrenia, substance abuse, history of suicide attempts or ideation, feeling of hopelessness, panic attacks, severe anxiety, and severe anhedonia. Most suicide terrorists are not subject to these risk factors, nor do they show suicidal intent, or demonstrate signs or backgrounds of mental illness (Hassan, 2010; Kavanagh, 2011; Merari et al., 2009; Townsend, 2007; Victoroff, 2005).

In contrast, suicide terrorists have been showing a varied demographic profile. Most Palestinian suicide terrorists have consisted mainly of late adolescent males (Merari, 2010). 9/11 suicidal terrorists were between 28 and 33 years married professional men with higher education from middle-class homes (Post et al., 2009). Many other Al-Qaeda members have been found to be at early adulthood, educated, and married with children (Hegghammer, 2007; Sageman, 2004). Additionally, terrorist groups usually try to weed out mentally disturbed recruits, as these could potentially be a security risk to the operations and the organization as a whole (Horgan, 2005; Silke, 2003). Instead terrorist organizations prefer to recruit those who appear ordinary, non threatening, and who can blend in the homogenic surrounding (Antonius, White-Ajmani, & Charap, 2012). This is one of the main reasons of such organizations to recruit women (Dearing, 2010).

Merari (2010) studied live suicide bombers who failed or survived suicide attacks for various reasons. These individuals were captured by Israeli security forces and were interviewed with consent by a clinical team in prison. An additional sample in his research consisted of the operators who planned, facilitated, and coordinated suicide attacks. Merari (2010) found that suicide dispositions were not detected in the majority of suicide candidates (60 percent). Additionally, the risk factors he found to be associated with suicidal terrorism were different compared to those of ordinary suicide. Specifically, most suicidal terrorists were not depressed, hopeless, impulsive, lonely, or helpless. They did not have diagnosable mental disorders, nor displayed previous self-mutilation. The strongest risk factor associated with suicidal terrorism was the personality of the candidate. That is an individual who was more susceptible to external influence (highly dependent–avoidant personality—which is usually not a typical risk factor for ordinary suicidal ideation). Such candidates are commonly shy, socially marginal, followers rather than leaders, loners, outsiders, with history of failing at school or feeling that they disappoint their parents and families (Merari, 2010). The focus of terrorist organizations on recruiting such individuals can also be seen in recent increase in recruitment of children and younger adults for suicide missions in Afghanistan and Pakistan by Al-Qaeda (Human Rights Watch, 2011).

The idea that suicide terrorists' personality consists of highly dependent–avoidant personality is corroborated by the fact that preparation for the act includes induction of various dissociative processes (e.g., tunnel vision, altered states of attention, detachment from feelings and the body, semi-hypnotic ecstasy, self-surrender, and coming closer to God). These processes could be self-induced, but frequently are manipulated and promoted by the terrorists' operators and spiritual guides (Orbach, 2004). There is a general tendency of people to obey authority, but some particularly sensitive individuals show even higher tendency to consent to commit actions that would harm others (Atran, 2003). This was demonstrated in Milgram's famous authority experiment in which participants executed orders that 'harmed' other participants (Milgram, 1974). Thus, terrorist organizations will often search for highly influenced individuals and recruit them as suicide bombers. A final corroboration to the notion that persuasion of the individual is a core aspect of suicide terrorist personality can be found in the manipulation of many female suicide attackers. Many women who join terrorist organizations do not join in order to become suicide bombers and are unwilling to commit suicide attacks. They are often pressured by other group members, cultural environment, peers, and extreme personal loss to commit such actions (Dearing, 2010; Victor, 2006).

DISCUSSION

Today, there is a growing consensus in the literature that the profile of suicide terrorists significantly differs from that of the profile of an individual who commits egoistic suicide (Merari, 2010; Pape, 2005; Post et al., 2009; Townsend, 2007). Most suicide terrorists do not have suicide dispositions, common risk factors, diagnosable mental disorder nor display previous self-mutilating behavior. The most common factor associated with suicide terrorists is susceptibility to external influence. And it appears that terrorist organizations are deeply interested in recruiting individuals with dependent/avoidant personality type. Furthermore, in contrast with egoistic suicide, there are additional elements that are important in the making of a suicide terrorist: (i) indoctrination to ideology, culture, atmosphere, mission, and group ideals; (ii) group commitment; (iii) personal commitment; and (iv) public support.

Therefore, in answer to the question 'Are suicide terrorists suicidal?' the answer in most cases is probably no; in particular when examined and compared to the common characteristics of egoistic and altruistic suicide. Townsend (2007) sees suicide terrorism as a different class of behavior than as another subgroup of egoistic suicide. This makes sense as some findings support that most suicide terrorists are not truly suicidal in the way suicide behavior is defined (Merari, 2010; Townsend, 2007). Merari views depression and suicidality "as an important contributing factor, but not as the main drive for undertaking a suicide mission in most cases" (Merari, 2012, p. 452). Considering all the above-mentioned factors, we share the opinion of Townsend (2007) and believe that suicide terrorism belongs to a different subtype of behavior than a form of suicide.

Despite the becoming opinion that suicide terrorists are not suicidal in nature, it is important to note that several authors claim that suicide terrorists actually do demonstrate some suicidal behavior and ideation (Lankford, 2010; Orbach, 2004). What we find mostly similar between suicide terrorists and egoistic suicide is the development of tunnel vision in the stage just prior to execution of the act (Orbach, 2004). Thus, there is a possible similarity in the process level rather than in characteristics of the individual or risk factors leading to the creation of a suicide attacker. However, considering the complexity of suicide terrorism, and the role that culture and organizations play in the indoctrination, preparation, training, and execution of these attacks, we find it difficult to explain the behavior of suicide terrorists by attributing the risk factors, and personality characteristics, which are widely accepted in the cases of egoistic suicide. Nevertheless, we share Lankford's (2010) call for researchers to promote work in the field of suicide terrorism and to leave room to answer this question as hopefully additional data will become available in coming years. What is needed is raw data including interviews with participants in all levels of suicide terrorism operations, in particular, recruitment, indoctrination, training, and execution. These participants should include: suicidal terrorists who survived attacks or were captured prior to the operation, commanders and decision-level operators, organizers of the attacks, facilitators, religious clerics, and trainers. Preferably, interviews with such participants will include clinical assessment and will be performed by clinical psychologists trained in assessments of suicide, personality disorders, and forensic psychology. As the raw data regarding suicide terrorism is hard to come by, advancement in this field will most definitely be slow. A possible pathway for acquiring access to this data might come from collaboration with the US military and intelligence agencies which are more likely to come by such information.

IMPLICATIONS

It is becoming evident that profiling individuals disposed to complete suicide attacks is a difficult task. Currently, psychologists and counterterrorism agencies lack a standardized measure that could indicate the possibility that an individual might fit the profile of a suicide terrorist. Additionally, it is becoming clearer that suicide terrorists have a diverse cultural, psychological, and economical background making this task even harder. The findings of Merari

(2010) reveal dependent/avoidant personality style as the single most common factor that could assist counterterrorism elements in locating potential suicide terrorists. As the profiling of potential suspects is already difficult and in consideration of the importance of the supporting system required to execute such an attack, it might be wise to consider dedicating counterterrorism resources to other areas than the profiling of the attacker. These areas should include: (i) recruiters—as potential suicide terrorists need to be individuals highly susceptible to external influences, so does their recruiter must be a person with a high capacity to influence people. Thus, counterterrorism assets should be dedicated to the detection of influential individuals involved in recruitment and maintaining such individuals under surveillance; (ii) recruitment setting—counterterrorism resources should be directed at settings where highly dependent individuals could be manipulated and recruited by operatives of terrorist organizations. Such locations could include madrasas (Islamic pre-school and school), mosques, youth groups and clubs, mourning gatherings, and prisons; (iii) organizational infrastructure—as suicide terrorism appears to be an organizational phenomenon rather than an individual one, it makes sense to target the organization. This is already partly done by NATO members as they target the financial resources of terrorist organizations such as Hezbollah, Al-Qaeda, Hamas, etc. and (iv) cultural-political—several researchers advice to focus the work of psychologists and counterterrorism resources on the social and political factors associated with suicide terrorism (Brym & Araj, 2012; Hassan, 2010). Lastly, if profiling of potential suicide attackers must be done, then it is recommended to follow the findings of Merari (2010) and search for an individual with avoidant/dependent personality style. Such an individual is commonly shy, socially marginal, a follower rather than a leader, a loner, an outsider, with history of failing at school, work, or feeling that they disappoint their parents and families.

REFERENCES

Abdel-Khalek, A. M. (2004). Neither altruistic suicide, nor terrorism but Martyrdom: A Muslim perspective. *Archives of Suicide Research*, 8(1), 99–113.

Aharonson, D. L., Klein, Y., & Peleg, K. (2006). Suicide bombers form a new injury profile. *Annals of Surgery, 244*(6), 1018–1023.

Antonius, D., White-Ajmani, M. L., & Charap, J. (2012). The behavioral profile of a terrorist: Theoretical and empirical observations. In U. Kumar & M. K. Mandal (Eds.), *Countering terrorism: Psychological strategies* (pp. 96–117). New Delhi: SAGE Publications.

Araj, B. (2012). The motivations of Palestinian suicide bombers in the second intifada (2000 to 2005). *Canadian Review of Sociology, 49*(3), 211–232.

Atran, S. (2003). Genesis of suicide terrorism. *Science, 299*(5612), 1534–1539.

Bongar, B. (2002a). The assessment of elevated risk. *The suicidal patient: Clinical and legal standards of care*, 2nd ed. (pp. 81–137). Washington, DC: American Psychological Association. doi:10.1037/10424-003

Bongar, B. (2002b). The knowledge base. *The suicidal patient: Clinical and legal standards of care*, 2nd ed. (pp. 3–38). Washington, DC: American Psychological Association. doi:10.1037/10424-001

Brym, R. J., & Araj, B. (2012). Are suicide bombers suicidal? *Studies in Conflict & Terrorism, 35*(6), 432–443.

Burnham, G. (2011). Suicide attacks—the rationale and consequences. *The Lancet, 37*(9794), 855–857.

Centers for Disease Control and Prevention. (2010). *Web-based injury statistics query and reporting system (WISQARS)*. Retrieved online on December 17, 2012 from www.cdc.gov/ncipc/wisqars

Crenshaw, M. (2007). Explaining suicide terrorism: A review essay. *Security Studies, 16*(1), 133–162.

Dearing, M. P. (2010). Like red tulips at springtime: Understanding the absence of female martyrs in Afghanistan. *Studies in Conflict & Terrorism, 33*(12), 1079–1103.

Durkheim, E. (1951). *Suicide*. New York, NY: Free Press.

Fields, R. M., Elbedour, S., & Hein, F. (2002). The Palestinian suicide bomber. In C. E. Stout (Ed.), *The psychology of terrorism: Clinical aspects and responses* (Vol. II, pp. 193–223). Westport, CT: Praeger Publishers/Greenwood Publishing Group.

Hassan, N. (2001, November 19). An arsenal of believers: Talking to the "human bombs." *The New Yorker*. Retrieved from http://www.newyorker.com/archive/2001/11/19/011119fa_FACT1

Hassan, R. (2010). Life as a weapon: Making sense of suicide bombings. *Dialogue, 29*(2), 5–9.

Hasso, F. S. (2005). Discursive and political deployments by/of the 2002 Palestinian women suicide bombers/martyrs. *Feminist Review, 81*(1), 23–51.

Hegghammer, T. (2007, February 05). *Saudi militants in Iraq: Backgrounds and recruitment patterns*. Retrieved from Oslo: Norwegian Defense

Research Establishment website: http://www.ffi.no/no/Rapporter/06-03875.pdf

Hicks, M. A. (2011). Casualties in civilians and coalition soldiers from suicide bombings in Iraq, 2003-10: A descriptive study. *Lancet, 378*(9794), 906-914.

Hirvikoski, T., & Jokinen, J. (2012). Personality traits in attempted and completed suicide. *European Psychiatry: The Journal of the Association of European Psychiatrists, 27*(7), 536-541.

Horgan, J. (2005). *Psychology terrorism*. London: Cass Publications.

Human Rights Watch. (2011, August 31). Afghanistan: Taliban should stop using children as suicide bombers. Retrieved from http://www.hrw.org/news/2011/08/31/afghanistan-taliban-should-stop-using-children-suicide-bombers

Israeli, R. (2003). *Islamikaze: Manifestations of Islamic martyrology*. Portland, OR: Frank Kass Publishers.

Kavanagh, J. (2011). Selection, availability, and opportunity: The conditional effect of poverty on terrorist group participation. *Journal of Conflict Resolution, 55*(1), 106-132.

Kruglanski, A., Gelfand, M., & Gunaratna, R. (2012). Terrorism as a means to an end: How political violence bestows significance. In P. Shaver & M. Mikulincer (Eds.), *Meaning, mortality and choice: The social psychology of existential concerns* (pp. 203-212). Washington, DC: American Psychological Association.

Kumar, U., Mukherjee, S., & Prakash, V. (2012). Sociocultural aspects of terrorism. In U. Kumar & M. K. Mandal (Eds.), *Countering terrorism: Psychosocial strategies* (pp. 47-73). New Delhi: SAGE Publications.

Kushner, H. W. (1996). Suicide bombers: Business as usual. *Studies in Conflict & Terrorism, 19*(4), 329-337.

Lankford, A. (2010). Do suicide terrorists exhibit clinically suicidal risk factors? A review of initial evidence and call for future research. *Aggression and Violent Behavior, 15*(5), 334-340.

Lankford, A., & Hakim, N. (2011). From Columbine to Palestine: A comparative analysis of rampage shooters in the United States and volunteer suicide bombers in the Middle East. *Aggression and Violent Behavior, 16*(2), 98-107.

Leenaars, A., Ben Park, B., Collins, P., Wenckstern, S., & Leenaars, L. (2010). Martyrs' last letters: Are they the same as suicide notes? *Journal of Forensic Sciences, 55*(3), 660-668.

Liem, M., Barber, C., Markwalder, N., Killias, M., & Nieuwbeerta, P. (2011). Homicide-suicide and other violent deaths: An international comparison. *Forensic Science International, 207*(1-3), 70-76.

Martinez, D. P. (2007). Kamikaze diaries: Reflections of Japanese student soldiers By Emiko Ohnuki-Tierney. *Journal of the Royal Anthropological Institute, 13*(3), 775-776.

Merari, A. (2010). *Driven to death. Psychological and social aspects of suicide terrorism.* New York, NY: Oxford University Press.
Merari, A. (2012). Studying suicide bombers: A response to Brym and Araj's critique. *Studies in Conflict & Terrorism, 35*(6), 444–455.
Merari, A., Diamant, I., Bibi, A., Broshi, Y., & Zakin, G. (2009). Personality characteristics of "self-martyrs"/"suicide bombers" and organizers of suicide attacks. *Terrorism and Political Violence, 22*(1), 87–101.
Milgram, S. (1974). *Obedience to authority.* New York: Harper & Row.
Moghadam, A. (2003). Palestinian suicide terrorism in the second intifada: Motivations and organizational aspects. *Studies in Conflict & Terrorism, 26*(2), 65–93.
Orbach, I. (2004). Terror suicide: How is it possible? *Archives of Suicide Research, 8*(1), 115–130.
Pape, R. A. (2005). *Dying to win: The strategic logic of suicide terrorism.* New York: Random House.
Pittel, K., & Rübbelke, D. T. G. (2012). Decision processes of a suicide bomber—the economics and psychology of attacking and defecting. *Defence and Peace Economics, 23*(3), 251–272.
Post, J., Ali, F., Henderson, S. W., Shanfield, S., Victoroff, J., & Weine, S. (2009). The psychology of suicide terrorism. *Psychiatry, 72*(1), 13–31.
Preti, A. (2008). School shooting as a culturally enforced way of expressing suicidal hostile intentions. *Journal of the American Academy of Psychiatry and the Law, 36*(4), 544–550.
Rosenberger, J. (2003). Discerning the behavior of the suicide bomber: The role of vengeance. *Journal of Religion & Health, 42*(1), 13–21.
Roy, A. (1988). *Risk factors in suicide.* Symposium of the Suicide Education Institute of Boston, in collaboration with the Center of Suicide Research and Prevention, at the American Psychiatric Association Annual Meeting, Montreal, Quebec, Canada.
Sageman, M. (2004). *Understanding terror networks.* Philadelphia, PA: University of Pennsylvanian Press.
Schirrmacher, C. (2012). They are not all martyrs Islam on the topics of dying, death and salvation in the afterlife. *Evangelical Review of Theology, 36*(3), 250–265.
Silke, A. (2003). *Terrorists, victims and society: Psychological perspectives on terrorism and its consequences.* West Sussex: Wiley Blackwell.
The National Counterterrorism Center (NCTC). (2011). *Annual Report on terrorism.* Washington, DC: Office of the Director of National Intelligence National Counterterrorism Center. Retrieved online on December 17, 2012 from http://www.nctc.gov/docs/2011_NCTC_Annual_Report_Final.pdf

Townsend, E. (2007). Suicide terrorists: Are they suicidal? *Suicide and Life-Threatening Behavior, 37*(1), 35–49.
Victor, B. (2006). *Army of roses*. London: Constable & Robinson.
Victoroff, J. (2005). The mind of the terrorist: A review and critique of psychological approaches. *Journal of Conflict Resolution, 49*(3), 3–42.
Wallace, B. (2004, September 25). They've outlived the stigma. *Los Angeles Times*. Retrieved from: http://articles.latimes.com/2004/sep/25/world/fg-kamikaze25

10

The Role of Military Psychologists and Psychiatrists in Understanding Suicide Terrorism

Uri Kugel, Laurie Black, Joseph Tomlins, Elvin Sheykhani, Bruce Bongar, Morgan Banks, and Larry James

Terrorism is generally described as an act of violence against a group of unsuspecting individuals, often *noncombatant* (e.g., civilians), to elicit fear within the greater target population in order to attain various goals. These goals are typically political and/or religious in nature (Faria & Arce, 2006). However, some argue that war is rooted in a "primordial violence, hatred, and enmity, which are to be regarded as blind, natural, force" (Clausewitz, 2008, p. 89). The US government defines terrorism as a "premeditated, politically motivated, violence perpetrated against noncombatant targets by subnational groups or clandestine agents, usually intended to influence an audience" (Title 22 of the US Code, Section 2656f). Such groups are thus considered to be non state actors.

The psychological effects of terrorism can be significant. Terrorism may elicit fear and anxiety that sometimes can extend far beyond the directly affected individuals. This is intensified by media coverage which directly influences large target audiences. Hoffman (2006) argued that it is designed to exert power where there is little to none. By using violence to generate publicity, terrorists seek to obtain the leverage, impact, and power they otherwise lack to influence political change on either a local or international scale. Victoroff (2005) stated, "Any effort to uncover the 'terrorist mind' will more likely result in uncovering a spectrum of terrorist minds" (p. 7). Moreover, this understanding might diverge one toward indulging in erroneous—though seemingly objective—beliefs such as, 'One man's terrorist is another man's freedom fighter.' In contrast, Martin Rudner eloquently highlights the misleading nature of this by stating: "It assesses the validity of the cause, when terrorism is an act. One can have a perfectly beautiful cause and yet if one commits terrorist acts, it is terrorism regardless" (Humphreys, 2007, p. 1).

Individuals who go as far as taking their own lives in order to induce change (*suicide terrorists*) likely take a different perspective and consider themselves martyrs rather than immoral terrorists. Therefore, suicide terrorism is more than just an act of violence in order to attain power. There are serious moral, cultural, and psychological effects involved that encourage people to commit suicide in order to manipulate political action via mass fear. Additionally, just like soldiers, suicide terrorists are often being used as a type of weapon by their leaders. As such, the suicide terrorist is manipulated to conduct an act in support of the political objectives of the terrorist group leader.

Suicide terrorism is not just a result of intense personal frustration or desperation, but an organizational imperative that, on the one hand, increases the likelihood of a successful terrorist attack and, on the other, is intrinsically appealing to terrorists because of its deeply unsettling psychological effects on the societies against which it is directed (Hoffman, 2006).

It is important to recognize the variability between general terrorism and suicide terrorism. Suicide terrorist attacks not only have lasting effects, they are often seen as foolproof. Planning a terrorist attack requires extensive knowledge on the range of methods to commit violence as well as on the targeted area of attack. However, with the added advantage of suicide terrorists, attacks no longer require intense training and shrewd attackers but instead may achieve their goal by simply calling upon an individual willing or made into ones who are willing to die for their cause.

Hoffman (2006) suggested that suicide bombers do not need to be sophisticated. They just need to be willing to end the lives of others as well as their own. After all, it is an easier task to strap a bomb to a belt and walk into a mall than to plan and plant a bomb in an undisclosed area and ensure it successfully detonates. In sum, it is the likelihood of success that attracts terrorists to suicide terrorism, in addition to the profound psychological effect it may have on its target.

Suicide terrorism is increasingly religious based. Between the years of 2001 and 2005, 78 percent of all suicide terrorist attacks were religious in nature (Hoffman, 2006). Moreover, from the 35 terrorist groups employing suicide missions in 2005, 86 percent were Islamic—who believe that following martyrdom, they will be presented with rewards in the afterlife (Hoffman, 2006). With shared belief systems, suicide terrorists are first and foremost members of the organizations that train them. These organizations often select their targets, supply the explosives, issue orders for launching an attack, and ultimately try to convince a larger population that their cause is just (Bloom, 2006). Thus, a longing for religious purity and/or a strong commitment to the welfare of the group may drive individuals to engage in suicide terror. Objectively, it is possible to grasp the concept that these people perceive themselves as *altruistic*, in that they are both furthering their organization's cause and ensuring a place for themselves and their families in heaven. Durkheim (1951) described this type of suicide as acute altruistic suicide; that is, the desire to die in order to combine with a deity as the conclusive expression of a religious belief (Merari, 2010).

A COMPARISON BETWEEN SUICIDE TERRORISM AND SPECIAL FORCES

This chapter examines the recruitment, selection, and training procedures for suicide terrorist organizations such as Al-Qaeda compared to the procedures employed by military organizations such as Special Forces (SF).

Initially, the contrast and comparison between SF and suicide terrorists seems a rather bold task. An initial assumption might be that any similarities are insignificant compared to the presumably greater differences. While this may be so, it is advised to examine one's own personal biases in order to objectively comprehend group differences and similarities. In this way, one may decipher legitimate implications to aid in counterterrorism efforts. Moghaddam (2005) compares the psychology that leads to terrorism as ascending of a narrow staircase, in which many people may stay on the ground floor, yet a rare minority will be successfully selected by recruiters from terrorist organizations. We will compare and contrast this rare minority with the 'rare minority' of individuals selected for Special Operations Forces (SOF) who are also asked to undertake extremely dangerous missions.

RECRUITMENT, SELECTION, AND TRAINING OF TERRORISTS

Selection and Recruitment

The demographics of suicide terrorists are highly varied regarding education, socioeconomic status (SES) (Atran, 2003), marital status, age (Post et al., 2009), and gender (Dearing, 2010). Jenkins (2006) describes the recruitment for terrorist organizations as a process of joining a missionary order rather than a military group. Terrorist organizations use different selection and recruitment procedures, in addition to different recruitment pools. For example, Hamas (in the Gaza Strip and West Bank) is usually based locally and recruit native Palestinians, whereas Al-Qaeda recruits both locally and internationally (Sparago, 2007).

In examining the case of Al-Qaeda and its affiliated networks, the following variables are often seen in most recruits: (i) devout Muslim; (ii) mostly male; (iii) young adults (adolescents and men in their 20s); (iv) various ethnicities, nationalities, and cultural backgrounds; (v) three quarters are married; (vi) two-thirds have children; (vii) in good physical condition; (viii) various SES levels; (ix) usually higher level of intelligence and education; and (x) no recruitment of individuals with mental instability or conditions (Sparago, 2007).

These characteristics were corroborated with Hegghammer's (2007) findings within a sample of 205 Saudis terrorists who died in Iraq between 2003 and 2005. Demographic features consisted of an average age of 23, nine with previous combat experience, and a diverse range of SES background. Most were recruited by top-down recruitment (recruiters within the group extend an invitation for the candidate to join their ranks), utilizing a pre-existing social link, and placed in private gatherings. Some were recruited in a bottom-up process (e.g., the Internet—candidates express interest in joining the group). In the latter method, recruitment was accomplished mostly through groups and friends who assembled for a united cause. Moreover, out of the 205, approximately 16 percent died as suicide bombers.

Recruitment for terrorist organizations usually takes place in the following settings: (i) prisons—especially where inmates are engaged in religious activity and bonding; (ii) madrasas, which are religious schools for lower levels of education—most recruits at this stage are very young (age: 8–10 years); (iii) mosques—where individuals with similar structure of socialization and religious extremity can converge, discuss, and interact; (iv) refugee camps—which contain populations with strong political grievance; and (v) the Internet—where a bottom-up recruitment is common (Post, 2005; Post & Pittas, 2012; Sparago, 2007). Internet recruitment relies strongly on videos of fallen Shahids and other successful suicide attacks that inspire interested individuals. Recruiters are often people with authority, imams, respected in their neighborhood, and/or people with strong interpersonal capacities (Jenkins, 2006; Post, 2004). Recruiters will frequently engage strong believers, and ridicule young targets, by invoking feelings of humiliation, shame, and guilt, and offer them a restoration of their dignity, manhood, duty, and honor by joining jihad (Daly & Gerwehr, 2006; Jenkins, 2006). Thus, recruiters are usually experts in human behavior and implement a variety of rewards and punishments to incite recruiters: "The brother who manages the agent should possess the qualifications of a perfect psychiatrist and an interrogator" (Post, 2004, p. 101).

Kavanagh (2011) determined that high education combined with poverty was a predictor for potential participation in martyrdom operations among Hezbollah recruits. As economic deprivation increases, the additional component of higher education raises the likelihood of participation fivefold. Therefore, in order to increase the chances of a successful mission, terrorist organizations show a preference for recruiting educated individuals because suicide attacks require a high level of intuition, the ability to adapt quickly, and a strong skill set. Once the recruit is selected and has accepted the invitation to join a terrorist organization, he or she will be initiated into its ranks. Initiation is usually performed by a high ranking member of the organization and a spiritual authority. Although indoctrination is often a gradual process, from the moment of official initiation, the recruit becomes a living martyr (*Shahid al-Chai*) and has been psychologically committed to execute his inevitable role (Orbach, 2004). For the followers of militant Islam, this is the highest honor as it signifies the irrevocable commitment to die in an attack against the organization's enemies. This is often a metamorphose of the individual's willingness to die for Allah (Orbach, 2004; Post, 2005).

MOTIVATION

There are several motivating factors for joining terrorist organizations, in particular Al-Qaeda (Kavanagh, 2011; Sparago, 2007): (i) social support—terrorist organizations provide a bonding structure where members with similar ideologies and beliefs can support each other; (ii) historical alliance—the organizations serve as a communal bond among members who fight a common enemy throughout time; (iii) political action—joining the organization signifies taking political action due to grievances and suppression; for many jihadi, a terrorist act is interpreted as a form of political action; (iv) the leader's charisma—many join due to the personal appeal of their military and religious leaders; and (v) religious beliefs—perhaps the strongest justification an individual joins the global holy-war (jihad), motivated to fight against the *infidel* sin in order to defend and protect Islam. Additionally, the likelihood of terrorist recruitment increases in areas with weak political and civil rights, high levels of repression, and government instability.

INDOCTRINATION

A major part in shaping a suicide terrorist is the indoctrination process (Jenkins, 2006). For many suicide attack recruits, the initial course of indoctrination lasts for years and takes place in mosques, in the culture where the individuals live, and in the media (Merari, 2010; Orbach, 2004). However, the most intensive part of the indoctrination occurs within the terrorist group: "The only way to understand this frightening demonstration of human readiness for self-sacrifice is to look at the group's influence on its individual members" (Merari, 2007, p. 109). The indoctrination process establishes the new recruit's position in the terrorist organization, provides education about the group and its missions, and develops the recruit's mindset toward executing an attack. Often this process is facilitated by the influence of a charismatic and powerful leader (e.g., Osama bin Laden, Zarqawi).Typically, indoctrination consists of ideological, political, and religious components; incorporating these emotionally charged elements tends to solidify and deepen an individual's commitment to the organization and its cause.

Indoctrination is carried out mostly in isolation and recruits are usually encouraged to severe ties with the outside world, in particular family members and friends, and especially those who oppose jihad, suicide missions, or care deeply about the recruit. In this period, the group becomes the new family for the recruit and a state of co-dependency between group members is established. The indoctrination process emphasizes themes, such as facing death, and builds the recruit's motivation by focusing on: (i) rewards—many recruits are convinced that, after death, they will enter paradise greeted by 72 virgins or that their families will receive a significant cash reward; (ii) dehumanization of the enemy—the enemy (both civilians and soldiers) are reduced to *subhumans* and *infidels* who oppose Islam and therefore should be destroyed; (iii) manipulation of religion and history—in which Islam and its cause are glorified while atrocities of the enemy and its ideology are inflated, manipulated, and often taken out of context; and (iv) promoting group allegiance—the social benefits of being a member are conditioned through the recruit's commitment to the cause and purpose of joining the organization (Sparago, 2007).

TRAINING

Training and preparation for missions are conducted differently between various terrorist organizations (Brynjar, 2008). Most terrorist groups distinguish between members who are vital to the group's survival and maintenance, and those who can be sacrificed for the cause and used as *cannon fodder*. The majority of suicide terrorists in Iraq between 2002 and 2008 were those without previous military experience or training (Tønnessen, 2008).

Nesser (2008) distinguishes between two generations of terrorists (particularly Islamic jihadis). The first was prior to the American invasion of Afghanistan (2003–2004) and the destruction of Al-Qaeda's training camps. During this period, the selection, recruitment, and training of terrorist operatives were top-down processes working within a hierarchical organization. In Iraq, the Zarqawi network and other terrorist groups provided training by ex-Iraqi military soldiers, officers, and militants with extensive previous experience obtained in Afghanistan. These trainers had strong backgrounds in preparing explosives, improvised explosive devices (IED), car-bombs, sniping, forging documents, and light weapons training (Tønnessen, 2008). Due to the destruction of terrorist training camps in Afghanistan and the weakening of Al-Qaeda affiliated networks in Iraq, the second generation of terrorists relied on a bottom-up process in which individuals independently sought action, recruitment, and training (Nesser, 2008; Tønnessen, 2008). Although many in this group traveled to other locations in the world (e.g., Pakistan) to attend training camps, others utilized improvised training, often complemented with Internet-based manuals. Camp training for the second-generation recruits usually included praying, physical exercises along with an obstacle course, theoretical lectures about arms and combat, Islamic indoctrination, and training in seizing buildings and the use of various types of weapons such as 60 mm mortar, RPGs, and explosives. Some of the trainees went on to specialize in IED and car bomb preparation, as well as sniping (Tønnessen, 2008).

In the last few years, online manuals have become more widespread (Stenersen, 2008). One major online training manual is The Encyclopedia of jihad (Mawsu'at al-jihad), divided into two sections. The first covers security and intelligence, organization, investigation, recruiting, operations, and protection. The second provides practical lessons in areas such as assassination, poison, invisible ink, explosives manufacture, and sniper training. There are also instructional videos available online to complement the above-mentioned topics. It is important to note that most of the available online materials are not directed toward a particular terrorist group nor produced by certain organizations such as Al-Qaeda, but rather by Internet-based sympathizers (Stenersen, 2008).

In general, training for suicide attack missions is often done in seclusion and varies greatly in time length according to the specific organization, the chosen target, and other details of operation (Orbach, 2004; Tønnessen, 2008). Orbach (2004) lists the following as common elements in training for suicide attacks: (i) physical fitness, explosives, and weapons training; (ii) indoctrination and strengthening of the recruit's motivation to execute the attack, usually including religious and political indoctrination; and (iii) preparation for facing death and the afterlife. The final days before the attack are highly structured in order to reduce anxiety and ensure that the recruit will not get cold feet. During this time, the behavior and mindset of the recruit is shaped in a way that promotes dissociative states, focuses intent, and establishes a tunnel vision that lasts until the actual attack and death of the recruit. This process is achieved by contemplating the importance and consequences of the mission, in addition to purification and religious practices such as praying, chanting, and fasting. Every minute detail becomes an important facet during this period. For instance, recruits often become preoccupied in ceremonies such as washing and cleaning their bodies, as well as carefully selecting the best garments for the occasion. Eventually, all but their act of martyrdom disappears from their minds and recruits optimally experience a transcendent state with the determination to carry out the attack.

RECRUITMENT, SELECTION, AND TRAINING OF SF OPERATIVES

Special Operations Force is an elite, covert unit comprised of soldiers, airmen, and Navy personnel within the US military. Special Operations is defined by the DoD as:

> *Operations requiring unique modes of employment, tactical techniques, equipment and training often conducted in hostile, denied, or politically sensitive environments and characterized by one or more of the following: time sensitive, clandestine, low visibility, conducted with and/or through indigenous forces, requiring regional expertise, and/or a high degree of risk.* (Department of Defense, 2010, p. 288)

The lineage of SF can be traced to commando groups in World War II such as the 5307th Composite Group (provisional), also known famously as 'Merrill's Marauders.' Merrill's Marauders fought in South East Asia, employing unconventional warfare and guerilla style tactics against the Japanese (Bank, 1986). The current SF community employs these same tactics, in cooperation with allied nations' military forces. They are deployed to hostile environments, usually where the deployment of conventional forces is not appropriate (Joint Chiefs of Staff [JCS], 2003). Special Operators ([SO] soldiers within special operations battalions) differ from regular forces in terms of candidate selection, training, mission variety, and command (Special Operations Command, SOCOM).

SOF work within various branches of the military, such as the Army Green Berets, Rangers, Navy Seals, Delta Force, and 160th Special Operations Aviation Regiment. Obviously, a complete inclusion of all Special Ops groups is beyond the scope of this chapter, so for purposes of comparison, we will focus on the Army Green Berets.

SF: GREEN BERETS

SOF can be found within all branches of the military, but the term 'Special Forces' technically refers to a particular type of army SOF sometimes known as 'Green Berets.' SF are driven by the credo 'De Oppresso Libre' meaning 'to free the oppressed' and currently operate within the seven SF groups (Bank, 1986; Joint Chiefs of Staff, 2003). Today, missions of SF include: "Unconventional Warfare (also known as guerrilla warfare), Foreign Internal Defense (training countries how to fight insurgencies), Direct Action (specific, aggressive, tactical operations, usually with strategic implications), Special Reconnaissance (the collection of tactical military information, often deep within enemy territory), and Counterterrorism" (Banks, 2006, p. 86). Green Berets go through a grueling recruitment, assessment, selection, and training process, lasting an average of two years. During this time, recruits are assessed on their operational capabilities, personalities, various aptitudes, and group cohesion. Once soldiers complete this process, they are placed within a team known as SF Operational Detachment Alpha (Banks, 2006; Diemer, 2001; Joint Chiefs of Staff, 2003; Russell, 1994).

RECRUITMENT

There are several ways to seek selection for SF. Within the army, recruits may express interest through Special Operations and enlist with a Military Occupational Specialty (MOS) as an 18x-Special Operations Candidate. This is not a formal enlistment occupational code, but it allows a soldier the chance to attend an SF Qualification Course (Diemer, 2001; Pleban et al., 1988).

Originally, to join SF, a candidate would have to at least hold a rank of E-4 (specialist/corporal) (Flin, 2001). Following the September 11th attacks, a study conducted by the DoD indicated that the current state of Special Operations was in dire need of staffing increases. Executive orders as well as regulation changes within the United States Armed Forces allowed a larger pool of potential soldiers to join the SF community (Department of the Army [DoA], 2006; Diemer, 2001). Permitting a larger group of candidates to potentially join SF serves two purposes: (i) allowing younger men (age 18) to join gives them a longer amount of time in the field; and (ii) increases the overall quality of potential candidates who wish to join (Bartone, Roland, Picano, & Williams, 2008; Diemer, 2001).

For a candidate to qualify for assessment, they must meet all SF requirements: (i) be at least 18 years of age; (ii) must be male (SF is not open to women); (iii) have a high school diploma; (iv) meeting requirement on the Armed Services Vocational Aptitude Battery (ASVAB); and (v) Combat Operation score of 98 (Diemer, 2001; U.S. Army Recruiting Command [ARC], 1999). Additional requirements must also be met, such as qualifying for secret level security clearance, taking the US military language battery, and meeting minimum physical requirements (Diemer, 2001). Candidates within SF are also given psychological batteries to ensure they are free of mental illness as it could hinder operational capabilities (Department of the Army, 2006; U.S. Army Recruiting Command, 1999). Minimum requirements for entering or passing the Special Operations Qualification Course change on a constant basis. It is important to note that only a small percentage of recruits pass all three phases of the course.

ASSESSMENT

Currently, within the US Army, approximately 1,800 service personnel positions are allotted for SF candidacy per year (these numbers change yearly due to various variables). Special Forces Qualification Course contains three phases. Phase one, known as the SF Assessment and Selection (SFAS) phase, is also referred to by recruits as *selection* (Diemer, 2001; Flin, 2001). This three-week course evaluates soldiers on a multitude of operational capabilities. Recruits are assessed on combat effectiveness, land navigation, skill with various weapons systems, as well as their emotional trauma and cognitive flexibility (U.S. Army Recruiting Command, 1999; U.S. Army Personnel Research Office, 1979).

Aptitude and intelligence. The US military states that the ASVAB is not a proper measure of intelligence. ASVAB scores of selected SF recruits were higher, on average, compared to regular army service members, ranging 8–10 points across all categories (technical, combat, field artillery). This information suggests that those chosen within the selection process may have more cognitive flexibility (Pleban et al., 1988).

Resiliency. A study by Bartone et al. (2008) examined psychological hardiness and successful selection within Special Operations Qualifying Course. A total of 1,138 candidates were given a psychological assessment that measures dispositional resilience in situations of extreme duress. On average, the failure rate during selection was 45–55 percent. Candidates, whose scores reflected emotional stability, likeability, and commitment, were determined to have high dispositional resilience and were more likely to graduate than those who scored lower on this measure. A similar study of US Navy Special Operations personnel found that candidates who were judged more social and emotionally stable had higher graduation rates than candidates who scored poorly on related measures (Mcdonald, Norton, & Hodgdon, 1990).

Personality assessment. The United States Special Operations Command (USSOCOM) advises that soldiers must be above average in mental flexibility, emotional stability, social cohesion, and physical fitness (Department of the Army, 2006). In addition to tests of physical endurance and aptitude (intelligence, agility, resourcefulness), SF candidates also receive personality assessments. Tests that were previously used for psychological screening included the Minnesota Multiphasic Personality Inventory (MMPI-2) and the Wonderlic Personnel Test (Banks, 2006). Candidates are assessed for mental flexibility, conformity, impulsivity, risk taking, energy level, interpersonal affect, among many other facets (Pleban et al., 1988). A study conducted by the U.S. Army Personnel Research Office (1979) found that attitudes of martyrdom, issues with authority, non compliance with orders, fear of injury, low social cohesion, and psychotic-like symptoms, were all negatively correlated to being chosen during the selection process. While no precise standard of the perfect SO exists, personality assessments are used and psychological profiles are conducted to screen out potentially unsuitable candidates during the selection phase of SFAS (Banks, 2006).

TRAINING

Training of SF is an extensive process which can last approximately two years. The training changes on a constant basis but commonly includes several elements such as: (i) a qualification course that covers land navigation and team building exercises (Department of the Army, 2006; Joint Chiefs of Staff, 2003); (ii) Survival, evasion, resistance, and escape (SERE) training which prepares soldiers to successfully survive captivity (Banks, 2006); (iii) intensive language training; (iv) small unit tactics courses; and (v) specialization training. Upon successful completion of the training, candidates graduate and report for duty to their respective SF groups (Hartmann, Sunde, Kristensen, & Martinussen 2003; Joint Chiefs of Staff, 2003; Russell, 1994).

DEMOGRAPHICS OF SF

SF vary in age, faith, and ethnic background. As noted previously, Congress established the requirement that all combat arms specialties are comprised solely of men (Banks, 2006). In comparison, suicide terrorists may be male or female. The Green Beret community consists of approximately 5,000 SO: 1,000 officers and 4,000 enlisted personnel (Harrell et al., 1997). Officers within the Green Berets are mostly Caucasian, or 90 percent of the total pool. The proportion of minorities is about 10 percent of all SF officers (3 percent African Americans, 2 percent Latino, and 5 percent others). Enlisted personnel within the Green Berets are 85 percent Caucasian and approximately 15 percent minorities (4 percent African Americans, 4 percent Latino, and 7 percent others) (Harrell et al., 1997). The average age of a Special Operations soldier is 32 years (this may be skewed due to previous requirements to be at least an E-4, and the extended amount of time it takes to advance from candidacy status). In comparison, the average age of an infantry man is 22 years (Kane, 2006).

MOTIVATIONS FOR JOINING SPECIAL OPERATIONS

Motivations for joining the Green Berets and the Special Operations community vary at large. However, SF often report intrinsic motivation as a deciding factor, expressing the desire to push oneself to the limit (Tucker & Lamb, 2007). There are extrinsic factors as well, such as extended leave, higher rank, and more privilege and prestige (Tucker & Lamb, 2007). SF are entitled to shorter deployments (on average six months versus the regular army's 12–15 month deployment), extended leave (at least one to two weeks following deployment), and bonuses (ranging from $1,300–$90,000 depending on rank, MOS, and length of service; Tucker & Lamb, 2007).

DISCUSSION

Although comparing suicide terrorists and US Army SF may seem peculiar at first by understanding the mechanisms involved in SF selection and training, military psychologists may, in turn, shed some light on the motivation, drives, and psychological mindset of suicide terrorists:

> The real purpose, most often, is for one group to get the other to do something it would not ordinarily do. In military terminology, we say that our purpose is to impose our will on the enemy.... Of course, what we are really talking about is behavior modification. Very rarely has the overall purpose of conflict been to annihilate another group of people. (Banks & James, 2007)

Interestingly, both suicide terrorists and SF are subjected to strong influences that, with time, empower them to execute actions that would be unimaginable to most individuals, including soldiers and people who have somehow habituated to the atrocities of war. However, SF are commonly very internally directed individuals who form a strong bond with their team members. As professional soldiers, they will often form and express their opinions over the plan handed to them. This is in contrast with suicide terrorists who often are made to be dependent on their leaders and operators for most things including how to end their lives.

Regarding recruitment, most SF candidates seek to join ranks through a bottom-up process, whereas suicide terrorists are often recruited in a top-down process and sometimes via a bottom-up one. Both sets of potential candidates are seen as above average, in terms of physical fitness, psychological hardiness, and aptitude, to ensure the operations will have the highest probability of completion (Joint Chiefs of Staff, 2003; Sparago, 2007). Terrorists and SF are screened by their prospective organizations and only a few are selected. Although terrorists have their own stringent admittance criteria, acceptance into SF appears to be much more competitive and exclusive in comparison, requiring superior physical and mental fitness determined by rigorous qualifications of aptitude and endurance that only a minority of individuals could pass, regardless of agility or motivation. Additionally, there are some similarities in psychological characteristics between SF and suicide terrorists. These include high motivation to participate in missions and intelligence. However, SF have an internal locus of control and independence of thought versus suicide terrorists' external locus of control and thought dependency on their leaders.

Training for SF differs from training for suicide terrorists in terms of duration, arms, contingency planning, and overall range of skill cultivation. For suicide terrorists, the focus is on indoctrination which takes place from the beginning of their recruitment through selection and eventual acceptance to the group. Suicide terrorists are immersed within the terrorist culture and infused with political and direct religious indoctrinations. They are prepared for death and the afterlife, the inevitability of a completed mission.

SF training is focused on perseveration and survival, and training on multiple contingencies, as "no battle plan ever survives the first encounter with the enemy" (Hughes, 1993, p. 45). While suicide terrorists are considered lower level expendable assets to carry out suicide attacks, SF are regarded as the polar opposite. SF's training is long and includes survival, resistance, escape, and evasion. SF is seen as indispensable assets used only for high-risk missions where stealth, tactics, and precision are vital for success. SF may die trying to achieve the objective, but they are provided with the knowledge, training, and equipment to best prepare them against all opposition. In a way, the objectives carried out by SF may seem to a distant outsider like 'suicide missions,' as they are commanded to perform inherently life-threatening endeavors. However, a major difference from suicide terrorists lies in SF's exceptional selection and training, which give a high priority to their safety and survival in missions.

Perhaps the most common misbelief about suicide terrorists is that they are uneducated, poverty-stricken, and/or depressed. This stereotype holds true for only a portion of suicide terrorists. Like SF, suicide terrorists have a wide range of within-group differences. For instance, through a series of interviews with volunteer suicide bombers, Hassan (2008) found that many were, in fact, middle class and educated. In this respect, both suicide terrorists and SF groups appear to have a large variance in their degree of education and economic status.

SF personnel are characteristically high in resilience (Bartone et al., 2008) and low in suicidality (Roy, Carli, & Sarchiapone, 2011). Assuming that resilience mitigates the suicide risk associated with trauma (Roy et al., 2011), there may be a possible connection between high occurrences of trauma, depleted resilience, and the success in cultivating suicidal behavior among suicide terrorists by their organizations. The etiology of suicide terrorism is an important area of study that requires more research by military psychologists.

Hassan (2008) argues that the propensity for suicide bombings may be found in broader social conditions rather than suicide bombers' individual profiles. He found a prevailing theme in that members of their families recounted histories of persecution, beatings, and torture, suffered at the hands of opposing forces. Therefore, he concluded that the driving force behind many suicide terrorists is revenge and humiliation.

In contrast, SF do not tend to join military organizations as a way to inflict vengeance. They join for a wide array of reasons such as an idiosyncratic way of proving oneself (Tucker & Lamb, 2007), financial gain (Department of the Army, 2006), patriotism, and altruism. Although suicide terrorists differ from SF in the first two motives mentioned, the latter two are arguably similar causes for joining their respective organizations.

One might argue that religion is a primary motivational force among suicide terrorists. Many cite jihad as their rationale for destroying America and its allies. Although religion may play a vital role in recruiting and motivating potential suicide bombers (Hassan, 2008), the driving force is usually not only religion but also a combination of politics, humiliation, revenge, retaliation, and perceived altruistic behavior.

This argument is consistent with other extent research examining the motivation behind joining terrorist organizations. As mentioned earlier, Sparago (2007) found that social support, historical alliances, political action, charismatic leaders, and religious beliefs all motivate suicide terrorists into joining their organizations.

Social support, political action, and historical alliances are seemingly parallel motivational forces within SF and suicide terrorists. The armed forces provide a bonding structure where members with shared ideology and belief systems can support each other. Similarly, terrorist organizations unite their members through their ideologies. Furthermore, joining either group represents taking a form of political action. The terrorist may join against political grievance and suppression, whereas SF may join to defend the homeland from prospective enemies. Lastly, both groups offer an alliance that bonds members who fight a common enemy throughout time—both SF and terrorists defend a nation, a culture, and a way of life in which they believe.

Although motivating factors for suicide terrorists and SF converge at times, they begin to depart in respect to their influential leaders and religious beliefs. Often terrorists join organizations to support influential leaders such as Osama bin Laden, whereas SF, who may feel inspired by certain individuals, would not join solely for that reason. Moreover, many suicide terrorists are often motivated to eradicate their enemies, whereas SF do not join to further religious movements. For both suicide terrorists and SF, their inspiration is stimulated by an over-arching cause—serving their community. This may be achieved in many ways: by liberating or protecting the homeland; by conveying religious or nationalistic beliefs; or by achieving vengeance or honor. Therefore, programs enabling individuals to serve the community might decrease the number of potential recruits for suicide terrorism. Additionally, publicizing the process in which terrorist organizations select, manipulate, and train suicide bombers might shine some light on the outcomes of potential recruits and consequently decrease willingness of candidates to join such organizations.

Literature integrating military psychology and research of suicide terrorism is scarce. This chapter presented several important factors and parallels that could be used in this important field of study. Evidently, much more work is needed in the integration of knowledge about SF with the research of suicide terrorism. We encourage researchers and military psychologists in particular to inspect the factors outlined in this chapter and enhance our understanding of suicide terrorism and its interception.

REFERENCES

Atran, S. (2003). Genesis of suicide terrorism. *Science, 299*(5612), 1534–1539.
Bank, A. (1986). *From OSS to Green Berets.* Novato, CA: Presidio Press.
Banks, L. (2006). The history of special operations psychological selection. In A. Mangelsdorff (Ed.), *Psychology in the service of national security* (pp. 83–95). Washington, DC: American Psychological Association.
Banks, L., & James, L. C. (2007). Warfare, terrorism, and psychology. In B. Bongar, L. M. Brown, L. E. Beutler, J. N. Breckenridge, & P. G. Zimbardo (Eds.), *Psychology of terrorism* (pp. 216–222). New York, NY: Oxford University Press.
Bartone, P. T., Roland, R. R., Picano, J. J., & Williams, T. J. (2008). Psychological hardiness predicts success in US army Special Forces candidates. *International Journal of Selection and Assessment, 16*(1), 78–81.
Bloom, M. (2006). *Dying dying to kill: The allure of suicide terror.* New York, NY: Columbia University Press.
Brynjar, L. (2008). Doctrines for jihadi terrorist training. *Terrorism and Political Violence, 20*(4), 518–542.
Clausewitz, C. V. (2008). *On war: A modern military classic.* (Col. J. J. Graham, Trans.). Radford, VA: Wilder Publications. (Original work published in 1832.)
Daly, S. A., & Gerwehr, S. (2006). *Al-Qaida: Terrorist selection and recruitment.* Santa Monica, CA: RAND Corporation. Retrieved online

on 15 December, 2012 from http://www.rand.org/pubs/reprints/ RP1214.
Dearing, M. P. (2010). Like red tulips at springtime: Understanding the absence of female martyrs in Afghanistan. *Studies in Conflict & Terrorism, 33*(12), 1079–1103.
Department of the Army. (2006). *U.S. special operations forces: Report 3-05-fm-100-25*. Department of the Army. Washington, DC: Headquarters, Department of the Army.
Department of Defense. (2010). *Department of Defense dictionary of military and associated terms: Joint publication 1-02*. Washington, DC: Federal Printing House.
Diemer, M. A. (2001). *Manning Special Forces in the 21st century: Strategies for recruiting, assessing, and selecting soldiers for Special Forces training*. Washington, DC: U.S. Army War College.
Durkheim, E. (1951). *Suicide*. New York, NY: Free Press.
Faria, J. R., & Arce, D. G. (2006). Terrorism support and recruitment. *Defense and Peace Economics, 16*(4), 263–273.
Flin, R. (2001). Selecting the right stuff: Personality and high-reliability occupations. In R. W. Roberts & R. Hogan (Eds.), *Personality psychology in the workplace* (pp. 253–276). Washington, DC: American Psychological Association.
Hassan, R. (2008). Global rise of suicide terrorism: An overview. *Asian Journal of Social Science, 36*(2), 271–291.
Harrell, M. C., Kirby, S. N., Sloan, J. S., Graff, C. M., McKlevey, C. J., & Sollinger, J. M. (1997). *Minority participation in special operations forces*. Washington, DC: National Defense Research Institute.
Hartmann, E., Sunde, T., Kristensen, W., & Martinussen, M. (2003). Psychological measures as predictors of training performance. *Journal of Personality Assessment, 80*(1), 87–98.
Hegghammer, T. (2007, February 05). Saudi militants in Iraq: Backgrounds and recruitment patterns. Oslo: Norwegian Defense Research Establishment. Retrieved from http://www.ffi.no/no/Rapporter/06-03875.pdf
Hoffman, B. (2006). *Inside terrorism*. New York, NY: Columbia University Press.
Hughes, D. (1993). *Moltke on the art of war*. Novato, CA: Presidio.
Humphreys, A. (2007, January 17). One official's 'refugee' is another's 'terrorist'. Retrieved from http://www.canada.com/nationalpost/news/story.html?id=a64f73d2-f672-4bd0-abb3-2584029db496
Jenkins, B. M. (2006). *Unconquerable nation: Knowing our enemy, strengthening ourselves*. Santa Monica, CA: RAND. Retrieved online on 15 December, 2012 from http://www.rand.org/pubs/monographs/2006/RAND_MG454.pdf

Joint Chiefs of Staff. (2003). *Joint publication 3-05: Doctrine for joint special operations.* Washington, DC: Government Printing Office.
Kane, T. (2006). *Who are the recruits? The demographic characteristics of U.S. military enlistment, 2003–2005.* Washington, DC: The Heritage Foundation.
Kavanagh, J. (2011). Selection, availability, and opportunity: The conditional effect of poverty on terrorist group participation. *Journal of Conflict Resolution, 55*(1), 106–132.
McDonald, D. G., Norton, J. P., & Hodgdon, J. A. (1990). Training success in U.S. Navy Special Forces. *Aviation, Space, and Environmental Medicine, 61*(6), 548–554.
Merari, A. (2007). Psychological aspects of suicide terrorism. In B. Bongar, L. M. Brown, L. E. Beutler, J. N. Breckenridge, & P. G. Zimbardo (Eds.), *Psychology of terrorism* (pp. 101–115). New York, NY: Oxford University Press.
Merari, A. (2010). *Driven to death. Psychological and social aspects of suicide terrorism.* New York, NY: Oxford University Press.
Moghaddam, F. M. (2005). The staircase to terrorism: Psychological exploration. *American Psychologist, 60*(2), 161–169.
Nesser, P. (2008): How did Europe's global jihadis obtain training for their militant causes? *Terrorism and Political Violence, 20*(2), 234–256.
Orbach, I. (2004). Terror suicide: How is it possible? *Archives of Suicide Research, 8*(1), 115–130.
Pleban, R., Thompson, T., Valentine, P. J., Dewey, G. I., Allentoff, H., & Wesolowski, M. (1988). *Selection and assessment of Special Forces course candidates: Preliminary issues.* U.S. Department of the Army.
Post, J. M. (2004). *The Al-Qaeda training manual: Military studies in the jihad against the tyrants.* Maxwell Air Force Base: USAF Counter Proliferation Centre.
Post, J. M. (2005). When hatred is bred in the bone: Psycho-cultural foundations of contemporary terrorism. *Political Psychology, 26*(4), 615–636.
Post, J. M., Ali, F., Henderson, S. W., Shanfield, S., Victoroff, J., & Weine, S. (2009). The psychology of suicide terrorism. *Psychiatry, 72*(1), 13–31.
Post, J. M., & Pittas, A. (2012). The role of strategic information operations in countering terrorism. In U. Kumar & M. K. Mandal (Eds.), *Countering terrorism: Psychosocial strategies* (pp. 96–117). New Delhi: SAGE Publications.
Roy, A., Carli, V., & Sarchiapone, M. (2011). Resilience mitigates the suicide risk associated with childhood trauma. *Journal of Affect Disorders, 133*(3), 591–594.
Russell, T. L. (1994). *Job analysis of Special Forces jobs.* Alexandria, VA: U.S. Army Research Institute for the Behavioral and Social Sciences.

Sparago, M. (2007). Terrorist recruitment: The crucial case of Al-Qaeda's global jihad terror network. New York: New York University Print. Retrieved online on December 15, 2012 from http://www.scps.nyu.edu/export/sites/scps/pdf/global-affairs/marta-sparago.pdf

Stenersen, A. (2008). The Internet: A virtual training camp? *Terrorism and Political Violence, 20*(2), 215–233.

Tønnessen, T. H. (2008). Training on a battlefield: Iraq as a training ground for global jihadis. *Terrorism and Political Violence, 20*(4), 543–562.

Tucker, G., & Lamb, C. J. (2007). *United States special operations forces.* New York, NY: Columbia University Press.

U. S. Army Personnel Research Office. (1979). Research on combat selection and Special Forces man power problems. Washington, DC: Department of the Army: Government Printing Office.

U.S. Army Recruiting Command. (1999). *Vision and transformation strategy.* Washington, DC: Department of the Army: Government Printing Office, 4–5.

Victoroff, J. (2005). The mind of the terrorist: A review and critique of psychological approaches. *Journal of Conflict Resolution, 49*(1), 3–42.

11

The Use and Abuse of Children/Youth in Terrorism and Suicide Bombing

Edna Erez and Anat Berko

In a recent Cable News Network (CNN) interview, Mia Bloom noted that "women and children are the new face of terrorism" (Bloom, 2012; see also Gray & Machin, 2008; Israeli, 2003). The use of children and youth (minors, persons under 18 years of age, hereafter children[1]) in terrorism has been documented in numerous conflict zones around the world. In the recent past, children have participated in insurgencies and wars, in Sierra Leone, Liberia, Congo, Sudan, Afghanistan, and Myanmar, and in terrorist operations in conflict zones such as Turkey, Iraq, Israel, and the Palestinian territories. They have served as camouflaged guerrillas, uniformed soldiers, warriors (Peters, 2005), and more recently as suicide bombers. According to Singer (2005a), there are about 300,000 children combatants (both boys and girls) under the age of 18, fighting in almost three quarters of the world's conflicts (see also BBC, 2012). The overwhelming majority (80 percent) of these conflicts include fighters who are children under the age of 15. Despite the UN convention prohibition against the use of persons less than 18 years of age in armed conflicts (see UNICEF [2012], Convention of the Rights of the Child), many government forces, paramilitary organizations, rebel groups, and terrorist organizations continue to recruit and employ children in military or terrorist activities.

This chapter reviews the ways in which children and youth are used and abused in military context and terrorism, with a focus on

---

[1] A common distinction is to refer to persons under 14-year old as children and from 14 to 18 as youth. We use children to address all persons under 18.

the misuse of children in the Palestinian[2] territories, where Hamas, Islamic jihad, and Fatah have routinely used children for military purposes including suicide bombings. While the topic of child soldiering has been examined extensively in recent studies (e.g., Rosen, 2005; Singer, 2005a, 2005b, 2006; Wessells, 2006), there is less scholarly work on the use of children in terrorism[3] in general, and by Palestinian terrorist organizations in particular. Our chapter examines these issues, focusing on the use and abuse of children and youth in advancing Palestinian interests, including activities of organizations such as Hamas, Islamic jihad, and Fatah.

We begin by describing the functions that children (both willing and unwilling participants) serve for insurgent and terrorist organizations, the motives behind recruiting (or forcing) children to engage in terrorist activities, the benefits organizations derive from using children in their operations, and the liabilities involved in such practices. We then examine the recruitment and indoctrination methods employed by groups or organizations, and the grooming and training of children for terrorist missions. The short- and

---

[2] It is important to make a terminological historical point here. Prior to Israel's establishment in 1948, the term 'Palestinian' referred to those who were living in Palestine and included the Jews living in the Yishuv (the Jewish community that continued to inhabit the land after the majority of its Jewish population was exiled), and those who immigrated to Israel prior to the establishment of the state. The Arabs living in the part of Mandated Palestine remaining after portion east of the Jordan River was given by the British to the Hashemites were commonly referred to as Arabs or South Syrians. The Palestinian Liberation Organization referring to Arabs as Palestinians did not come into existence until 1964 under Ahmed Shukhairy, a time tellingly when Jordan still controlled what they called the West Bank (Judea and Samaria) and Egypt still controlled Gaza. Using the term 'Palestinians' to refer to the Arabs in mandated Palestine, is then of relatively recent origin (since 1964). Many of the Israeli Jews today are descendants of the Jewish Palestinians up to 1948. Many others are descendants of those who were exiled.

[3] The terminology and overlap between war and terrorism has been the topic of debates in academic writings and political discussions. In this chapter, we refer to the role, functions, and experiences of children who are used or abused in military and related context. Delving into a discussion of the overlap or differences between war and terrorism, or listing the factors that distinguish the two phenomena or concepts (e.g., issues of size or number of participants, purpose, targets, tactics, sponsors, applicable rules) is beyond the scope of this paper.

long-term social and psychological effects that living in conflict areas have on children are discussed, and the impact of participation in military or terrorist activities on children are reviewed. We then describe the experiences of Palestinian youngsters who serve time in prison for their involvement in terrorist activities, the reasons they joined terrorist organizations or participated in military activities, and their perspectives on their involvement. The chapter concludes with discussion of public policy implications of the use of children in terrorism.

THE BENEFITS OF USING CHILDREN IN WAR AND TERRORISM

Children provide various strategic and tactical benefits to the insurgent groups or terrorist organizations that employ them. First, the recruitment of children into combat and terrorism is easier, compared to recruiting adults. The distinctive vulnerabilities of children—their limited physical, social, mental, and cognitive development—make their recruitment, both as willing and unwilling participants, a relatively easy task. These developmental features also assist in keeping children compliant, obedient, and loyal to the organization and its cause.

The authority that adults have over children, and the universal norms that children should respect adults and obey their orders, provide rebel groups and terrorist organizations an advantage in recruiting minors. Children usually do not question adults' orders or requests for favors, often agreeing to honor them with little or no returns. In the context of Palestinian terrorism, a 16-year-old child volunteered to become a suicide bomber for a sum of 100 shekel (the equivalent to $25) because an adult has asked him to do it (Berko & Erez, 2005). For a similar sum of money, another 16-year-old child agreed to carry a bag and bring it to the other side of a checkpoint. Unknown to the child, the bag contained explosives, and the organization's operative intended to detonate the explosives as the child approached the guards at the checkpoint (Erez, 2006).

Children represent an asset for terrorist organizations as they can fulfill diverse roles and functions that adults may not be able or willing to do. Inside terrorist organizations or armed groups, children serve as lookouts, bodyguards, guards, porters, domestic laborers, medics, messengers, cooks, spies, mine sweepers, recruiters, sex slaves, human shields, fighters, and suicide bombers. Roles may vary by age and gender, with girls more often expected to provide sexual or domestic services, and younger boys and girls serving as spies (Wessells, 2006). In the Palestinian context, children have been utilized in perpetrating attacks on Israeli citizens, attending violent demonstrations, confronting Israel Defense Forces (IDF) soldiers, smuggling bombs and weapons, and maintaining security of or guarding over terrorist meetings and operations. In some cases, children were involved in terrorist activities without their knowledge or consent. In one case, a 12-year-old Palestinian boy was unknowingly given a bomb to smuggle into Israel. But in other terrorist operations, children enthusiastically took part in various aspects of the operation, contributing to its success by virtue of being minors, thus fending off attention to their actions.

Children who provide support services for organizations are likely to escape authorities' attention, having clear advantages over adults. Children's physical size, mental condition, together with prevailing social attitudes toward children as innocent, naïve, or gullible, help them escape surveillance and avoid suspicion. These assumptions and beliefs also make children's excuses and justifications for their actions or presence in specific locations often go unquestioned. The first US soldier to be killed by hostile fire in the Afghanistan war represents a case in point. He was shot in an ambush by an unsuspected 14-year-old boy (Singer, 2005a).

Children's participation in resistance and terrorist activities bestows an important symbolic advantage. During the first *Intifada* (uprising) in the Palestinian territories (1987–1993), well-organized Palestinian youths who confronted Israeli soldiers by throwing stones at them received much media attention. Their aims were to gain sympathy from the international community as well as from segments of Israeli society, who watched daily on their television screens Israeli soldiers fighting and arresting children (Rigby, 1990). The images of children throwing stones and confronting uniformed armed soldiers amplified perceptions of Palestinian vulnerability (Rosen, 2005) and sent a message about the depth of the conflict and the extent of the resistance. As Israeli soldiers often have orders not to shoot children, Palestinian children felt immune to retaliation, allowing them to continue the practice of stone throwing.

The docile characteristics of children as naïve, impressionable, compliant, and respectful of adult orders, have led to their recruitment by various regimes, insurgent groups, or terrorist organizations facing urgent manpower shortage. The child recruits are then quickly trained to become fighters or fulfill other military functions. For instance, in the Iran–Iraq war, following some years of fierce fighting, both sides suffered significant losses of (adult) manpower, weakening them tactically and strategically. Subsequently, both countries began recruiting children, ignoring their own domestic conscription laws, which prohibit the use of children in war. In Iran, President Ali-Akbar Rafsanjani decreed in 1984 that "all Iranians from 12 to 72 should volunteer for the Holy War" (Brown, 1990, p. 2). Numerous children were then pulled out of schools; indoctrinated in the glory of martyrdom and sent to the front lines. Iranian commanders used these children in their first waves of attacks, to clear paths through minefields, and overwhelm Iraq's defenses (Brown, 1990). Iraq also used children in this war, sending them to the front with minimal training. Following the Gulf War, Iraq under Saddam Hussein continued to use children for military purposes. The Saddam's Lion Cubs, a paramilitary force of children between the ages of 10–15, was created, and its members received training in arms and combat tactics (Singer, 2006). American troops who participated in the Second Gulf War also reported facing children in battles across Iraq. The view that children are a potential pool of fighters and the practice of using them in military operations characterizes other armed conflicts (see Singer, 2006 discussions of the use of children by organizations such as the Liberation Tigers of Tamil Eelam [LTTE] in Sri Lanka, Partiya Karkerên Kurdistan [PKK] in Turkey or in Liberia).

In the Arab/Palestinian case, first during the British Mandatory rule, and later, following the Six-Day War in 1967, the Arab Palestinian leadership resorted to children and youth to conduct religious war and further nationalist goals through violence and armed encounters (Rosen, 2005). In fact, the radicalization of Arab/Palestinian population during these periods developed out of the radicalization of its youth (Rosen, 2005), who through schools and youth movements were indoctrinated and trained in military tactics. During the first *Intifada* (uprising), the established Palestinian Liberation Organization leadership was in exile in Tunis. Thus, the daily operation of the uprising was handled by youth organizations and educational or civil institutions that mobilized children (Hilterman, 1991). In the second *Intifada*, the involvement of children was also high: young teens made up almost three quarters of the participants (Singer, 2006).

MOTIVATION TO PARTICIPATE AND RECRUITMENT METHODS

Motivation to join organizations and partake in military or terrorist activities is often intertwined with the recruitment tactics employed by insurgent groups and terrorist organizations. The local context of the conflict, its respective push and pull factors, and the lived realities of the recruits, together, explain children's motivation to join and participate in armed activities.

Generally, children who grow up in conflict zones or deeply divided societies are acutely affected by the violence around them (e.g., Pine, Costello, & Masten, 2005; Masten & Narayan, 2012; Women's Commission for Refugee Women and Children, 2000). These traumatic experiences provide children and youth with motivation, inspiration, and justifications to join rebel groups or terrorist organizations, and fight for a group's cause. Living in conflict areas also leads to the normalization of violence (Masten & Narayan, 2012), predisposing children to be interested and willing to join and participate in armed undertakings. Experiences such as witnessing the death of relatives, destruction of homes, displacement, and other hardships resulting from hostilities can be powerful influences on children (Somasundaram, 2002). Push factors such as personal and familial difficulties, economic necessities, or political oppression and harassment may also play a role in motivating children to join terrorism. But children may also become involved in militant activities for thrill and excitement (Venhaus, 2010), and for adolescent males, participation may comprise a way to prove their manhood (Berko & Erez, 2005).

Methods of recruitment of children extend from persuasions and to promises for material well-being, adventure, or salvation, to threats, force and other illegal means to enlist young recruits. In some conflict areas (e.g., Sierra Leone or Congo), large numbers of children are recruited by force, through abduction, or credible threats. Children were subject to threats, deprivation, beatings, forced labor and ingestion of drugs, and tasked with dangerous and onerous jobs. Girls were overwhelmingly subject to sexual violence, or becoming 'bushwives' (Singer, 2005b). For some children, military involvement provides a form of employment, for others who are neglected or abandoned (because they were orphaned, have HIV, etc.), it is a form of survival (Doek, 2008).

The majority of children who join armed groups or terrorist organizations, however, 'choose' to do it, although under various constraints. Children's choices to join such groups are sometimes made within contexts of personal or familial hardships, poverty or economic necessity, and the normalization of violence or war. The political, cultural, and ideological environments may also be accompanied by need for personal security or peer group pressures. Many of these reasons are the same for which adults choose to join military groups or organizations (Wessells, 2006).

Children who lost family members or close friends in hostilities, or have experienced violence and victimization related to a political conflict, often endorse violence and revenge as legitimate responses. Palestinian youth who joined the ranks of Fatah or Hamas and volunteered to perpetrate suicide bombing spoke of relatives or significant others who were killed or maimed during encounters with the IDF, listing revenge as the reason for their involvement in terrorist acts (Berko & Erez, 2005, 2007).

To encourage children to join military activities and terrorism, organizations make various promises and lure children by providing them opportunities that children facing social and material dire conditions, or living in poverty, cannot imagine. For instance, the LTTE promises children that they would learn how to drive vehicles or motorcycles. Another method that organizations employ to attract children is to offer them and their families material benefits and assurances about their financial welfare (e.g., Hamas, LTTE).

An important method to motivate and recruit children is making promises about spiritual and religious rewards waiting for those who would join and pursue the goals of the organization. Throughout the world, a common thread that transcends culture and religion, race and ethnicity, tribe or clan, is honor, valor, and a noteworthy label placed on male children (and more recently female) for enlistment and participation in military operations. For instance, in

Palestinian towns posters of *shaheed*s (martyrs) glorifying their suicide bombing attacks appear on walls of schools and other public areas, and many public buildings, children camps, or educational institutions are named after them (Hafez, 2006; Palestinian Media Watch, 2012b, 2012c). In addition, cards portraying the photographs of *shaheed*s accompany purchases of chewing gum, the way baseball cards do in North America. Palestinian television has time and time again broadcasted songs that call children to sacrifice themselves for the national cause, to become martyrs, and glories those who have been engaged in such acts. Palestinian TV also aired interviews of children who declare their wish to practice *shahada* (submission, sacrifice) and become *shaheed*s (Palestinian Media Watch, 2012a, 2012b). It also showed Palestinian Authority leaders applauding children who were singing "I shall saturate you with my blood, redeem you with my life," or narrated a report in which a girl has insisted on singing *Intifada* song about the 'Martyr who loved death,' despite the Palestinian Authority Television (PA TV) host expressing a preference for a song about life (Palestinian Media Watch, 2012a, 2012b).[4]

The recruitment of children is often facilitated by collective institutional efforts and activities aimed at injecting children with ideology and praising those who convey the message through their action. Various countries and groups in many conflict zones have established 'youth wings' that inculcate children with ideological directions, and provide them with armed training, in preparation for military or terrorist activities. Recruitment may take place through educational institutions, in places of worship, or by creating special programs for youth. The LTTE used to visit schools and screen films of the government's attacks and destruction, and their own successful counterattacks. In other cases, they have showed off well-dressed children in uniform, boots, and medals, causing the children who observed them to envy and subsequently join the group (Singer, 2006). In the Palestinian context, the creation of various youth groups or paramilitary troops consisting of children has been evident during the British Mandatory rule and continues to date (Rosen, 2005). Children have been recruited through the educational system, in the context of leisure activities after school, and through the religious establishment.

---

[4] The honored martyr (*shaheed*) is distinguished from the person committing suicide (*Istishhad*), who is considered to have broken Islamic law.

Terrorist organizations have begun to employ the Internet and cell-phone texting as tools for indoctrinating and recruiting children. An example of a clip that was broadcast on PA TV over several years, at times twice a week, features a child actor playing Muhammad al-Dura—a Palestinian child whose death in crossfire while his father was holding him was broadcast to the entire world[5]—calling to other Palestinian children to follow him to Child Martyrs' Heaven. Marcus and Crook (2006) describe the child in this clip as follows:

> *I am waving not to part but to say, 'Follow me,' is Dura's invitation on the TV screen. The children watching this video are then shown what awaits them if they join Dura in death. The video follows the child actor—"Dura"—joyously frolicking in heaven. He romps on the beach, plays with a kite and runs toward a Ferris wheel. The children are being told that death in conflict with Israel will bring them into a child's paradise. Muhammad al-Dura is already in this paradise, tranquil and fun-filled.* (Marcus & Crook, 2006, p. 1)

Organizations have created websites which use the Internet to target children by applying 'narrowcasting' (Weimann, 2008). Using modern marketing and advertising tactics, these special websites include programs to indoctrinate children in the ideology of the organization, and free computer games that provide them virtual practice in acts of terrorism. For example, the *Al-Fateh* site has a link to the official Hamas site. Also, in addition to its graphics, drawings, children's songs, and stories, some of which are written by children, the site includes messages promoting suicide terrorism. It presented the picture of a decapitated head of young female suicide bomber who in 2004 detonated an explosive belt in

---

[5] The death of Muhammad al-Dura, a 12-year-old boy, while his father was shielding him from the crossfire between Israelis and Palestinians in Gaza in 2000, was first thought to be caused by Israeli fire. Following an investigation, it was found that the child was not killed by the Israelis, and that the scene may have been staged or manipulated by the French TV reporters. Nonetheless, the picture of the child and his father during crossfire was transmitted around the world, becoming a powerful message about the presumed brutality of the Israelis toward children, a message that has been repeated in several high profile cases of terrorism.

Jerusalem, killing two policemen and wounding 17 civilians. The text accompanying the picture praises the act, stating that she is now a *shaheeda* (martyr) in paradise, like her male comrades. Another posting is the last will of a Hamas suicide bomber, who, in 2001, carried out a suicide bombing attack at a teen club in Tel Aviv, killing 21 youth. Both acts were glorified and set as examples to follow (Weimann, 2008).

PALESTINIAN CHILDREN, TERRORISM, AND SUICIDE BOMBING

The use of children and youth in the Palestinian context, as noted above, dates back to the early stages of the Israeli–Arab/Palestinian conflict, prior to the establishment of the State of Israel (Rosen, 2005). More recent attempts by Palestinian nationalist and terrorist organizations (such as Fatah, Hamas, and Palestinian jihad) to attack Israeli citizenry and disrupt daily life, continue to be marked by efforts to influence, recruit, and employ youngsters. Educational institutions, from kindergarten through high school, instill 'resistance' ideology that endorses and glorifies sacrifice and suicide bombing. Books and learning materials, games, toys, awards, recreational activities, naming of facilities, and promoting role models constructed through these means—all revolve around military activities, suicide bombing, and the valor, significance and contribution of the *shaheed*s for Palestinian pride and goals (Hafez, 2006). Perusal of websites, TV programs, and other mass media communications, reinforces the centrality of violence and sacrifice in Palestinian youth education (Palestinian Media Watch, 2012c; Weimann, 2008).

Recent research on the involvement of Palestinian youth in armed operations and terrorism suggests that they fit the profile of children who willingly participate in other conflict areas. Palestinian children who partake in terrorism are not immune to the influence of the cultural milieu in which they grow up, and the realities of the armed conflict they experience. Yet, recruitment, obedience, and partaking do not emanate from fear, threats, or physical coercion. Although the cultural and social milieu, which emphasizes a quest for national identity, liberation, and a homeland, and glory for those who have sacrificed their lives for these goals is a major factor in their participation (Hafez, 2006), and although they may not always be aware of the scope or implications of their involvement (e.g., Berko & Erez, 2005), they are considered willing participants (Rosen, 2005). Also, as the ideology of liberation in struggles that are influenced by strong religious beliefs, as is the case in some aspects of the Israeli–Arab/Palestinian conflict and their attempts to delegitimize Israel and the Jews (e.g., preaching in mosques), Palestinian Islamic youth view the national cause as having divine sanction, a part of their devotion to higher authorities (Wessells, 2006).

Palestinian society has glorified armed 'resistance,' teaching children from an early age to view military activity as glamorous and desirable. Pictures of toddlers with explosive belts are displayed in ceremonies and places where children congregate, sending a message that these are paths for fame and prestige. Militaristic values and focus on martyrdom are transmitted via parades, ceremonies, educational programs, theme parks, media images, songs and posters that honor warriors and suicide bombers. Children in such contexts learn to associate military activity and sacrifice with respect, prestige, and glory—all captivating attractions for children who otherwise may feel unimportant, vulnerable, or powerless. Mothers who express pride in seeing their sons partaking in military actions or suicide bombing (e.g., Hugi, 2005),[6] together with peer pressure to perpetrate political violence, make children who do not subscribe to these values to feel as outsiders, as being feel left out—situations that children would avoid at any cost.

Interviews of Palestinian children and youth serving prison time for partaking in terrorist attacks or failed suicide bombing confirm the influence of various tangible and intangible rewards on the decision to participate. Dispatchers who sent youngsters on suicide bombing missions listed such rewards as effective incentives to prompt children to volunteer for suicide missions. These rewards included not only glory and fame but also cash money,

---

[6] There is evidence, however, that mothers of suicide bombers, who are presented as having encouraged their children to die as *shaheed*s, are subject to pressures to appear in public as if they celebrate the death. The mothers mourn the loss of their children and suffer tremendously from their demise (Shalhoub-Kevorkian, 2003). They are also likely to lose the financial support of the terrorist organizations if they do not cooperate in celebrating the death of their children.

financial support for the family, adventures, reaching paradise, and spending time with 70 virgins, as powerful influences. An important consideration for some of the recruits was to appear as 'real men'—someone who is not afraid to die for the cause (Berko & Erez, 2005).

But there are other sets of motives to partake in terrorism, particularly suicide bombing. They consisted of using the suicide mission as a way to resolve mundane problems the children faced at the time, such as getting out of difficult circumstances at home, evading the grip of family control, extricating themselves from demanding school expectations, or avoiding fights and insults by fellow students (Berko, 2012). In some cases, youngsters were pressured to volunteer, and in extreme cases, some were threatened that if they do not agree, embarrassing details about them or their family, particularly information related to the modesty of female members of their family, would be revealed (Berko, 2012).

It is important to note, however, that the use of children in terrorism is debated within Palestinian society, and stakeholders are divided on this issue as well. While the Palestinian leadership promotes armed hostilities by all age groups, and terrorist organizations continuously look for young volunteers, parents of children who were sent to suicide missions generally express anger that their children were selected for such missions. All the youngsters interviewed stated that they concealed their plans and activities related to suicide bombing from their parents, knowing that they would object to their becoming suicide bombers (Berko & Erez, 2005, 2007).

Interviewed dispatchers also expressed some reservations about the use of children. Some felt that sending children on suicide missions may be less effective in fighting the enemy than dispatching adults, as children are "underdeveloped in their capabilities to inflict maximum casualties" (Berko, 2012). Others, however, confirmed that children have tactical advantages over adults, such as their ability to evade surveillance, or provide other benefits for their handlers (Berko, 2012).

Interviews of incarcerated youngsters also revealed that many were pressured by dispatchers or their proxies to volunteer for suicide missions. Repeated appeals and incessant requests to become famous *shaheeds* were accompanied by promises for material support of their family, or the pleasures of paradise. Some of the youth who ended up in prison expressed resentment that Palestinian leaders and functionaries in terrorist organizations do not recruit their own children for suicide bombing missions, but send other people's children to death. Others complained that they were told by their dispatchers that, in case they are caught, they would receive lenient sentences, when in reality they received much longer prison sentence than promised (Berko, 2012).

Some of the children interviewed were known in their neighborhoods to have developmental problems, low self-esteem, and persons who are eager to please others. In other cases, the children interviewed admitted being envious of and wanting to emulate their older peers in the neighborhood (*shabab*) who were carrying or involved in hiding weapons. In still other cases, volunteering for suicide missions started as a joke, but soon became a fait accompli from which the children could not get out without losing face. Youngsters, who did not want to disappoint their friends, show signs of fear, or be ridiculed for lack of masculinity and 'not being a man' soon found themselves in preparation for the mission and on their way to the target (Berko & Erez, 2005). Most were afraid to share their associations or whereabouts with their parents, who, as the interviewees stated, warned them to avoid socializing with persons known for their involvement in terrorism (Berko & Erez, 2005, 2007). Other children reported that they were asked to join various operations to shield adults from blame—in case things go wrong. They noted that they were informed that youngsters, as minors, would be exonerated for their involvement in terrorist operations, thereby helping the adults involved to avoid serious repercussions (Berko, 2012).

A concern related to the abuse of children in Palestinian terrorism has been the use of children as human shields, the designation and use of areas around schools as places to store and stock weapons, and firing missiles from public places adjacent to educational institutions, hospitals, or mosques (all of which are likely to include children). In other cases, civilians, particularly children, were summoned to places in which terrorist operatives were hiding to protect them from likely attacks. Children were also used to surround operatives in order to facilitate their escape from combat zones.

Whereas our earlier examples described how terrorist organizations make use of children qualities such as size, obedience, mental development or naiveté, ability to avoid surveillance or other tactical benefits, these latter examples demonstrate how terrorist organizations exploit conventions and rules of war designed to avoid or minimize civilian, particularly children casualties that tend to attract heightened international media attention.

CONCLUSION

The use of youth in military activities and terrorism continues to be a subject of scholarly and political debates on domestic and international levels. Researchers and human right observers have referred to it as one of the worst forms of institutionalized child-abuse practices—whether physical, psychological, or sexual.

It is commonly argued that prevention or reduction of child participation in military activities and terrorism is dependent on understanding why children choose to join such activities in the first place (e.g., Somasundaram, 2002). At the core of the debates are questions about how to approach children who participate in military missions, how to view or define their responsibility when they cause death and injuries, and what political and legal measures to adopt for preventing children from joining armed conflicts. Legal scholars, social science researchers, and human rights organizations do not agree on whether children engaged in war and terrorism are innocent victims or fighters fully responsible for their actions. The question has no clear-cut answer, but is dependent on the circumstances of children participation, including the local context, the history of the conflict, the way in which children are recruited or their loyalty maintained, the level and type of compulsion exerted, and alternative options available for survival.

International conventions, treaties, and protocols set the age of adulthood at 18. The discourse of many NGOs and humanitarian organizations presents children (i.e., persons younger than 18) as vulnerable, helpless, and in need of protection. According to many of these organizations, children who participate in combat or terrorism are victims of adult manipulation and criminal exploitation. While in many conflicts this may be the case, in many others these images do not represent accurate characterization of the majority of participants. Further, there is no consensus on the age at which childhood is thought to end, the competencies or presumed characteristics of children, and the customs and norms about what is appropriate for children to do. Anthropologists contend that definitions of children and childhood are not universal but vary considerably and are culturally specific (Rosen, 2005, 2007). Further, much of the literature questions the assumption that children are helpless, dependent, and incompetent, noting that these views and approaches constitute a social construction rather an objective description of youngsters (e.g., Park, 2010). In examining various cases of children participating in wars and terrorism around the world conflict areas, one can find evidence to support both of these contrasting views.

Recruitment, loyalty to the group, and compliance with the organization's orders may be sustained by various means, ranging from measures indicating free will to those demonstrating coercion, or total lack of agency in the matter. In various conflicts around the world, and in a most pronounced manner in Palestinian society, the forces that influence children and motivate them to participate in terrorism are all encompassing, penetrating every aspect of children's daily lives. Educational institutions, religious establishments, media, information technology, and popular culture exert influence by glamorizing military actions, and creating and sustaining subversive spaces for acts of violence and terror. In such environments, children can easily become active participants who feel empowered by partaking in the world of military activities and terrorism. Children who do not participate in such activities may feel left out and disempowered. Although some of the children may have specific grievances about unfulfilled promises, strong pressures, or certain degrees of exploitation by adults, by and large, most do not consider themselves victimized by their environment. Nor do they resist the identity of fighters or potential martyrs; on the contrary, they enthusiastically embrace these identifies. These circumstances make the problem of combating the use of children in terrorism and suicide bombing a complex and multilayered enterprise, one that requires concerted efforts on the familial, institutional, and political (state) levels.

Review of the cases discussed in this chapter also demonstrates the limitations of current efforts to end the use of children in armed conflicts by passing international law that targets the unscrupulous recruiters of children, and by sponsoring advocacy campaigns that denounce the cruelty of armed conflict and its harmful effects on children compelled to participate. Such calls, made mostly by humanitarian agencies, assume that participating children are victims, have no agency, with universal motives for involvement and not contingent on the specific sociopolitical contexts in which they live. They also ignore the harmful effects of the normalization of violence on children, and its predominance in predisposing youth to become involved in political violence. Several cases discussed in this chapter demonstrate the impact of environment on children's participation in terrorism; yet these cases also demonstrate that participating youngsters are often not passive victims but rather active participants who have voluntarily joined armed conflicts.

The Palestinian case reviewed in this chapter well reflects the many shades of children's involvement in armed conflicts and suicide terrorism, the overt and more subtle compulsion experienced by youngsters to join political violence and perpetrate suicide bombing, and other uses of children in terrorism, such as being human shields in hostilities. In considering public policy designed to prevent using children in armed conflict and terrorism, all facets of children existence in the particular society need to be examined and addressed, from the conditions that normalize political violence, encourage participation, and glorify martyrdom, whether they originated in educational institutions, religious indoctrination, mass communication, leisure time activities, economic conditions, or in the political and social history of the particular conflicts.

REFERENCES

BBC. (2012). *Children in conflict*. Retrieved online on October 12, 2012 from http://www.bbc.co.uk/worldservice/people/features/childrensrights/childrenofconflict/soldier.shtml

Berko, A. (2012). *The smarter bomb: Women and children in terrorism*. Lanham, Maryland: Rowman & Littlefield.

Berko, A., & Erez, E. (2005). 'Ordinary people' and 'death work': Palestinian suicide bombers as victimizers and victims. *Violence and Victims, 20*(6), 603–623.

Berko, A., & Erez, E. (2007). Gender, Palestinian women and terrorism: Women's liberation or oppression? *Studies in Conflict and Terrorism, 30*(6), 493–519.

Bloom, M. (2012, August 6). Analysis: Women and children constitute the new faces of terror. *CNN*. Retrieved from http://security.blogs.cnn.

com/2012/08/06/analysis-women-and-children-constitute-the-new-faces-of-terror/
Brown, I. (1990). *Khomeinis forgotten sons: The story Iran's boy soldiers*. London: Grey Seal Books.
Doek, J. E. (2008). *Republic of Sierra Leone. Child soldiers: Global report 2008*. Retrieved online on February 16, 2013 from http://www.childsoldiersglobalreport.org/content/sierra-leone
Erez, E. (2006). Protracted war, terrorism and mass victimization: Exploring victimological/criminological theories and concepts in addressing terrorism in Israel. In U. Ewald & K. Turkovi (Eds.), *Large-scale victimisation as a potential source of terrorist activities—regaining security in post-conflict societies*. NATO Security through Science Series, E: Human and Societal Dynamics (Vol. 13, pp. 89–102). The Netherlands: ISO Press.
Gray, D. H., & Matchin III, T. O. (2008). Children: The new face of terrorism. *International NGO Journal, 3*(6), 108–114.
Hafez, M. (2006). *Manufacturing human bombs: The making of Palestinian suicide bombers*. Washington, DC: United States Institute of Peace.
Hilterman, J. R. (1991). *Behind the intifada*. Princeton, NJ: Princeton University Press.
Hugi, J. I. (2005). I raised my son to be suicide bomber: I encourage all my children to die as martyrs. *Maariv*, September 8, 2005.
Israeli, R. (2003). Palestinian women and children in the throes of Islamikaze terrorism. ACPR Policy Paper No. 139.
Marcus, I., & Crook, B. (2006). Seducing children to martyrdom. *Palestinian Media Watch Bulletin, 6*. Retrieved online on December 10, 2012 from http://www.jerusalemsummit.org/eng/pmw.php?pmw=16
Masten, A. S., & Narayan, A. J. (2012). Child development in the context of disaster, war, and terrorism: Pathways of risk and resilience. *Annual Review of Psychology, 63*, 227–257.
Palestinian Media Watch (PMW). (2012a). *Palestinian kids created as "fertilizer," to saturate the land with blood*. Retrieved online on January 31 2012 from http://www.palwatch.org/main.aspx?fi=157&doc_id=6255
Palestinian Media Watch (PMW). (2012b). *Success of Shahada promotion*. Retrieved online on January 17, 2013 from http://palwatch.org/main.aspx?fi=415
Palestinian Media Watch (PMW). (2012c). *Glorifying terrorism and terror*. Retrieved online on January 18, 2013 from http://www.palwatch.org/main.aspx?fi=448
Park, A. S. J. (2010). Child soldiers and distributive justice: Addressing the limits of law? *Crime, Law, and Social Change, 53*(4), 329–348.
Peters, L. (2005). *War is no child's play: Child soldiers from battlefield to playground*. Occasional Paper No. 8. Geneva: Geneva Centre for the Democratic Control of Armed Forces.

Pine, D. S., Costello, J., & Masten, A. (2005). Trauma, proximity, and developmental psychopathology: The effects of war and terrorism on children. *Neuropsychopharmacology, 30*(10), 1781–1792.
Rigby, A. (1990). *The living intifada*. London: Zed Books.
Rosen, D. M. (2005). *Armies of the young: Child soldiers in war and terrorism*. Piscataway, NJ: Rutgers University Press.
Rosen, D. M. (2007). Child soldiers, international humanitarian law, and the globalization of childhood. *American Anthropologist, 109*(2), 296–306.
Shalhoub-Kevorkian, N. (2003). Liberating voices: The political implications of Palestinian mothers narrating their loss. *Women's Studies International Forum, 26*(5), 391–407.
Singer, P. W. (2005a). The new children of terror. In J. Forest (Ed.), *The making of a terrorist* (pp. 105–119). Retrieved online on January 5, 2013 from http://www.brookings.edu/views/papers/singer/chapter8_20051215.pdf
Singer, P. W. (2005b). *Terrorists must be denied child recruits*. Brookings Institute. Retrieved online on January 2, 2013 from http://www.brookings.edu/research/opinions/2005/01/20humanrights-singer
Singer P. W. (2006). *Children at war*. Los Angeles, CA: University of California Press.
Somasundaram, D. (2002). Child soldiers: Understanding the context. *British Medical Journal, 324*(7348), 1268–1271.
UNICEF. (2012). *Children and armed conflict*. Retrieved online on October 19, 2012 from http://www.unicef.org/emerg/index_childsoldiers.html
Venhaus, J. M. (2010). *Why youth join Al-Qaeda*. Special Report 236. Washington DC: United States Institute of Peace. Retrieved online on October 14, 2013 from http://www.usip.org/sites/default/files/resources/SR236Venhaus.pdf
Weimann, G. (2008). Narrowcasting: The trend in online terrorism. *Gazette, 70*(3), 9–15.
Wessells, M. G. (2006). *Child soldiers: From violence to protection*. Cambridge, MA: Harvard University Press.
Women's Commission for Refugee Women and Children. (2000). *Untapped potential: Adolescents affected by armed conflict*. Retrieved online on October 10, 2012 from http://www.unicef.org/emerg/files/adolescents_armed_conflict.pdf

12

Deterring Suicide Terrorism

Dushyant Singh

Terrorism is a weapon of the weak. Terror group in its initial stages suffers from tremendous asymmetrical force disadvantage. However, the group also enjoys a considerable information or intelligence advantage. This generates a tendency to exploit respective strengths by each side (Basilici & Simmons, 2004; Dyke & Crisafulli, 2006). As the terrorist has information, he normally achieves strategic and tactical surprise quite easily in their attacks. This invites a severe clamp down by the security forces. In the ensuing competition, whenever the terrorists are squeezed for resources or losing the fight or wish to send a message of ultimate commitment to their cause or simply outbid the other terror groups may resort to suicide terror attack. 9/11 incident in the US, killing of former Indian Prime Minister Mr Rajiv Gandhi, 26/11 Mumbai terror attacks, 2002 Akshardham temple terror attack, attack on Indian Parliament in India are a few recent examples of suicide terror attacks. The preference of this form of strategy by terrorists can also be appreciated from the fact that Pakistan alone has faced over 329 attacks and suffered over 5,119 fatal and 10,830 nonfatal casualties since 2002 (South Asian Terrorism Portal, 2012, November 11).

There has been a dramatic rise in the quantum of suicide attacks since the decade of 1980s. A total of 36 countries are affected by suicide terrorism with Iraq, Afghanistan, Pakistan, and Sri Lanka having suffered the most. The magnitude of the problem can be understood from the intensity of growth of suicide attacks and their relative lethality. Hassan citing Department of Defence has enumerated that while number of terrorist incidents worldwide fell from its peak of 665 in 1986 to 208 in 2003, incidence of suicide bombing increased from an annual average of 31 in the 1980s to 98 in 2003 (Hassan, 2009). Chicago Project data indicates a total of 2,297 attacks since 1981 to 2011 leading to 29,951 fatal and 76,332 nonfatal casualties.

Of even greater concern is the average death per suicide attack which has been 13.1 and average wounded per attack stands at 33.3. In fact from 2004 to 2010, the average attack per year has been 273.43 with maximum being 469 in the year 2007. India too has been adversely affected by it and has suffered 13 suicide bombings since 1981 (University of Chicago, 2011).

The geometric rise of suicide terrorism has forced various states to evolve workable counterterrorism strategies. As part of counter suicide terror, strategy deterrence has also been suggested by many analysts and security operatives. However, given the nature of a suicide attack, there are many experts and analysts who suggest that it is almost impossible to deter suicide terror attack because it is firstly rooted in irrationality; secondly, the bombers lack fear of punishment as they are so highly motivated that they are willing to die and so not deterred by fear of punishment or any other reason and finally they lack a return address or a fixed/defined location where effective retaliation can be effected (Bar, 2008; Trager & Zagorcheva, 2005–2006). In fact, Nason states, "Deterrence is counter-productive and that counter-terrorism regimes are imbalanced towards coercive and punitive deterrents at the expense of a focus on addressing root causes and undercutting popular support for terrorists" (Nason, 2010, web page). These differing views do have some merit and need to be factored while formulating a deterrence strategy but to suggest that deterrence has no place, may not be entirely true. There are many security experts who emphasize that suicide terrorism can be deterred (Almog, 2004; Bar, 2008; Department of Defence, USA, 2006; Morral & Jackson, 2009; Tippet, 2009; Trager & Zagorcheva, 2005–2006). Suggestions and strategies postulated by these scholars/security experts range from adopting military options to preventive measures. It is argued that deterring suicide terrorism is complex but not impossible. It only requires a comprehensive approach encompassing both passive and active measures aimed at shrinking disruptive options of a terror group and pushing them toward political/non-military solutions. The chapter selects a definition of suicide attack based on available literature, thereafter evolve a framework of deterrence to deal with suicide terrorism and then suggest few strategies for deterrence of suicide terrorism.

HISTORICAL PERSPECTIVE OF SUICIDE TERRORISM

While suicide attack is an age old phenomenon, it was first used in its modern format by Hezbollah. Subsequently, it became a strategy of choice of other groups such as Hamas, Palestinian Islamic jihad (PIJ), Tehrike Taliban-e-Pakistan, Taliban, Al-Qaeda, Lebanese Baath Party, and Al-Aqsa Martyrs Brigades, Marxist and Arab nationalist organizations, Liberation Tigers of Tamil Elam, Al-Qaeda, Chechens, Taliban and Kashmiri Militants (Hassan, 2009). In the past, suicide attacks were used very sparingly and quite often by state actors. Suicide attacks were first used by the Zealots of Jewish sects during the Roman Era. Subsequently, they have been employed during the Crusades by both sides in the Middle East. Similarly, the Russian anarchist's movements also saw emergence of suicide terrorism in the nineteenth century. Even the Japanese Pilots carried out suicide attacks to destroy American Forces in the Pacific (Hassan, 2009; Moghadam, 2006; Pape, 2003). Hassan quoting Axell and Kase has stated that "in April 1945 during the Battle of Okinawa some 2000 Kamikaze rammed their fully fuelled fighter planes into more than 300 ships, killing 5000 Americans in the most costly naval battle in U.S. history" (Hassan, 2009). This attack probably may have been the inspiration for 9/11 attack where in the Suicide Squads of Al-Qaeda flew into the World Trade Center twin towers and the Pentagon.

In between this phenomenon became less popular since better methods of disruption and attacks were available to non state actors/terrorists. However, as the state developed effective countermeasures to conventional forms and modes of terror attacks, the counter state elements/groups have adapted and innovated to evolve more virulent forms of disruption, attacks, detonation, and explosion against the state forces. Suicide attacks represent the most virulent form of means in this escalatory ladder of conflict between the state and the counter state. This form of attack in the repertoire of terrorist or counter state groups has become a serious concern due to its unprecedented use. Table 12.1 illustrates this concern quite vividly. Number of suicide attacks which stood at 6.9 attacks per year from 1981 to 2000 jumped to 12.6 per year for the period 2001 to 2003 and stands at 265.14 per year in case of most bombed countries as per data held by University of Chicago. However, what remains constant is the lethality of suicide attacks.

Table 12.1
Suicide attacks from 2004 to 2010 of most bombed countries

Year	Attacks	Killed	Wounded	Lethality (killed/ attacks)
2004	130	1,706	4,739	13.1
2005	190	2,554	5,927	13.4
2006	268	2,290	4,470	8.5
2007	458	5,322	10,971	11.6
2008	325	2,857	6,804	8.8
2009	262	3,301	8,061	12.6
2010	223	2,726	6,598	12.2
Total	1,856	20,756	47,570	11.46
Average attack per year	265.14	2,965.14	6,795.71	11.46

Source: Database of Chicago Project on Security and Terrorism, University of Chicago (2011).

The data in Table 12.1 pertain to Iraq, Afghanistan, Pakistan, Israel, Lebanon, Palestine, Sri Lanka, Russia, Indonesia, Somalia, Kenya, and India.

Lethality of suicide attacks has remained constant at around 12.6 from 1981 to 2010 thus highlighting the potency of this form of terror attack (University of Chicago, 2011). As far as popular weapons used by terrorists are concerned, the preferred weapons of choice amongst these are car and belt bombs. However, lethality wise airplanes are the most lethal but this fact may be skewed as the data are biased due to the mother of all terror attacks, the 9/11 attacks (Figures 12.1 and 12.2).

Suicide terrorists usually attack a variety of targets such as the security forces, politicians, and civilians. An important inference that one can make from the data on distribution of attacks by target and corresponding lethality reveals that while the number of attacks are maximum on the security forces, the lethality of attacks is most on civilian targets (Figures 12.3 and 12.4). The implication is

Attacks by Weapon

- Airplane: 0.1%
- Belt Bomb: 30.7%
- Car Bomb: 51.3%
- Other: 8.3%
- Unknown: 9.6%

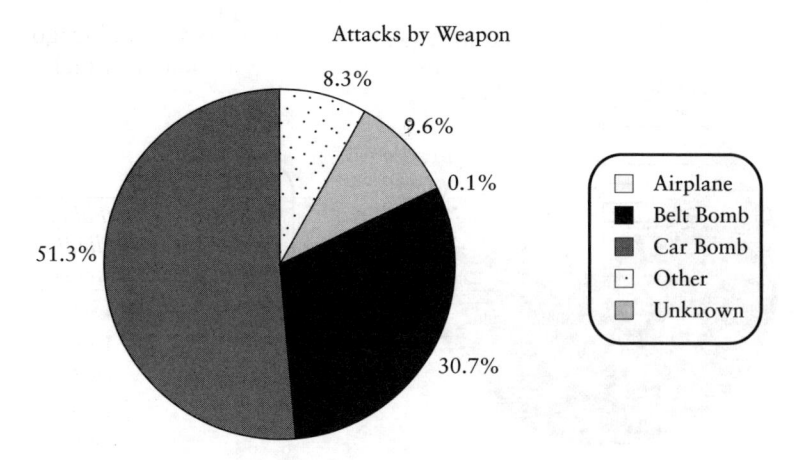

Chicago Project on Security and Terrorism

Figure 12.1
Attack by weapons

Source: Database of Chicago Project on Security and Terrorism, University of Chicago (2011).

Lethality by Weapon

Chicago Project on Security and Terrorism

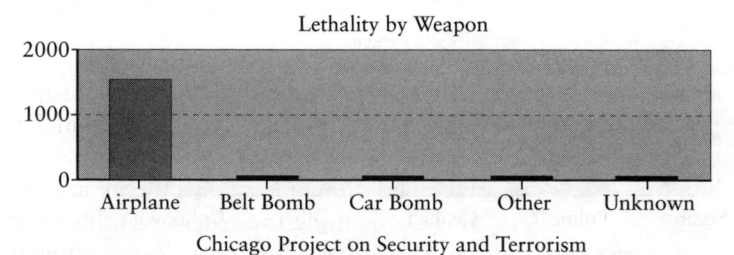

Figure 12.2
Lethality by weapon

Source: Database of Chicago Project on Security and Terrorism, University of Chicago (2011).

that since the security forces and politicians are very well protected they suffer relatively lesser casualties despite being attacked more. This therefore could be one of the reason for the terrorists to target civilians as they are least protected and hence suffer maximum casualties. Therefore, while evolving a deterrence strategy, this aspect needs to be factored.

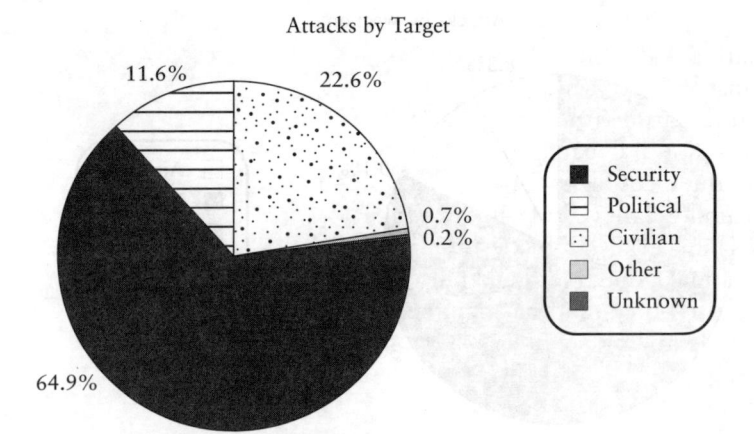

Attacks by Target

- 11.6%
- 22.6%
- 0.7%
- 0.2%
- 64.9%

Legend: Security, Political, Civilian, Other, Unknown

Chicago Project on Security and Terrorism

Figure 12.3
Distribution of suicide attacks by targets

Source: Database of Chicago Project on Security and Terrorism, University of Chicago (2011).

Lethality by Target

Target	Value
Security	~8
Political	15
Civilian	~20
Other	~5
Unknown	~4

Chicago Project on Security and Terrorism

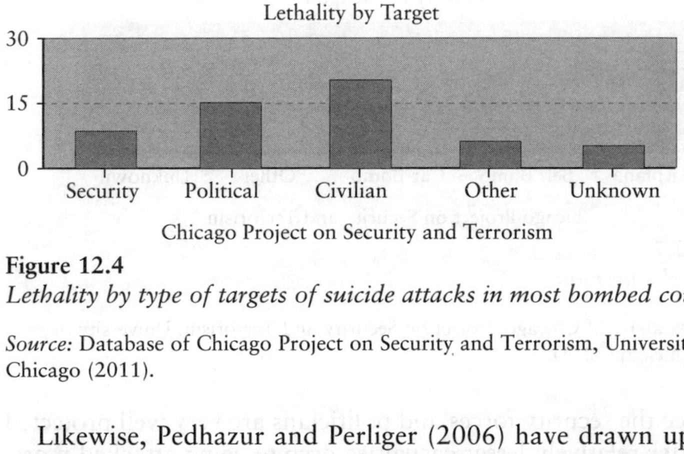

Figure 12.4
Lethality by type of targets of suicide attacks in most bombed countries

Source: Database of Chicago Project on Security and Terrorism, University of Chicago (2011).

Likewise, Pedhazur and Perliger (2006) have drawn up a correlation between suicide attacks and the nature of strategic aims that is whether suicide attacks were conducted by a terror group in the context of a territorial or ethnic conflict or against moderate Islamic regimes or against occupation forces in percentage terms according to years. Their finding reveals that while in the 1980s the attacks were mostly directed against occupation forces mainly against Western Military operating in Lebanon; in the 1990s, once the international forces withdrew Hezbollah continued its attack against South Lebanon Army and Israel over continuing territorial and ethnic conflicts. Other groups such as the Liberation Tigers of Tamil Eelam (LTTE) in Sri Lanka, Partiya Karkerên Kurdistan (PKK) in Turkey and Palestinians also conducted a number of suicide attacks due to ethnic and territorial conflicts. However, they have also noted that the common perception that terrorists mostly target democratic regimes may not be entirely correct. As per their finding, only 37 percent of the targeted regimes are democratic and 41 percent are non democratic and about 21 percent countries have restricted democratic practice. The trends of the last three decades indicate that suicide attacks are a strategic option chosen by various groups to signal their seriousness of commitment to their cause. The data on suicide attack highlight the need to ensure a workable deterrence strategy. However, to do so it is essential to understand the definition and various elements of suicide terrorism only then we can address the dimensions of suicide terrorism which would then help derive an effective deterrence strategy.

DEFINITION OF SUICIDE TERRORISM

Correct definition of a term helps one to focus in the correct direction. Unfortunately, security experts have still not arrived at a commonly accepted definition of suicide terrorism. The debate on the definition of suicide terrorism has been captured well by Assaf Moghadam (2006a) who has formulated two typologies: the first being narrow and the second being broader in scope. The broader typology encompasses attacks where the death of the attacker may not be necessary for the outcome of the suicide attack but the death of the perpetuator is almost certain (Moghadam, 2006a). Narrow suicide attack is commonly defined as attack whose success is contingent upon the death of the perpetuator (Hassan, 2009; Moghadam, 2006a). While these definitions do encompass most of the suicide terror attacks today in the world, a similar formulation has been done by Pape who defines suicide terrorism as:

A suicide attack can be defined in two ways, a narrow definition limited to in which an attacker kills himself and a broad definition that includes any instance when an attacker fully expects to be killed by others during an attack. (Pape, 2003, p. 3)

Examples of narrow definition of suicide attacks are killing of former Prime Minister of India Mr Rajiv Gandhi and that of broad definition would be the Mumbai 26/11 attacks and Indian Parliament attack. Most scholars prefer to work with the narrow definition such as Moghadam, Bloom, Gambeta, and Hafez on the grounds that ensured sacrifice must be distinguished from an attack in which there may be high risk but still there is a chance albeit tiny one that the attacker may survive the attack (Moghadam, 2006a). Likewise, Pape too prefers to work with the narrow definition on the ground that this is the common practice in literature (Pape, 2003). Crenshaw (2007) quoting analysts such as Pape, Bloom, Pedzahur and colleagues has also highlighted numerous other explanations for suicide terrorism that range from terming suicide attacks as suicide terrorism, suicide bombing, martyrs, suicide attacks, and so on. For the purpose of this work in keeping with the existing practice, the narrow formulation has been taken as the definition of suicide attacks.

WHAT MOTIVATES A SUICIDE ATTACKER?

If we accept that self-destruction is a precondition for a suicide attack, then the next issue that has agitated the minds of various security experts is the motivation for a person to indulge in such attacks. The theory of mentally deranged or people with psychological disorders indulging in such acts has since long been rejected by security experts and scholars. Sheehy-Skeffington (2009) state quoting various researches on the psychology of terrorism that terrorism is a fundamentally social act. Hoffman and McCormick (2001) quoting Nasra state that none of the 250 suicide attackers and their handlers which Nasra interviewed conformed to the suicidal personality type. Atran (2003), as quoted by Hassan, has also come to similar conclusion (Hassan, 2008).

As to possible causes, Sheehy-Skeffington (2009) suggests that when an entire community perceives itself to be suffering unjustly to the extent that suicide terrorism is seen as a valid response and is normalized within the community's value system, it only remains for a terrorist group to select willing and vulnerable recruits who could act with minimal training and psychological preparation. Bloom (2006), on the other hand, suggests many reasons for individuals to indulge in suicide attacks such as spiritual rewards in afterlife, responsibility with God for the attackers' families, celebrity status, and even cash bonuses. He also goes on to quote Stern to state that people indulge in suicide attacks that are driven by a sense of humiliations or injustice. Bloom has cited the following excerpts of an interview with a failed suicide attacker in support of his argument:

> Pictures of dead kids had a major affect on me.... I had to carry the kid in my own arms.... After the istishhad (martyrdom) of a friend of mine ... made me think that human life is threatened every moment without good cause ... without distinction between those [of us] who are soldiers, civilians, adults or kids. (Bloom, 2006, p. 36)

Revenge has also been a prime motivator in driving individuals to suicide terror. Widows or bereaved siblings seeking revenge have been recruited in Chechnya, Sri Lanka, and Palestine with regular frequency (Bloom, 2006).

Religion and nationalism too play a significant role in motivating individuals to resort to suicide terror attacks. Hafez (2006) says in respect of Palestinian bombers that religious and nationalist appeals that equate self-sacrifice with martyrdom and national salvations are instrumental in producing volunteers for suicide attacks. He has quoted examples after examples of Hamas, Al-Aqsa and Islamic jihadi lessons to support his theory (Hafez, 2006). Similarly, Crenshaw has also suggested the role of religion in motivation of a suicide attacker or bomber. She has highlighted number of terrorist groups such as Hezbollah in the 1980s, Hamas, Islamic jihad, Al-Qaeda and Islamic group in Egypt since the 1990s of using Islam to recruit, motivate, and sustain suicide attacks. Likewise, other religious dispensation such as Christian groups, Buddhist groups, and Sikh groups have also exploited religious texts and sentiments to recruit, prepare, and sustain suicide terrorism (Crenshaw, 2000). Sali (2010) too suggests the articulation of suicide attacks as the gateway to heaven by terror groups as one of the primary reasons for individuals resorting to such attacks. Hoffman and McCormick also state that groups which employ suicide attacks draw explicitly on a well-developed tradition of shahada or martyrdom (Hoffman & McCormick, 2001). Durkheimian analysis extends both religious and economic reasons for people to undertake suicide attacks and suggests that while the people are recruited in the name of God they are purely used for promoting political interest of the group and in helping them to recruit more suicide terrorists (Bakken, 2007). Hoffman and McCormick also suggest that secular terrorist draw upon the ethos of hero to recruit and motivate their suicide attackers. Example of LTTE black tigers and bomber of West Bank and Gaza supports this argument (Hoffman & McCormick, 2001).

MULTICAUSAL MOTIVATION

The aforementioned arguments suggest that there could be many reasons for an individual to undertake a suicide attack. Hassan (2009) quoting Pape suggests that while religion may play an important role in recruiting and motivating a would-be suicide attacker, the driving force of a suicide attacker is not religion but a cocktail of motivations including politics, humiliation, revenge, retaliation, and altruism. Carrying the idea of multiple causes of suicide attacks forward, Moghadam (2006b) has developed an excellent multicausal framework for analyzing suicide attacks. It is pitched at three levels namely the individual level, organizational level, and the environmental level.

The individual level or the L1 level is designed to identify the personal motivations that motivate a person to indulge in suicide terror. However, while doing so the act must be seen as a system in which the role of other individuals such as the bomber, recruiter, foot soldiers, and spiritual leaders must also be analyzed and decomposed to identify the cause of their indulging in suicide terrorism. To highlight this level of analysis, Moghadam (2006b) says that in the case of Palestinian bombers the motivations include a combination of factors such as seeking of revenge, posthumous benefits in heaven, material or immaterial benefits, personality types such as exploited suicide bomber, psychological reasons due to traumatization and humiliating treatment, tribal mentality of avenging defeat to the bitter end that is prevalent in Arab world, and culture of martyrdom. Some of these reasons can be attributed to Chechen bombers as well.

Organizational level (L2) analysis is probably the most important level at which suicide terrorism can be tackled most effectively. Although there are occasions when individual bombers acting on their own have perpetuated suicide attacks, for any meaningful suicide attack organizational backup is not only necessary but also essential to cater for functions such as training, finances, explosives, reconnaissance of target, preparation and motivation of potential suicide bombers (Moghadam, 2006b). Organization use rationalization technique to continue attracting new recruits for example, Baken says that organizations attract recruits and push them into suicide terrorism due to sociocultural environment that honors those who sacrifice themselves in the name of larger collective (Bakken, 2007). Further, organizational level analysis into the causes of suicide attacks is also important since it is relatively easier to identify organizational level motives. More often than not organizational motives for suicide attacks are quite different and are rational in nature hence subject to negotiation. Organizations are driven by issues such as outbidding the other terrorist groups, for example LTTE and other groups operating in North and East Sri Lanka, Hamas and Islamic Jehadi Party in Palestine (Moghadam, 2006b), political power (Bloom, 2006) and strategic signaling to the target audience, and security forces/state forces/agencies (Hoffman & McCormick, 2001). In fact, Hoffman and McCormick say that:

> *suicide tactics have been adopted by a growing number of terrorist organizations around the world because they are shocking, deadly, cost effective, secure, and very difficult to stop. There are only two basic operational requirements that an organization must be able to satisfy to get into the game: a willingness to kill and willingness to die.* (Hoffman & McCormick, 2001)

Similarly, Hassan has quoted Pape's study which offers the theory that suicide attacks follow a strategic logic specifically designed to coerce modern liberal democracies to make significant political and territorial concessions (Hassan, 2009). Such aims can only be espoused by organizations or counter state organizations. A careful analysis of organizational motives clearly indicates that at the organizational level there is ample scope for deterrence. These arguments clearly establish that such attacks cannot be launched without a proper organization that is able to recruit, train, indoctrinate suicide attackers, provide detailed target information, and direct them to their targets. Similarly, Moghadam gives other reasons such as creating fear in the minds of target audience, garnering of international support and for internal moral boosting. He also cites suicide attacks being resorted to due to a number of tactical advantages such as accuracy, high lethality, cost efficiency, and irrelevance of planning an escape route (Moghadam, 2006b).

Environmental level analysis (L3) is essential for the simple reason that they serve as facilitators for organizations and individuals to indulge in suicide attacks. For example, a territory under foreign occupation may breed conditions that push people to join organizations that indulge in suicide attacks. Similarly, poverty and government repression may encourage suicide attacks but by themselves they are not necessary conditions for suicide attacks. Likewise

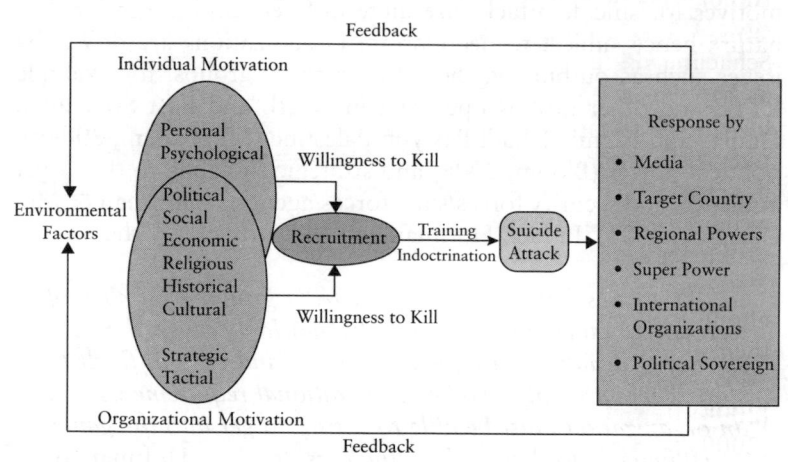

Figure 12.5
Moghadam's suicide terrorism cycle

Source: Adapted from Moghadam (2006b).

religious, ethnic, and nationalist groups may also encourage the culture of martyrdom as is the case in Palestine, LTTE, West Bank, and Gaza (Moghadam, 2006b).

The idea of highlighting the multicausality of possible causes of suicide attacks was to establish the fact that demystifying suicide attacks is a very complex problem. The multicausality of suicide terrorism has also been represented in a model by Moghadam (2006b) as shown in Figure 12.5. This model establishes the importance of combating suicide terrorism by addressing the problem at all three levels but more importantly at the organizational and environmental levels as it is relatively more difficult to deter individual terrorists due to the problem of locating potential individual suicide terrorists.

CAN SUICIDE ATTACKS BE DETERRED?

There are many analysts who suggest that suicide attacks cannot be deterred. Problems such as lack of return address of a suicide attacker and irrational behavior are a few reasons. For example, Almog's claim of reduction in suicide attacks in Israel to the strategy of cumulative deterrence (Almog, 2004) is countered by Schachter on the ground that it is merely a tactical pause and can at best be described as tactical deterrence and hence unlikely to have a lasting impact (Schachter, 2010). Similarly, Sebastiano Sali puts forth the logic that new terrorism as he refers to the current day manifestation of terrorism is extremely difficult to deter, although he does suggest some countermeasure to deal with the problems such as negotiations and role of the community (Sali, 2010). Likewise, Bakken says that, "the most frightening thing about suicide bombers is that there is no deterrence that can stop them (suicide bombers) from completing their mission" (Bakken, 2007, p. 9). On the other hand, there are analysts such as Almog (2004), Trager and Zagorecheva (2005–2006), Morral and Jackson (2009), and Tippet (2009) who believe that suicide terrorism can be deterred. Without going any further into the debate of whether suicide attacks can be deterred or not, this chapter attempts to identify strategies that may help in preventing recurrence of suicide terrorism through past experiences in Israel.

Combating suicide attacks at the tactical level does not differ much from that of combating a conventional terror attack except that it needs far more rigorous implementation of the security plans, sensitization of possible targets, and enhancing the degree of difficulty of accessing a high-value target by a potential suicide attacker. However, the nature of attack which calls for supreme sacrifice from an individual and the phenomenal impact that it creates on the common public and to some extent on the security forces makes suicide attack seem incapable of being deterred. While this perception may appear true it is not entirely borne by facts as has been suggested by Almog (2004), Tippet (2009), Trager and Zagorecheva (2005–2006), Morral and Jackson (2009) that there are ways and means to deter such a threat but before proposing methodology of achieving deterrence it will be prudent to identify a correct definition of deterrence and the desired framework within which we can assess that deterrence can work against suicide terrorism. This is essential as the classical understanding of deterrence was evolved in the context of cold war where its applicability was tested between two rational and probably more responsible state actors. On the other hand, deterrence in the context of suicide terrorism or conventional terrorism is more often than not between non state and relatively less accountable actors.

DEFINING AND IDENTIFYING ELEMENTS OF DETERRENCE IN THE CONTEXT OF SUICIDE TERRORISM

A permanent solution primarily lies in identifying systemic solutions to prevent support to organizations indulging in terrorism and also identifying effective deterrence measures. Like the debate over commonly accepted definition of suicide terrorism, lessons on common understanding of deterrence in the context of suicide terrorism do not exist. This debate stems from basic difference in applicability of the concept of deterrence to terrorism.

Classically, deterrence is a factor of image or perception in the mind of the entity being deterred and is formed by a number of factors such as the capability of the deterring entity and its will to use that capability when required. It is also dependent on the behavioral pattern and will of the organization or the entity being deterred. It is in this backdrop that analysts state that deterrence was applicable in the context of cold war between two rational state actors or power blocks where consequences of a nuclear conflict were properly analyzed and understood and then decisions arrived at. Cuban missile example is an excellent example of playing out of a classical deterrence. However, in the context of terrorism or suicide terrorism it is more often than not a non state actor often believed to be irrational and unpredictable that is one of the parties to the conflict. In such a conflict scenario, classical deterrence may not work.

Above notwithstanding, there are many scholars and practitioners of counterterrorism strategy who believe that deterrence is workable and only its dimensions in the context of suicide terrorism need to be redefined. Commonly, deterrence means avoiding, preventing someone from taking a particular course of action, which implies that it works in the cognitive domain of the actors involved in a conflict situation. Nason (2010) has discussed two broad definitions of deterrence: narrow formulation and broad formulation. He has referred to Ross and Gurr's (Ross & Gurr, 1989 as cited by Nason 2010) definition as being the narrow formulation of deterrence which is achieved by increasing the risks for terrorists and people who might join or support them, generally by the risk of punishment or operational failure. The threat of punishment, operational failure, and coercive reprisal are understood to deter terrorists from making attacks (Nason, 2010). Similarly, Morral and Jackson (2009) from RAND corporation, Almog (2004) from Israel, Tippet (2009) and Trager and Zagorcheva (2005–2006) support this view. Essentially, narrow formulation can be identified as following the hard options of employing stronger security forces, better intelligence, better cooperation amongst security forces at the national and international levels and hardening of soft and high priority targets against possible terrorist attacks, and prompt punitive action against a suicide terror attack.

Nason (2010) defines broader formulation of deterrence as addressing the root cause of suicide terrorism. It could include anything that deters terrorists from undertaking attacks. Whilst not losing the potential for coercive measures, these policies could range from the provision of inducements to join the political process to attempts to tackle the root causes of terrorism. Nason quotes Davis and Jenkins who argue that "a broader conceptualisation of 'deterrence' could include an influence component [...] that has both a broader range of coercive elements and a set of plausible positives" (Nason, 2010, web page). Nason supports the broader formulation of deterrence arguing that terrorists cannot be deterred by threat of punishment or operational failure and that deterrent policies are counterproductive, creating a negative-sum game in which all parties stand to lose (Nason, 2010). However, commonly understood framework of deterrence in the security community is that of narrow formulation. The US strategic command manual also lays down the hard option to achieve deterrence against terrorism despite the difficulty in achieving credible deterrence against a non state actor due to reasons such as identification and location, differing perception of cost-benefit analysis, range of sensitive targets to be protected, and difficulty in imposing cost on non state actors. Another factor that differentiates state from non state actors involves the manner in which they value things: they have different goals/objectives and employ different means to achieve them (USSTRATCOM, 2006). What is evident from the preceding discussions is that both the form of deterrence strategies are essential for dealing with suicide attacks, however, its application has to be carefully orchestrated to achieve deterrence.

STRATEGIES TO ACHIEVE DETERRENCE

A terrorist group looks for a particular result after a suicide attack, if the impact of the attack is prevented by stopping a suicide attack even before it is mounted through sound intelligence or the damage is minimized through effective security measures, the group may get de-motivated. Repetitive failure in achieving the desired result is likely to convince the terrorist group of the futility of undertaking a suicide attack. We also need to bear in mind that continued failure of high-value events such as a suicide attack may force the terrorist groups to discard suicide bombing or attack as a preferred form of waging a war with a state. Building on this concept, Almog has cited the Israeli approach of building a bank of victory against a terror group to dissuade it from undertaking further terror attack or in other words deterring the group. As per him, Israeli security forces were able to intercept 142 would-be bombers, most of whom were en route to destinations deep within Israel which has contributed to achieving deterrence (Almog, 2004). In a prolonged conflict with a non state actor, Almog says that the approach to deterrence has to be cumulative in nature where in the use of threats and military force has to go on simultaneously. Assets in a victory bank produce moderate behavior in adversary/terrorist group. This may lead to near absence of direct conflict and may also lead to political negotiation even peace agreements (Almog, 2004). Almog has identified several factors that have contributed to success of cumulative deterrence in the context of Israel. These are as follows:

The strengthening of territorial defensive shields through the establishment of multilayered systems (including electronic fences, high-technology sensors, special rules of engagement, security buffer zones, and various delaying obstacles that slow would-be terrorists from reaching their targets) and an increasing number of professional units trained specifically to oppose the terrorist threat. Ongoing improvements in intelligence capabilities as a major force multiplier. Consistent emphasis on infrastructure operations, such as demolishing the homes of terrorists' families; destroying the terrorists' weapon factories, storage facilities, and tunnels; and eliminating the terrorists' financial networks. Continued application of high technology to maintain Israel's relative advantage. (Almog, 2004, p. 10)

This strategy of cumulative deterrence is successful. In the case of Israel, it is evident from the fact that from 2008 to 2010 there have been very minimal suicide attacks in Israel, in fact in the year 2008 there was no suicide attack in Israel (Schachter, 2010). Although Schachter (2010) goes on to express his doubt whether this success could be attributed to Israeli strategy, the fact that it has produced moderation and caution on the behavior of various terrorist groups operating against Israel should suggest that the cumulative deterrence strategy is working. The essential elements of cumulative deterrence strategy are defeat, deny, diminish, and defend. Analysis in the context of Indian experience would also suggest that this strategy works. India has also built a series of victory banks that has provided it with success in deterring suicide terrorism. Successful counterterror campaign in the Indian context are: against Punjab terrorist groups, resolve to deal with LTTE in Sri Lanka, intervention in male, success in Kargil, effectively dealing with terrorism in Jammu and Kashmir, success in combating and eliminating 26/11 terrorists, and systemic tracking/booking of a number of terrorists involved in various terror attacks in India. Resolve to deal with terrorism employing the hard option along with the soft approach to a great extent has resulted in absence of suicide terrorist attacks in India. This deduction is supported by the fact that as per University of Chicago data base on suicide terrorism, there have been only 13 suicide attacks in India between 1980 and 2011, which is extremely low as compared to countries reeling under suicide terror attack such as Iraq, Afghanistan, and Pakistan (University of Chicago, 2011).

Having established the fact that hard option is essential for achieving deterrence, it is essential to identify points of intervention. In this context, the Moghadam (2006b) model suggests three levels of intervention namely individual, organizational, and environmental. While the endeavor of any state should be to intervene with cumulative deterrence strategy at all the levels, as discussed earlier it is relatively easier to deter an organization than an individual suicide bomber (Almog, 2004). In fact, Trager and Zagorcheva (2005–2006) go on to state that while it may be difficult to deter a suicide bomber it is relatively easier to deter the financier, bomb maker, resource provider, and other elements in a terror group who form part of a terror organization (Trager & Zagorcheva, 2005–2006). Therefore, cumulative deterrence should focus on the organizational level of intervention. The aim should be to deter organizations because organization besides being sensitive to the life of the operative is also sensitive to any information that compromises the organization and its goals. Conceptually, the strategy of deterring suicide terrorism could be represented as shown in Table 12.2. In this strategy, means of deterrence would comprise of passive and active measures to either deny access of suicide terrorists to sensitive targets or proactively intervene and render any suicide terror attack attempt unsuccessful and if the attack does take place then to effectively neutralize the support base of suicide attackers so as to send a strong message to the terror group indulging in suicide attack.

Table 12.2
Figurative representation of deterrence strategy for suicide terror attack

Levels and Points of Intervention	Methods of Intervention

• **Individual Level:**
  ▪ Suicide attackers—extremely difficult
  ▪ Family of the suicide bombers if they can be identified
• **Organizational Level:**
  ▪ Leadership
  ▪ Bomb makers
  ▪ Financing sources
  ▪ Resource providers
  ▪ Terrorist networks
  ▪ Recruitment networks
• **Environmental:**
  ▪ Socioeconomic condition
  ▪ Religious, political, and cultural extremism
	• **Denial:**
	  ▪ Hardening of target
	  ▪ Protection measures
	  ▪ Raising of Special Forces
	  ▪ Intelligence and surveillance
	  ▪ International alliance
	  ▪ Endeavor to make a terrorist group as close as possible like a state
	• **Punitive:**
	  ▪ Deterrence through punishment
	  ▪ Target the individuals
	  ▪ Exercise control on resources such as explosives, arms, and munitions
	  ▪ Support elements can be such as bomb makers, financiers, trainers, and leaders

Source: Compiled by the author himself.

Above formulation suggests that while soft actions such as addressing environmental factors will have to be addressed in the long term, for these actions to be implemented hard options will have to be taken in the short term. As discussed earlier, concept of deterrence in the classical sense cannot be applied to suicide terrorism, Almog's concept of cumulative deterrence (Almog, 2004) can be effectively employed against suicide terrorism.

DETERRENCE BY DENIAL STRATEGIES

Denial strategies essentially focus on raising the cost of operation of suicide terror groups through passive protective measures. Protection of targets, security, and secrecy related to deployment and employment of security forces contribute toward achieving deterrence by denial. Lowering the density of passengers at air-line counters reduces the pay-off in the event of a terror attack which may deter a terror group from indulging in undertaking a suicide attack (Almog, 2004). Likewise, hardening of security measures to protect possible targets with bollards, armed guards, or security-credentialing systems may increase the attacker's sense that any given operation will be more difficult to execute (Morral & Jackson, 2009). Similarly, pay-offs can be reduced by efficient response and recovery mechanism in the country such as action by special forces like National Security Guard in the case of India. Other countries that have raised highly potent Special Forces to deal with terror attacks are the Delta Forces and Navy Seals of the United States, Groupe d'Intervention de la Gendarmerie Nationale of France (GIGN), Grenz Schutz Gruppe 9 of Germany (GSG 9), and Seriyat Matakal of Israel. Morral and Jackson (2009) also suggest that it may be prudent to enhance the uncertainties about the capabilities of counterterrorism security systems through the use of partial or complete secrecy surrounding their properties or even, when deception is viable, through deceptive disclosures about their characteristics. For example, it might be advantageous for the defender to increase attacker's uncertainties by broadcasting the deployment of face-recognition systems, watch lists, and informants, but obscuring the details of where these assets are deployed and how effective they are (Morral & Jackson, 2009). Offer of amnesty can also cause uncertainty amongst the terrorists (Trager & Zagorcheva, 2005–2006). Offering of alternatives especially if groups have political ambitions that can be accommodated will also fall in this strategy. For example, of the 42 organizations banned by the US, most of them fall in groups that have goals which can be accommodated (Trager & Zagorcheva, 2005–2006).

Developing a sound intelligence and surveillance system will help thwart attacks even before they are launched or when they are in process of being launched. An important component of deterrence against terrorism is the perception by the terrorist organization that the deterring state enjoys 'intelligence dominance.' Israel has enjoyed an image of an intelligence superpower with the ability to target terrorist leaders (and even state targets) at will. Israel has achieved temporary and fragile deterrence vis-à-vis Hezbollah and the Palestinians over the years (Bar, 2008). In this context, it may be noted that since September 2000, Israeli authorities have prevented more than 340 suicide bombings from advancing beyond the planning stages. In addition, they have intercepted 142 would-be bombers, most of whom were en route to destinations deep within Israel (Almog, 2004). International alliances too have contributed toward achieving deterrence as it helps create an image of greater strength and reach. Backing of Israel by the US and the UK is a case in point (Bar, 2008).

DETERRENCE BY PUNISHMENT

At the apex of deterrence strategy should be the decision-making elements which essentially would mean eliminating the leadership and or disrupting their command and control mechanism through covert and overt means. While it may be very difficult to deter a determined and a motivated suicide bomber or attacker, it is relatively easier to deter the group to which he belongs as it is the group that has aims and goals that are negotiable. If the aims and goals of these groups are threatened, then the group would be forced to negotiate. Bar says:

> The more a terrorist organization takes on the attributes of a state, the more susceptible it becomes to deterrence. A threat of punishment of unknown proportions looms darker than a punishment meted out on a regular basis. The Palestinian Authority has "preferred" to remain a failed state, unable or unwilling to control its terrorist components. Syria and its proxies know that Israel has had no interest in risking a full-fledged war with Syria over acts of terror. (Bar, 2008, web page)

Targeting of a terror group's leadership has been a fairly effective method of achieving deterrence. Some well-known examples are targeting of Guzman the Shining Path leader in Peru which signaled the end of Shining Path. Similarly, the Kurd militancy took a severe beating when its leader Abdulla Öcalan was captured and publically humiliated which went as a deterrent message in the ranks of PKK (Singh, 2009).

Accessibility to financial and material resources is an important component in the system of suicide terror. A tight control over this supply chain contributes very effectively toward raising cost of conducting an operation by a terror group. Most effective example of this is targeting of the Noorodin network, an Al-Qaeda franchise and a breakaway faction of the terror group Jemaah Islamiyah (JI) of Indonesia. This group was responsible for series of suicide bombings in Indonesia including the famous Bali and Marriott hotel bombing. The Indonesian Police specifically targeted the bomb makers, financiers, and explosive providers to crack the terror organization (International Crisis Group, 2006). Schonhardt (2012) also says the terror group has been crippled by a police crackdown and rifts within the organization. And all the major suspects who participated in the 2002 Bali attack have been killed or imprisoned (Schonhardt, 2012). It may therefore be safely concluded from the long stretch of peace in Indonesia post 2009 to the strong deterrence message that was sent in the environment post the targeted manner in which most of the key elements of Noordin Mohammed's terror network were eliminated. This may have dissuaded other splinter groups that still remain active in Indonesia from resorting to more suicide attacks. Another punitive method to dissuade suicide bombers is to threaten the family members of a suicide terrorist. For example, an Israeli Agent managed to stop a would-be suicide bomber Ahmad from going through a suicide bombing by threatening his father Mustafa a wealthy Palestine merchant in Gaza of dire consequences if he did not stop his son (Ahmad) from carrying out suicide bombing (Almog, 2004). While one may say that such tactics cannot be applied in all conditions but where feasible it must be utilized especially if a terror group operates within the territory controlled by the state forces. The moral and ethical virtues of such a strategy may be questionable but in the larger interest of the society such measures may be resorted to.

CONCLUSION

The chapter has highlighted that suicide terrorism is not always a work of a deranged personality. It is a deliberate act by a highly motivated person often recruited, trained, and launched by rational terror groups with the aim of achieving their stated goals. Since security forces enjoy greater force advantage, a terror group tries to overcome this disadvantage through deception and unconventional tactics such as suicide attacks. The chapter also established that while classical concept of deterrence cannot be applied in case of suicide terrorism, deterrence in a modified form has always been practiced by various state forces in the past. Deterrence of terrorist organizations has been based—when it existed—mainly on tactical deterrence through day-to-day actions, which add up to an ever-shifting perception of the object of deterrence (Bar, 2008). Almog makes this concept even clearer in his formulation of cumulative deterrence where victory bank in favor of the security forces over time against terror groups creates an image of invincibility and thus puts caution and refrain in the minds of terror groups from resorting to suicide terror (Almog, 2004).

There are multiple reasons for individuals to resort to suicide terror which had been amply established by Moghadam (2006a, 2006b). Causalities for suicide terror exist at different levels that is, at the individual, group, and the environmental levels. These levels help identify the levels of intervention which state forces can adopt in evolving a deterrence strategy. The means to intervene can be either through hard (military options) or soft (nonmilitary options). While hard options cannot be part of the permanent solution to deal with suicide terror, they do create the necessary conditions to apply the soft options. Keeping these arguments in mind, the strategy suggested is a mix of deterrence by denial which essentially means passive security measures and deterrence by punishment which entails pre-attack foiling of a suicide attack through sound intelligence by addressing the potential suicide bombers at various stages such as recruitment, training, targeting financial, material support base, and post-attack to quickly locate and eliminate the key players involved in organizing and conducting of the attack so as to send a strong deterrence message in the environment. Hence, the strategy to deal with suicide terror has to perforce be a mix of hard and soft options with the soft option comprising the need to address root causes that create the condition for emergence of suicide terrorism. A balanced offensive defensive approach is a must for ensuring deterrence against such a threat.

REFERENCES

Almog, D. (2004). Cumulative deterrance and war on terrorism. *Parameters, US Army War College, 34*(1), 4–19.
Atran, S. (2003). Genesis of suicide terrorism. *Science, 299*(5612), 1534–1539.
Bakken, N. W. (2007). *The anatomy of suicide terrorism: A durkheimian analysis.* Newark, NJ: University of Delaware.
Bar, S. (2008). *Deterring terrorists.* Retrieved online on August 23, 2012, from Hoover Institution Stanford University: http://www.hoover.org/publications/policy-review/article/5674
Basilici, S. P., & Simmons, J. (2004). *Transformation: A bold case for unconventional warfare.* Retrieved on November 21, 2012, from Fas. Org: http://www.fas.org/man/eprint/bassim.pdf
Bloom, M. (2006). Dying to kill: Motivation for suicide terrorism. In A. Pedahzur (Ed.), *Root causes of suicide terrorism* (pp. 25–53). New York: Routledge Taylor & Francis Group.
Crenshaw, M. (2000). The psychology of terrorism: An agenda for the 21st century. *Political Psychology, 21*(2), 405–420.
Crenshaw, M. (2007). Explaining suicide terrorism. *Security Studues, 16*(1), 133–162.
Department of Defence, USA. (2006). *Global deterrence joint operating concept.* Retrieved online on August 23, 2012 from www.dtic.mil/futurejointwarfare/concepts/do_joc_v20.doc
Dyke, J. R., & Crisafulli, J. R. (2006). *Unconventional counter insurgency in Afghanistan.* Retrieved online on August 23, 2012 from http://www.dtic.mil/cgi-bin/GetTRDoc?AD=ADA451756
Hafez, M. M. (2006). Dying to be martyrs: The symbolic dimension of suicide terrorism. In A. Pedahzur (Ed.), *Root causes of suicide terrorism* (pp. 54–80). New York: Routledge Taylor & Francis Group.
Hassan, R. (2008). Global rise of suicide terrorism: An overview. *Asian Journal of Social Science, 36*(2), 271–291
Hassan, R. (2009). *What motivates the suicide bombers.* Retrieved online on November 21, 2012, from Yale Global Online: http://yaleglobal.yale.edu/content/what-motivates-suicide-bombers-0
Hoffman, B., & McCormick, G. (2001). Terrorism, signaling, and suicide attack. *Studies in Conflict and Terrorism, 27*(4), 243–281.
International Crisis Group. (2006). *Terrorism in Indonesia Noordin's network: Asia report No. 114–115 May 2006.* Brussels & Jakarta: International Crisis Group.
Moghadam, A. (2006a). Defining suicide terrorism. In A. Pedahzur (Ed.), *Root causes of suicide terrorism* (pp. 13–21). New York: Routledge, Taylor & Francis Group.

Moghadam, A. (2006b). The roots of suicide terrorism: A multi causal approach. In A. Pedahzur (Ed.), *Root causes of suicide terrorism* (pp. 81–107). New York: Routledge Taylor & Francis Group.

Morral, A. R., & Jackson, B. A. (2009). *Understanding the role of deterrance in counterterrorism security.* Santa Monica, CA: RAND Corporation.

Nason, A. (2010). *Deterrence and terrorism in the modern era.* Retrieved online on October 05, 2012, from E-International Relations: http://www.e-ir.info/2010/05/24/deterrence-and-terrorism-in-the-modern-era/

Pape, R. A. (2003). The strategic logic of suicide terrorism. *American Political Science Review, 97*(3), 1–19.

Pedhazur, A., & Perliger, A. (2006). *Middle Eastern terrorism (roots of terrorism).* New York: Chelsea House Publications.

Ross, J. I., & Gurr, T. R. (1989). Why terrorism subsides: A comparative study of Canada and the United States. *Comparative Politics, 21*(4), 405–426.

Sali, S. (2010). *Deterring terrorists and deterring states: Fundamentally different tasks?* Retrieved online on August 12, 2012, from E-International Relations: http://www.e-ir.info/2010/02/19/deterring-terrorists-and-deterring-states-fundamentally-different-tasks/

Schachter, J. (2010). Unusually quiet: Is Isreal deterring terrorism? *Strategic Assessment, INSS, Israel, 13*(2), 19–27.

Schonhardt, S. (2012). *Bali bombings: 10 years later, progress and some bumps ahead.* Retrieved online on January 24, 2013, from Indonesia Digest: http://www.indonesia-digest.net/2700terrorism.htm

Sheehy-Skeffington, J. (2009). Social psychological motivations of suicide terrorism. *Paper presented at the annual meeting of the ISPP 32nd Annual Scientific Meeting, Trinity College, Dublin, Ireland Online.* Retrieved online on August, 2012, from academic.com: http://www.allacademic.com/meta/p314683_in

Singh, D. (2009). *Al-Qaeda as a charismatic phenomenon.* Monterey, California, USA. Retrieved online on January 24, 2012, from Calhoun: http://calhoun.nps.edu/public/bitstream/handle/10945/4735/09Jun_Singh.pdf?sequence=1

South Asian Terrorism Portal. (2012, November 11). *Fidayeen (suicide squad) attacks in Pakistan.* Retrieved from SATP: http://www.satp.org/satporgtp/countries/pakistan/database/Fidayeenattack.htm

Tippet, M. D. (2009). *Deterring terrorism: A framework for making retaliatory threats credible.* Retrieved online on October 7, 2012, from Naval Post Graduate School Dudely Knox Library: http://edocs.nps.edu/npspubs/scholarly/theses/2009/Dec/09Dec_Tippet.pdf

Trager, R. F., & Zagorcheva, D. P. (2005–2006). Deterring terrorism: It can be done. *MIT Press Journals—International Security, 30*(3), 87–123.

University of Chicago. (2011). *Chicago project on security and terrorism*. Retrieved online on November 18, 2012 from CPOST Suicide Attacks in India: http://cpost.uchicago.edu/index.php

USSTRATCOM. (2006). *Deterrence operations joint operations concept version 2.0*. Retrieved online on October 12, 2012, from Future Joint Warfare: www.dtic.mil/futurejointwarfare/concepts/do_joc_v20.doc

About the Editors and Contributors

THE EDITORS

Updesh Kumar, Ph.D., is a Scientist 'F' and in the chair of the Head, Mental Health Division at Defence Institute of Psychological Research, R&D Organization, Ministry of Defence, Delhi, India. Dr Kumar obtained his Doctorate degree from Punjab University, Chandigarh. With more than 23 years of experience as a scientist in R&D organization, he specializes in the area of suicidal behavior, personality assessment, and personnel selection and has developed a number of psychological tests and assessment tools. Dr Kumar has been a psychological assessor (psychologist) in various services selection boards for eight years for the selection of officers in Indian Armed Forces. He is a certified psychologist by The British Psychological Society with level 'A' and level 'B' Certificate of Competence in Occupational Testing. He has to his credit many important research projects relating to the Armed Forces. Dr Kumar has edited four quality volumes on *'Recent Developments in Psychology,' 'Counseling: A Practical Approach,' 'Suicidal Behaviour: Assessment of People at Risk'* (SAGE Publications), and recently *'Countering Terrorism: Psychosocial Strategies'* published by SAGE Publications, *'Positive Psychology: Applications in Work, Health and Well-being'* (in press, Pearson Publication) and *'Suicidal Behaviour: Underlying Dynamics'* (in press, Routledge Publication, UK). Dr Kumar has authored manuals on *'Suicide and Fratricide: Dynamics and Management'* for defense personnel, *'Managing Emotions in Daily Life & at Work Place'* for general population, *'Overcoming Obsolescence & Becoming Creative in R&D Environment'* for R&D organizations, and *'Self-Help Techniques in Military Settings.'* He has authored more than 50 other academic publications in the form of research papers, journal articles, and book chapters and represented his institute at national and international level. He has been the recipient of Defence R&D organization's (DRDO) Technology Group Award in 2001 and 2009, and Professor Manju Thakur Memorial Award 2009 by Indian

Academy of Psychology (IAAP). He was also conferred with the *DRDO's Best Popular Science Communication Award 2009* by Hon'ble Defence Minister of India and *DRDO Technology Day Award, 2012* by Hon'ble Scientific Advisor to Defence Minister. Dr Kumar has been recently conferred upon with the prestigious DRDO's Scientist of the Year Award 2013 by the Government of India.

Manas K. Mandal, Ph.D., is currently Director General (Life Sciences), Defence R&D Organization (DRDO), Ministry of Defence, Government of India, Delhi. Dr Mandal obtained his postgraduate and Doctorate degrees from Calcutta University in 1979 and 1984, respectively. He has completed his Postdoctoral Research Program at Delware University (Fulbright Fellow), USA in 1986–1987 and at Waterloo University (Shastri & NSERC Fellow), Canada in 1993–1994. Dr Mandal was a Professor of Psychology at Department of Humanities & Social Sciences, Indian Institute of Technology, Kharagpur. He was also a visiting professor at Kyushu University, Japan in 1997. During 2003, he was a Fulbright Visiting Lecturer, Harvard University, USA. He has been awarded various Research Fellowships and Scientific Awards such as International Scientific Exchange Award (Canada), Seymour Kety Grant (USA). Recipient of four prestigious awards from the Prime Minister of India, Young Scientist Award (1986), Agni Award for Excellence in Self-Reliance (2005), Scientist-of-the Year Award (2006), Technology Spin-Off Award (2007). Dr Mandal has to his credit seven books, and over 100 research papers/chapters published in peer-reviewed journals/books. These researches are cited in more than 125 international journals and books.

THE CONTRIBUTORS

Farhana Ali is a terrorism analyst, a writer, and sought-after public speaker on conflicts in the Muslim world. For years, she has traveled to South Asia, particularly throughout Pakistan to understand the domestic and foreign policy challenges in the country. Along with regional expertise, she has focused on women's activism in mass sociopolitical movements and terrorist networks. She is among the few female scholars, and the only Muslim woman, who examines closely the female suicide bomber trend in Iraq and other conflicts. Ms Ali appears regularly on diverse media outlets, including the BBC world radio and television, CNN headline and world news, Al-Jazeera English, Voice of America, Canadian television, National Public Radio, and on foreign broadcast television and newspapers, such as Europe, the Middle East, and South Asia. Ms Ali is a former international policy analyst with the RAND Corporation (2005–2008) and a political analyst with the US Government (2000–2005). She is currently a senior fellow at the Center for Advanced Studies on Terrorism (CAST).

Morgan Banks, Ph.D., is a psychologist, author, and retired Colonel from the United Stated Army after putting in 37 years of service, with over 27 of those years as a Clinical Psychologist. Dr Banks was involved in establishing the psychological screening program for US Army Special Forces personnel and prior to his retirement was the Army's senior operational psychologist. Dr Banks has worked extensively in the field of counterterrorism and was deployed in both Afghanistan and Iraq. He is the author or co-author of several book chapters on Operational Psychology.

Anat Berko, Ph.D., is a Research Fellow at the International Institute for Counterterrorism (ICT) and a lecturer at the Lauder School of Government, Diplomacy and Security at the Interdisciplinary Center (IDC) in Herzliya, Israel. Her research focuses on terrorism, particularly suicide bombers and their handlers, and she has conducted studies for the Israel's Counterterrorism Team and Israel's National Security Council. She also serves as an advisor to senior government officials. Dr Berko has been a visiting professor at George Washington University and she has delivered lectures on various aspects of counterterrorism at NATO, the US Congress, the State Department, the Federal Bureau of Investigation (FBI), the military forces, and various universities. She frequently appears on international media commenting on terrorism incidents throughout the world. Dr Berko received her doctoral degree in criminology from Bar-Ilan University and is the author of two books, The Path to Paradise, and The Smarter Bomb, as well as several articles in scholarly journals. Until 2003, she served in the

Israel Defense Forces, where she achieved the rank of Lieutenant Colonel.

Laurie Black, M.S., is currently a candidate for Ph.D. in clinical psychology at Palo Alto University (PAU), where she earned her M.S. in clinical psychology. She is a member of Clinical Emergencies and Crises Research Group at PAU led by Dr Bruce Bongar. Her research interests include examining military and veteran suicide, suicide risk assessment practices, and trauma and resiliency as consequences of catastrophic events. She is involved in research within the Veterans Affairs Health Care System, focused on improving the lives of deployed veterans by investigating war-related stressors, as well as research that will contribute toward improvement in the diagnosis and treatment of veterans with Posttraumatic stress disorder (PTSD) and traumatic brain injury (TBI).

Bruce Bongar, Ph.D., ABPP, FAPM, is the Calvin Professor of Psychology at Palo Alto University and a Consulting Professor of Psychiatry and the Behavioral Sciences at Stanford University School of Medicine. Dr Bongar received his Ph.D. from the University of Southern California. Past clinical appointments include service as a senior clinical psychologist with the Division of Psychiatry, Children's Hospital of Los Angeles, and work as a community mental health/senior clinical psychologist on the psychiatric emergency team of the Los Angeles County Department of Mental Health. He is past president of the Section on Clinical Crises and Emergencies of the Division of Clinical Psychology of the American Psychological Association, and is also the winner of both the Shneidman and Dublin awards for outstanding career contributions to suicide research from the American Association of Suicidology. Since 2001, he has also become interested in the psychology of mass casualty events and suicide terrorism.

Mark Dechesne obtained his Ph.D. (cum laude) in 2001 on the effects of fear on social behavior. His subsequent research has increasingly focused on the motivation of terrorists, the workings of terrorist organizations, and reactions to terrorism. From early 2006 until September 2008, he worked at the Department of Homeland Security (DHS) Center of Excellence NC-START (National Consortium for the Study of Terrorism and Responses to

Terrorism) of the University of Maryland in the United States. Since 2008, he has been connected to Leiden University Campus, The Hague. He is a frequent contributor to public and policy debates on issues related to terrorism and counterterrorism. He also served on the editorial board of the *Journal of Personality and Social Psychology: Attitudes and Social Cognition, and Interpersonal Relations and Group Processes*.

Edna Erez is a Professor in the Department of Criminology, Law, and Justice at the University of Illinois at Chicago. She has L.L.B. from the Hebrew University Law School and M.A. in Criminology and Ph.D. in Sociology from the University of Pennsylvania. Professor Erez received around two million dollar grants from state and federal grants in the US and overseas to study various topics related to victimization and the justice system. She was a visiting professor and research fellow in universities and research centers in Australia, Germany, Poland, and Israel. Her publication records include over 100 referred articles, book chapters, and grant reports. She is past editor of Justice Quarterly, and she is currently a co-editor of International Review of Victimology and Violence and Victims. She also serves on editorial board of several other journals in criminology and legal studies. Her research areas include violence against women, victims in transnational crime, the use of the Internet for jihadist activities, and women in crime and terrorism.

Riaz Hassan, Ph.D., is a Visiting Research Professor at the Institute of South Asian Studies, National University of Singapore and Emeritus Professor of Sociology at Flinders University, Adelaide, Australia. His recent books include: suicide bombings (Routledge, 2011), Life as weapon: The global rise of suicide bombings (Routledge, 2010), Inside Muslim minds (Melbourne University Press, 2008), and Faithlines: Muslim conceptions of Islam and society (Oxford University Press, 2003). He is a Fellow of the Academy of the Social Sciences in Australia and Member of the Order of Australia.

Schuyler W. Henderson is an Associate Training Director, New York University Department of Child and Adolescent Psychiatry, Columbia University, New York. Schuyler has spent several years working in India, Romania and with refugee communities in

Chicago, attended University of Illinois at Chicago College of Medicine. He completed his internship in pediatrics at Yale, and then moved to New York University/Bellevue for a residency in adult psychiatry, followed by a fellowship in child and adolescent psychiatry at Columbia, where he also completed a postdoctoral fellowship in Public Child Psychiatry and received his Masters in Public Health. He has published papers in *Literature and Medicine* and *Journal of Medical Humanities* as well as shorter pieces and book reviews for other journals, including *Journal of the American Medical Association, New England Journal of Medicine,* and *Academic Medicine.* He has published chapters in three books, writing about case formulation in child and adolescent psychiatry, trauma mental health research, and the question of resistance and defiance in medical narratives. He was the inaugural John F. McDermott Assistant Editor in Residence of the *Journal of the American Academy of Child and Adolescent Psychiatry.*

Luis de la Corte Ibáñez, Ph.D., is a Professor in the Department of Social Psychology and Methodology of the Autonomous University of Madrid, Spain and member of the Governing Board of the Institute of Forensic Science and Security at the same university. His main research topics are terrorism, political violence, and organized crime. He is an author of numerous academic papers and chapters and several books on those topics. In turn, he is a part of the editorial boards of the *Terrorism Research Journal*. His publications include *La lógicadelterrorismo* (The Logic of Terrorism, 2006, Alianza Editorial), *La yihadterrorista* (Terrorist Jihad, written together with Professor Javier Jordán, 2007, Síntesis), and *Crimen.org. Evolución y claves de la delincuenciaorganizada* (Crime.org. Key Developments and organized crime, 2010, Editorial Ariel).

Larry James, Ph.D., is a psychologist, author, and former Colonel in the United States Army. Dr James is notable for serving as Joint Task Force Guantanamo's chief psychologist in 2003, and as Abu Ghraib's chief psychologist in 2004. Dr James is currently the Dean, School of Psychology at Wright State University in Dayton, Ohio. Dr James' research interests include military psychology, development of behavioral services in primary care, obesity and eating disorders. He is also an expert on global war on terrorism.

ABOUT THE EDITORS AND CONTRIBUTORS

Victoria Kendrick is currently pursuing her Ph.D. in Clinical Psychology with an emphasis in Forensic Psychology at Palo Alto University in Palo Alto, California. Victoria's main areas of research interest involve Clinical Emergencies including Suicide Terrorism as well as research on rehabilitation of violent offenders. Specifically, Victoria is interested in Serious Mental Illness (SMI) within prison populations and how suicidal thinking is related to offender's recidivism rates as well as rehabilitation potential.

Uri Kugel, M.S., is a Ph.D. clinical psychology student at the Palo Alto University in Palo Alto, California. Uri earned his M.S. in clinical psychology from the Leiden University in the Netherlands. He is a member of Clinical Emergencies and Crises research group at PAU led by Dr Bruce Bongar. Uri's main research interests include clinical emergencies and in particular suicide in the US Military, within the US veteran population, and suicide terrorism. Additionally, Uri conducts research in the field of evidence-based Internet assessment, and clinical-oriented artificial intelligence.

James R. Liddle is a doctoral student in the evolutionary psychology Ph.D. program at Florida Atlantic University. He is a member of Dr David F. Bjorklund's evolutionary developmental psychology lab and is co-advised by Dr Todd K. Shackelford at Oakland University. His research interests focus primarily on the origin and development of religious belief systems as well as superstitious beliefs. He is currently investigating the societal factors that influence religiosity.

Jonathan Matusitz, Ph.D., is an Associate Professor in the Nicholson School of Communication at the University of Central Florida (UCF). His academic interests include the study of globalization, terrorism, culture, technology, health communication, and social networks. One of his particular emphases is the threat that terrorist groups pose to Western civilization. Another focus of his research is the Wal-Martization and the Disneyfication of the world. On top of having 95 academic publications and more than 100 conference presentations, Dr Matusitz taught at a NATO-affiliated military base in Belgium in 2010. In 2012, he was honored with a prestigious teaching award by the College of Sciences at UCF.

Swati Mukherjee is a Scientist 'D' at Defence Institute of Psychological Research (DIPR), Delhi. She has obtained her M.Phil. degree from University of Delhi. She has been a Gold Medalist throughout her undergraduate and postgraduate study in applied psychology. She is involved in many major research projects of the Institute. She has to her credit a few publications in the form of journal articles and book chapters. She has been the associate editor of a volume on *Recent Developments in Psychology* and has co-authored a manual on *Suicide and Fratricide: Dynamics and Management* for the Armed Forces personnel and a manual on *Overcoming Obsolescence & Becoming Creative in R&D Environment* for R&D organizations. Her areas of interest are social psychology and positive mental health practices. She has been a recipient of Defence Research & Development Organization (DRDO) Best Performance Award in the year 2008. She is currently pursuing her doctoral research from Tata Institute of Social Sciences, Mumbai.

Jerrold M. Post, M.D., is a Professor of Psychiatry, Political Psychology and International Affairs and a Director of the Political Psychology Program at The George Washington University. Dr Post has devoted his entire career to the field of political psychology. Dr Post came to George Washington after a 21-year career with the Central Intelligence Agency where he was the founding director of the Center for the Analysis of Personality and Political Behavior. He initiated the US Government program in understanding the psychology of terrorism. He served as expert witness in five terrorism trials, and, since 9/11, has testified on the psychology of terrorism before the Senate, House, and the United Nations. He chaired the committee on the Psychological Roots of Terrorism for the International Summit on Democracy, Terrorism, and Security in 2005. He is the author of *The Mind of the Terrorist: The Psychology of Terrorism from the IRA to Al-Qaeda*.

Todd K. Shackelford received his Ph.D. in evolutionary psychology in 1997 from the University of Texas, Austin and his M.A. in psychology from the University of Michigan in 1995. He is a professor and chair of the Department of Psychology at Oakland University, where he is a director of the evolutionary psychology lab. He has published more than 250 peer-reviewed articles and chapters in edited volumes and has co-edited 10 volumes. Much of Shackelford's research addresses sexual conflict between men and women, with a special focus on testing hypotheses derived from sperm competition theory. Since 2006, Shackelford has served as an editor of Evolutionary Psychology.

Stephen Shanfield, M.D., is a Professor Emeritus at University of Texas Health Science Center at San Antonio (UTHSCSA) and Clinical Professor of Psychiatry. Dr Shanfield graduated from University of California, Los Angeles (UCLA) and received his M.D. from the Keck School of Medicine, University of Southern California. He trained in psychiatry at Yale School of Medicine where he also had a fellowship in Social and Community Psychiatry. After military service at Wilford Hall USAF Medical Center in San Antonio, Dr Shanfield joined the faculty at the medical school at the University of Arizona where he reached the rank of Professor.

Elvin Sheykhani is a Ph.D. clinical psychology student at Palo Alto University in Palo Alto, California. Elvin's main research interests include Crisis management and Military Psychology. Elvin is interested in working with the US Veteran population, within the domain suicide prevention within active duty and reservist personnel. Elvin conducts research on suicide prevention within the US military and assessment of Special Operations personnel.

Major General Dushyant Singh is serving in the Indian Army since December 1981. He has rich experience in the areas of Military Operations including conduct of Counterterrorist Operations against Islamic, Communist, and Secessionist terrorist groups in India including a year-long tenure in UN as Military Observer to monitor Civil War peace treaty mechanism in Liberia, Africa. He has a distinguished career record with Masters in Defense Studies from Madras University, Masters in Management from Osmania University, Masters in Defense Analysis with specialization in Terrorist Operations and Financing from Naval Postgraduate School, Monterey, California, USA. His thesis at NPS, Monterey California dealt with various theories of charisma and its exploitation to facilitate early decapitation of a terrorist movement. He has published a number of articles dealing with human resource development, anti-terrorist operations and military operations in various professional magazines of Indian Defense Forces. He has also handled counterterrorist operations at the strategic and operational levels in an elite counterterror organization.

Anne Speckhard, Ph.D., is an Adjunct Associate Professor of Psychiatry at Georgetown University Medical School. Dr Speckhard has been working in the field of posttraumatic stress disorder since the 1980s and has extensive experience working in Europe, the Middle East, and the former Soviet Union. She has provided expert consultation to European and Middle Eastern governments as well as the US Department of Defense (DoD) regarding programs for prevention and rehabilitation of individuals committed to political violence and militant jihad. In 2006–2007, she worked with the US DoD to design and pilot test the Detainee Rehabilitation Program in Iraq. Since 2002, she has collected more than 400 research interviews of family members, friends, close associates and hostages of terrorists and extremists in Palestine, Israel, Iraq, Lebanon, Morocco, Jordan, Russia, Chechnya, Belarus, Netherlands, United Kingdom, Belgium, and France. Dr Speckhard consults to governments and lectures to security experts worldwide.

Joseph Tomlins is a Ph.D. graduate student in clinical psychology at Palo Alto University in Palo Alto, California. Joseph's research currently centers on clinical emergencies. Within this domain, he focuses on suicide risk assessment in the US military, suicide terrorism, and lesbian, gay, bisexual, and transgender (LGBT) issues. Joseph has experience researching the efficacy of Exposure, Relaxation and Re-scripting Therapy (ERRT) in a randomized clinical trial for the treatment of posttraumatic nightmares. Additionally, he has researched disaster mental health responders and their feelings of optimism, coping, and preparedness for future deployments.

Jeff Victoroff received his Masters in Social Science from the University of Chicago and his M.D. with honors from Case Western Reserve University School of Medicine. After residencies in both neurology and psychiatry in Harvard hospital programs, he completed his fellowship in Neurobehavior at University of

California, Los Angeles (UCLA). Since then, he has been at the University of Southern California, Keck School of Medicine where he now serves as Associate Professor of Clinical Neurology and Psychiatry. He is interested in human aggression, especially the root causes of political violence. In addition to his studies of the neurobehavioral bases of violent behavior, he has edited two books on the psychology of terrorism, serves on the UN roster of Terrorism Experts, advises US Government agencies, and conducts empirical studies of the social psychology of terrorism.

Stevan Weine is a Professor of Psychiatry and Director of the International Center on Responses to Catastrophes, at the University of Illinois at Chicago. His scholarly work focuses on the personal, familial, social, cultural, and historical dimensions of trauma and migration. In 1999, he was awarded a Career Scientist Award from the National Institute of Mental Health on 'Services Based Research with Refugee Families' for which he conducted ethnography of Bosnian adolescents and their families. He was principal investigator of a National Institute of Mental Health funded research study called 'A Prevention and Access Intervention for Survivor Families' that is investigating the Coffee and Family Education and Support intervention with Bosnian and Kosovar families in Chicago. Weine is author of two books. When History is a Nightmare: Lives and Memories of Ethnic Cleansing in Bosnia-Herzegovina (Rutgers, 1999) is based upon survivor's oral histories. Testimony and Catastrophe: Narrating the Traumas of Political Violence (Northwestern, 2006) is a narrative inquiry of diverse testimony readings from within four different twentieth century sociohistorical occurrences of political violence.

Author Index

Abdel-Khalek, A., 107
Abdel-Khalek, A. M., 12–13, 178, 183
Abdul-Khaliq, 123
Abou El Fadl, K., 122
Abualrub, J., 121
Aharonson, D. L., 174
Akhmedova, K., 34, 149, 151–152, 163
Alcorta, C. S., 47
Alexander, Y., 118
Almog, D., 232, 243–253
Antonius, D., 183
Apter, A., 94
Araj, B., 180, 183, 187
Arce, D. G., 192
Arendt, H., 100, 110
Argo, N., 97
Asad, T., 96, 99, 104, 110
Ataturk, M. K., 122
Atran, S., 5, 9, 21, 30, 44–45, 52, 64, 107, 184, 195, 238
Aunger, R., 48

Bakken, N. W., 240–241, 243
Ballif-Spanvill, B., 3
Bandura, A., 31, 35–36, 135
Bank, A., 200–201
Banks, L., 201, 203–205
Barlow, S. H., 3
Barraclough, B., 95
Barrett, J. L., 44–46
Bar, S., 232, 250–251, 253
Bar-Tal, D., 32
Bartone, P. T., 202–203, 207
Basilici, S. P., 231

Baweja, H., 77
Bering, J. M., 44–45, 47
Berko, A., 93, 129, 131, 137–139, 213–228
Berkowitz, L., 7
Berlo, D. K., 61
Berry, D., 45
Beutler, L. E., 48
Bibi, A., 173
bin Laden, Osama, 122, 124, 208
Blackmore, S., 48
Blackwell, A. D., 50–51, 54
Bleske, A., 47
Bliss, D. E., 47
Bloom, M., 4, 20–21, 28, 30, 35, 97–98, 100–102, 107, 127, 194, 213, 238–239, 241
Bloom, P., 45
Bongar, B., 48, 173–187, 192–209
Bonger, B., 151
Borum, R., 42
Bourke, J., 103, 105
Boyer, P., 44–46
Brachman, J. M., 72
Brannan, D. W., 13
Breckenridge, J. N., 48
Brodie, R., 48
Broshi, Y., 173
Brown, L. M., 48
Bru, E., 47
Brym, R. J., 187
Brynen, R., 10
Brynjar, L., 198
Burnham, G., 173
Buss, D. M., 47, 50

AUTHOR INDEX

Campbell, R. J., 12
Campione-Barr, N., 129
Canetti-Nisim, D., 43
Caracci, G., 64
Carli, V., 207
Carlson, J. R., 62
Castells, M., 26
Charap, J., 183
Cherrington, D. J., 63
Clausewitz, C. V., 192
Clayton, C. J., 3
Coleman, J. S., 20
Coll, S., 76, 82
Comer, J. S., 69
Cooper, J. M., 7
Costello, J., 218
Crenshaw, M., 4, 109, 118, 174, 238–240
Crisafulli, J. R., 231
Crook, B., 221
Crumley, B., 76, 88
Csibra, G., 45

Dabbagh, D., 94
Dabbagh, T. S., 94–95
Dalgaard-Nielsena, D., 24
Daly, S. A., 196
Darwin, C., 44
Dawkins, R., 48–49
Dearing, M. P., 181, 183, 185, 195
de Catanzaro, D., 9
De La Corte, L., 18–38
Della Porta, D., 23, 26, 31
De Miguel, J. M., 18
Dennett, D. C., 42, 48
Denny, L., 120
Diamant, I., 173
Diani, D., 31
Díaz, D., 18
Diaz, T., 70
Diemer, M. A., 201–202
Diener, E., 137
Doek, J. E., 219

Dollard, J., 7
Doob, L., 7
Dougherty, B. J., 71
Douzinas, C., 65
Durkheim, E., 9–10, 118, 175, 194
Durodi, B., 68
Dweck, C. S., 13
Dyke, J. R., 231

Eckstein, J., 74
Elias, N., 108
Elster, J., 21, 30
Erez, E., 213–228
Erlanger, E., 132
Esler, P. F., 13

Faria, J. R., 192
Fenster, J. R., 47
Feshbach, S., 7
Fields, R., 22
Fields, R. M., 180
Fincher, C. L., 48
Finnegan, C. A., 67
Fishman, S., 13, 19, 33
Fisk, R., 72
Flin, R., 202
Freud, S., 7

Gambetta, D., 18, 23, 30, 107
Gandhi, Rajiv, 231
Ganor, B., 5, 18, 20–21
Gelfand, M., 175–176
Gergely, G., 45
Gerwehr, S., 196
Gill, P., 27, 33–34
Giménez-Salinas, A., 29
Ginges, J., 49, 54, 107
Goetze, G. B., 51
Gould, S. J., 47
Gray, D. H., 213
Greenberg, J., 33
Gressang, D. S., 69
Grimland, M., 94

Gunaratna, R., 175
Gupta, D. K., 20
Gurr, T. R., 245
Guthrie, S. E., 44

Hafez, M., 13, 20, 23, 25–26, 31, 36, 67–68, 107, 121, 130, 134, 220, 222–223
Hafez, M. M., 238–239
Hakim, N., 176
Hamilton, W. D., 50
Hamlin, J. K., 45
Hammel, E., 70
Hansen, I., 49
Harrell, M. C., 204
Harris, C., 95
Harris, S., 43, 49, 53
Hartmann, E., 204
Haselton, M. G., 47
Hassan, N., 107, 139–140, 178, 180–183
Hassan, R., 93–112, 187, 207–208, 231, 233, 237–238, 240–242
Hasso, F. S., 181
Hatemi, P., 8
Hayden, T., 76, 89
Haykel, B., 125
Hegghammer, T., 183
Hicks, M. A., 174
Higgins, E. T., 13
Hilterman, J. R., 218
Hirsch, C. S., 95
Hirvikoski, T., 176
Hodgdon, J. A., 203
Hoffman, B., 42, 118, 192–194, 238, 240–241
Hope, D. S., 67
Horgan, J., 28, 118, 183
Horowitz, M. C., 72
Hronick, M. S., 42
Hughes, D., 206
Hugi, J. I., 223
Humphreys, A., 193
Hussein, Saddam, 217

Ibrahim, A., 124
Ismayilov, M., 6
Israeli, R., 6

Jaber, H., 70
Jackson, B. A., 232, 243–245, 250
Jacobson, P., 127
Jacuch, B., 153
James, P., 51
James, W., 23
Jayyusi, M., 99
Jenkins, B. M., 195–197, 246
Johnson, K., 10
Jokinen, J., 176

Kahneman, D., 21
Kalyvas, S., 30
Kane, T., 205
Kasab, Ajmal, 79–81
Kavanagh, J., 183, 196–197
Kelley, J., 127–128
Kelly, R., 81
Kelly, R. C., 95, 105–107
Kendall, P. C., 69
Keniston, K., 129, 132
Kerkhof, A., 94
Khetan, A., 80–81
Klandermans, B. M., 26
Klein, Y., 174
Kriesberg, L., 32
Kristensen, W., 204
Krueger, A. B., 19
Kruglanski, A. W., 13, 18–19, 21, 33, 87, 175–176
Kubler-Ross, E., 108
Kumar, U., 173
Kurlantzick, J., 140
Lahkvi, Zaki-ur Rehman, 81
Lamb, C. J., 205, 207
Lankford, A., 27, 174, 176–177, 182–183, 186
Laqueur, W., 118
Lavine, H., 33

AUTHOR INDEX

Lester, D., 6, 13
Lewis, D., 5
Lia, B., 148
Liddle, J. R., 42–56
Liem, M., 6, 176
Lodge, M., 33
Louis, W., 24

Machluf, K., 49
Magid, I. M., 121
Makki, A. R., 84–86
Maleckova, J., 19
Marcia, J. E., 13
Marcus, I., 221
Martinez, D. P., 179
Martinussen, M., 204
Marwah, V., 82
Marzuk, P. M., 95
Masten, A., 218
Masterson, J. F., 65
Matusitz, J., 60–73
McCauley, C., 118
McCormick, G., 238, 240–241
McDermott, R., 8
McDonald, D. G., 203
McKinley, W., 63, 66
Medin, S., 107
Menon, S., 5
Merari, Ariel, 5–6, 11, 23, 30, 129–130, 134–135, 138, 173, 175–177, 182–187, 194, 197
Metzger, A., 129
Milgram, S., 184
Miller, C., 61
Miller, N., 7
Moghadam, A., 20, 25, 28, 180, 233, 237–238, 240–243, 248, 253
Montuori, A., 34
Morral, A. R., 232, 243–245, 250
Mowrer, O., 7
Mukherjee, S., 173
Mundra, K., 20
Murberg, T. A., 47

Murray, S., 63
Mursheda, S. M., 24

Narayan, A. J., 218
Nason, A., 232, 245–246
Nesser, P., 198–199
Newman, B., 70
Nieuwbeerta, P., 6, 176
Nisbett, R., 135
Nordstrom, C., 103
Norenzayan, A., 47, 49
Norton, A. R., 70
Norton, J. P., 203
Nyhof, M. 46

Ocalan, A., 120
O'Connor, T., 4
O'Donovan, O., 105
O'Hair, D., 61
Oliver, A. M., 107
Olson, L. C., 67
Opotow, S., 36
Orbach, I., 177–178, 182, 184, 186, 196–197, 199
Otterbein, K. F., 95, 105, 107

Palermo, G. B., 7
Pape, R. A., 20, 24–25, 28, 30, 35, 64, 107, 185, 233, 237–238, 240
Park, C. L., 47
Pavan, S., 24
Paz, R., 148
Pedahzur, A., 9–11, 28, 43, 50, 52, 63, 66
Peleg, K., 174
Perliger, A., 9, 43, 236
Peters, L., 213
Pine, D. S., 218
Pittas, A., 196
Pittel, K., 182
Pleban, R., 201, 203
Polichak, J., 33
Poole, J. J., 72

Poole, S., 118
Post, J. M., 8, 13, 117–143, 183, 185, 195–196
Postmes, T., 137
Prabhakaran, Vellupillai, 120, 136
Prakash, V., 173
Preti, A., 177

Rabasa, A., 79, 84, 86–87
Rafsanjani, Ali-Akbar, 217
Ranstorp, M., 71
Rantisi, Abdul Aziz, 97
Reader, W., 42
Ricolfi, L., 21, 35
Riemer, W. J., 10
Rigby, A., 216
Roberts, M., 107
Rosenberger, J., 180
Rosenberg, S. W., 20
Rosen, D. M., 214, 216–217, 220, 222–223, 227
Ross, J. I., 42, 245
Ross, L., 135
Roy, A., 174–175, 207
Rübbelke, D. T. G., 182
Ruby, C. L., 9
Rudner, R., 192
Russell, T. L., 201, 204

Saad, R., 67
Sabucedo, J. M., 18
Sageman, M., 22–23, 64, 132, 138–139, 183
Sali, S., 240, 243
Sánchez Cuenca, I., 30
Sarchiapone, M., 207
Saunders, D., 62
Sayeed, H., 80–81
Schachter, J., 243, 247
Schafer, R. M., 62
Schimel, J., 33
Schirrmacher, C., 176
Schmid, A., 3, 119

Schmid, A. P., 61
Scholl, B. J., 45
Schonhardt, S., 252
Schweitzer, Y., 64, 153–154
Sears, R., 7
Segal, M., 118
Shackelford, T. K., 42–56
Shalhoub-Kevorkian, N., 223
Shariff, A. F., 47, 49
Sheehy-Skeffington, J., 238–239
Shermer, M., 120
Shikaki, K., 107
Shneidman, E., 151
Silberman, I., 13
Silke, A., 22, 118, 183
Simmons, J., 231
Simon, B., 26
Simon, H. A., 21
Simon, L., 26
Simonson, P., 60, 62
Singer, P. W., 213–214, 216–220
Sirriyeh, H., 10
Smetana, J., 129
Smith, D., 68
Somasundaram, D., 218, 226
Sosis, R., 47
Sparago, M., 195–198, 206, 208
Spears, R., 137
Speckhard, A., 34, 138, 147–171
Speckhard, Anne, 34, 138, 147–171
Sprinzak, E., 120
Stack, S., 10
Steinberg, L., 129
Steinberg, P., 107
Stenersen, A., 199
Stern, J., 49, 54
Stevens, M. J., 13
Strenski, I., 98
Strindberg, N. T. A., 13
Sunde, T., 204
Suresh, D. P., 47

AUTHOR INDEX

Taber, C., 33
Tajfel, H., 26
Tankel, S., 81–82
Tardiff, K., 95
Taylor, D. M., 24
Taylor, M., 28
Taylor, S., 10
Thornhill, R., 48
Timmermans, S., 108
Tippet, M. D., 232, 243–245
Tønnessen, T. H., 198–199
Townsend, E., 94, 107, 174, 176–177, 183, 185
Trager, R. F., 232, 243–245, 248, 250
Tremoulet, P. D., 45
Tucker, G., 205, 207
Tuck, R., 96, 108
Tuman, J. S., 65–66
Turner, J. C., 26

Vanrompay, V., 153
Vasilenko, V. I., 70
Venhaus, J. M., 218
Venzke, B., 124
Victor, B., 185
Victoroff, J., 3, 50, 117–143, 183, 192
Volkan, V., 136

Wallace, B., 179
Walzer, M., 93, 96, 102, 105, 110
Wardlaw, G., 3
Weimann, G., 221–222
Weinberg, L., 9, 43
Wessells, M.G., 214, 216, 219, 223
White-Ajmani, M. L., 183
Williams, G. C., 46
Williams, J. J., 61
Williams, T. J., 202
Wilson, D. S., 46
Workman, L., 42
Wright-Neville, D., 68
Wright, Q., 95
Wynn, K., 45

Yassin, S. A., 136
Yonghe, Y., 5
Yoshihara, S., 71
Young, L., 10–11

Zagorcheva, D. P. 232, 245, 248, 250
Zakaria, F., 80
Zakin, G. 173
Zayat, M., 124
Zimbardo, P., 136–137
Zimbardo, P. G., 49
Zuckerman, P., 49, 54

Subject Index

Abdel-Khalek martyrdom, 12
Abu Graib prison, Iraq, 104
Abu Nidal terrorist, 128–129
accomplished suicide bombers, 154–155
active planning suicide, 152
act of terrorism, 66
actual killers, 106
acute altruistic suicide, 10, 175
acute hopelessness, 183
adolescent psychology, 129–132
Afghanistan
   freedom for terrorist groups in, 181
   recruitment of children and younger adults for suicide missions in, 184
   U.S. and coalition military operations in, 120
   women as suicide bombers in, 181
aggressive behaviors, 7
Ahl-e-Hadith (People of the Hadith), 81
Akshardham temple terror attack (2002), 231
Al'Aqsa Martyrs Brigades, 98
Al-Fateh site, 221
Allah, 68, 120, 196
Allah Akbar (God is great), 128
Al-Qaeda, 5, 22–23, 25–26, 51–52, 71–72, 120, 130, 132, 148, 169, 183, 187, 194–195
Al-Qaeda version 1.0, 133
Al-Qaeda version 2.0, 133–134
altruistic behavior, 50

altruistic suicide, 9–12, 118, 175, 178
al-Zawahiri, Ayman, 124
announcement effects, 182
anomic suicide, 175
armed assault, 83
armed resistance, 119
attack by weapons, 235
attempted suicide bombers, 153–154
audience
   definition of, 69
   Hezbollah suicide attacks on US Marines (1983) [see Hezbollah suicide attacks on US Marines (1983)]
   public character of terrorism, 70
authoritarian societies, 13

bad death, 107–109, 111
Baghdad Sniper, 68
Berlo model of communication, 61
biopolitics, 63
bloody counterterrorist strategies, implementation of, 34–35
bombers, suicide, 21–23, 35, 63, 107, 110, 117–118, 129, 132, 137, 193
   euphoria in hypothetical, 152–153
   and Kamikaze pilots of Japan, difference between, 179–180
   live, 184

SUBJECT INDEX

bombings, suicide, 64–65, 94–95, 107, 109–110, 151–152, 214
  acts of public performance, 111
  death of civilians in Palestine due to, 97–98
  as murderous killing, 93
  and Palestinian children, 222–226
  propensity for, 207
Bonger, Bruce, 151
Bourke, Joanne, 103

Caliphate, 72, 121–124
campaigns on suicides, 20–21, 28
capital punishment, 105–106
Casa Blanca suicide bombers, 168–169
causalities in war, 107
charismatic leader–follower relationships, 136
Chechen separatist groups, 120
Chechen suicide bombers, 138, 159
children
  benefits of using in war and terrorism, 215–218
  serve for military and terrorist organizations, xvii–xviii
  use in terrorism, 213–214
  motivation to participate and recruitment methods, 218–222
Christianity, 52
collective identity, 126
Committee on the Psychological Roots of Terrorism, 125–126, 129, 137
communicating suicide terrorism model, 65–66
communication of terrorism, 61–63, 89
communicative act, terrorism as, 61

conflictive ethos, 32–34
conflict zones, 148–149, 160
  dissociation in, 167–168
  victims in, 164
congestive heart failure (CHF), 47
conventional terrorist attacks, 83, 87–88
conviction role in terrorism, 85
coordinated attacks, 86–87
countering dissociative states with anger, 157–158
counterterrorism agencies, 186
culture diffusion, frames death of human bombers, 36
culture of martyrdom, 36

death
  brokering, 108
  good and bad, 107–109
  living (see living death)
  nature assertion over culture, 111
  penalty, 106
defection effects, 182
Defence Institute of Psychological Research (DIPR), xviii
Defence Research and Development Organization (DRDO), xviii
dehumanization, 35
  of enemy, 135
deindividuation, concept of, 136–137
demonization discursive, 35, 135
Department of Defense, US, 118–119, 200
depersonalization, 26–27
deterrence strategy against terrorism, xviii, xix, 232, 244–249
  by denial strategies, 249–251
  by punishment, 251–252
  for suicide terror attack, 249
die, being prepared to, 12–14

dissociation, 150–153. *See also* posttraumatic stress disorder (PTSD)
  in conflict zones (*see* conflict zones, dissociation in)
  and euphoria in accomplished suicide bombers, 154–155
  and euphoria in attempted/failed suicide bombers, 153–154
  in terrorist assassin, 158–159
  in terrorist sender of suicide bombers, 157
  in volunteers for suicide missions, 155
domestic violence, 176
dying process, 108

egoistic suicide, 175, 177–178, 181, 183, 185
encoding process, 65
enemies of Islam, 53
ethnic antagonisms in Sri Lanka, 100
euphoria
  in accomplished suicide bombers, 154–155
  in attempted/failed suicide bombers, 153–154
  in hypothetical suicide bombers, 152–153
evolutionary psychological science of suicide terrorism, xiv
  directions for future research, 53–55
evolutionary psychology, 43–44
  applicability to suicide terrorism, 48–53
extreme Islamism, 173

failed suicide bombers, 153–154
Fatah movement, 130, 214, 222
fatalistic suicides, 10–11

FBI, 118
fedayeen attacks, 76, 82, 84, 86
female suicide attackers, 185
foreclosure of identity, 13
frustration–aggression hypothesis, 7
fugitive terrorist, 163

Gaza Community Health Program, 141
good death, 107–109, 111

Hamas, 5, 26, 66, 94, 97–98, 127, 130–131, 187, 214, 222
Hezbollah suicide attacks on US Marines (1983), 5, 63, 69–72, 125, 130
historical alliances, 208
holy war, 121, 217.
  See also jihad
home grown terrorists, 133
homicidal, 109
  behaviors, 7
homicide, 105
homicide–suicides, 177
hostile aggression, 7
human bombers, 36
human bombs, 127
humiliation role in suicidal terrorists life, 182
hypersensitive agent detection device (HADD), 44–48
hypothetical suicide bombers, 152–153

immoral killing, 109
improvised explosive devices (IEDs), 77–79, 84
incarcerated terrorists from Middle East, 131
indoctrination process, 197–198, 206
in-group influence effects, 27

SUBJECT INDEX

in-group *vs* out-group enmity, 136
injury, 151
intergroup relations theory, 136
International Laws of War, 111
International Summit on Democracy, Terrorism, and Security (2005), Spain, 137, 125
Inter-Services Intelligence (ISI), Pakistan, 81–82
Intifada (uprising), Palestinian, 64, 129, 155, 158, 164, 167, 216–218, 220
intractable conflicts, 32–34
Iranian Revolution, 99
Iraq
  civilian death from 2003 to 2010, 174
  suicide attacks by women between 2003 and 2010, 181
  US and coalition military operations in, 120
  use of children in war, 217
Iraqis suicide volunteers, 25
Islam, 52
Islamic beliefs, 53
Islamic jihad, 94, 98, 131, 214
Islamie revolution (1979), Iran, 122
Islamikaze, suicide terrorists, 179
Islamist sniper, 68
Islamist sniper, 68
Israel Defense Forces (IDF), 216
Israeli–Arab/Palestinian conflict, xviii
Israeli–Palestinian conflict, 102
Istishhad, Islamic notion of, 4

Jemaah Islamiyah (JI), Indonesia, 140, 252
Jewish Sicarii, xi
jihad, 121–122, 127
jihadi Salafi networks, 25

jihadis threat, 76
jihadist martyrdom videos, 68
jihadist terrorists generate social noise, 68
Judaism, 52
judicial killing, 108
just war, 119

Kamikaze pilots of Japan act in World War II, 5, 179–180
Khalifah, 122
kill enemy, 109
killing, 95–97, 151
  of innocents by taking one own life, 110
  in war and terrorism, 103–107
kin selection theory, 50–52
Koran, 121, 140
Kurdish nationalism, 136
Kurdistan Workers Party (PKK), Turkey, 120, 251

Lashkar-e-Taiba (LET), 77, 80–82, 84–85
Lebanese Muslims, 72
legality of war, 97
lethality by weapon, 235
lethal violence, 105
liberal democracies, 110
liberal doctrine, 107
Liberation Tigers of Tamil Eelam (LTTE), 5, 49, 82, 101, 120, 217. *See also* Tamil Tigers
live suicide bombers, 184
living death, 155–156, 158
London transit bombings of 7/7/2005, 133
loss, deficits of psychological assistance for, 167–168

madrasas, 195–196
Madrid train station bombing (2004), 133

male suicides, 183
Markaz al-Dawa was-Irshad (Center for Preaching and Guidance), 81
martyrdom, 53, 73, 156, 168, 194. *See also* suicide terrorism
　definition of, 176
　dissemination of culture of, 36
　ideology, 149, 162–163
　missions, 171
　mythology, 13
　operations, 138, 140
　as social noise, 66–68
　suffering of death, 175
mass-mediated images, 60, 72–73
meme, 48
mental faculties of religious belief, 44
mental pain, 182
militant jihadi ideology, xvi, 147–148
militant jihadi terrorists groups, 170–171
military psychology, 209
minimally counterintuitive (MCI), 45–46
Minnesota Multiphasic Personality Inventory (MMPI-2), 203
modern-day terrorism, 3, 76
Moghadam suicide terrorism cycle, 242
moral appropriateness, 105
moral disengagement mechanism, 135–136
moral legitimacy, doctrine of, 97
mortality salience, 33–34
motivation(s)
　to children to terrorists organizations, 218–222
　for joining special operations, 205
　for joining terrorist organizations, 197
　for suicide attacks, 182
multicausal motivation, 240–243
Mumbai style suicide attacks, xv, 76–77, 82–83, 90
　characteristics of, 88
　contingency planning, 89–90
　importance of attribution, 88–89
　suicide terrorist and terrorist, critical difference between, 86
Mumbai terror attacks of 26/11, xv, 76, 231. *See also* Kasab, Ajmal
　background of, 79
　combination of attack methods, 84–85
　communication role in, 85, 87–88
　coordination of, 84
　individual perpetrator, 80
　recorded conversations between militants in Mumbai and their handlers in Pakistan, 80
　sixty hours of, 77–79, 90
　style of attack, 82
　willingness of perpetrators, 83–84
murder, 104–107, 109
Muslims, 68, 72, 127, 170, 195
　adolescents, 129–130
　assassins, xi
　clergy, 122
　Koran against killing of, 121
　moderate, 53
　Ummah, 125

nationalism, definition of, 24
NATO, 187
neurobiological approach, 8–9
new terrorist methods, xi
NGOs, 226
Nobel, Alfred, 62

SUBJECT INDEX

noncombatant, 192
non conflict zones, xvi, 148, 168–171
non religious groups, 47
non suicide terrorism, 85
normal dissociation, 150
normal suicide, 151–152

obligatory altruistic suicide, 175
online videos, 60, 67, 73
optional altruistic suicide, 10, 175
organized violence, 96, 105
Oslo accord, 99–100
Ottoman Empire, 123
out-group enmity, 136

Palestine, 109
  study of suicides in, 94
  suicide bombers
    and 9/11 suicidal hijackers, contrast between, 132–133
    motivation for suicide attacks, 182
  suicide bombings, 98–99
  suicide terrorism in, 63
  terrorist organizations employing suicide bombings, 97
  terrorists in, 127
  violence option to achieve independent state, 97
Palestinian, 214n2
  children and terrorism, 222–226
  jihad, 222
  suicide terrorists, 54
Palestinian Authority Television (PA TV), 220–221
Pape's nationalist theory of suicide terrorism, 25

Partiya Karkerên Kurdistan (PKK) in Turkey, 217
Pew Global Attitude Survey, 133
philosophy of the bomb, 62
pious predecessors, 123n4
PLO, 128
political action, 208
political community, 107
political polarization to suicide terrorism, 31
political theory, 109
political violence, 8, 147
posthumous effects, 182
posttraumatic hyper-arousal, 162–163
posttraumatic stress disorder (PTSD), 129, 149–151, 156, 159–163
  identification with aggressor, 163–166
  and increased fanaticism, 163–166
potential martyrs, sense of foreshortened future among, 155–156
potential suicide bombers, 139
pre-traumatic dissociation, 150
Prevention of Terrorism Act (PTA) 1979, Sri Lanka, 101
prison, 159–162
psychache, 151–152, 156
psychological assistance, deficits for trauma and loss, 167–168
psychological infrastructure, 32
psychology
  of charismatic leader–follower relationships, 136
  of terrorism, 125–126

Qur'an, 53, 121, 124n5

radicalization process to suicide terrorism, 31–36
recruitment
  of children in terrorists organization, 218–222
  of special forces, 200–201
  for terrorist organizations, 195–196
religion
  evolution of, 44–48
  influence on suicide campaigns, 24–25
  invokes authority of divine covenants, 108
  primary motivational force among suicide terrorists, 208
religious
  beliefs, 46, 49–50, 52, 55
  extremism, 180
  individuals, 47
  polarization, 31
  sects, 52
Research Department Explosive (RDX), 77
Revolutionary Armed Forces of Columbia (FARC), 87
Rezaq, Mohammed, 128–129
righteous, 123n4
right to kill, 96, 108

sacrifice, 9, 32, 84, 222
Salafi-Jihadi ideology, 124
Salafi-Jihadis, 123, 125, 133
Salafism, doctrine of, 121, 123–125
sausalities for suicide terror, 253
school shooting, 176
scrutiny of world over suicide terrorism events, 10
Second Gulf War, 217
selection
  of special forces, 200–201
  of terrorism, 195–196

self-destruction
  by suicide terrorism, 178
  in egoistic suicide, 178
self-destructive behavior, 9
self-mutilation in egoistic suicide, 178
sense of empowerment, 152–153
September 11, 2001 terrorist attacks, 64, 117
SF Operational Detachment Alpha, 201
shaheeda (martyr), 222
shaheed heroes, 139
*shaheed*s (suicide bombers), 63, 223n6, 224
Shining Path, Peru, 87
Shinto religion, 179
shooting-rampages, 176
shuhada (martyrs), 66
signature method, 63
Sinhalese nationalism, 100
smart bombs, 117
social cohesion, 27
social identification, 37
social identity matters, 23–27
social interaction, 22–23, 37
socialization of soldiers, 135
social noise method, 62, 66–68
  suicide terrorism as, 63–64
social process models, 134–137
social psychological theory, 134–137
social psychologists, 35
social psychology, 23–24, 87, 118
social support, 208
sole reliance, 7
special forces (SF), 194
  assessment of, 202–204
  demographics of, 204–205
  Green Berets, 201
  internally directed individuals, 206

SUBJECT INDEX

missions of, 201
motivation for joining, 205
personnel high in
   resilience, 207
recruitment of, 200–202, 206
selection of, 200–201
training of, 200–201, 204,
   206–207
Special Operations Command
   (SOCOM), 201
Special Operations Forces (SOF),
   194, 201
Special Operators (SO) soldiers,
   200–201
Sri Lanka, 100–102, 109
stigmatization, 35
suffering, 182
9/11 suicidal hijackers, 132–133
suicidal/suicide(s), 42, 65–66,
   94–95, 119–120
   altruistic suicide (*see* altruistic
      suicide)
   attackers, motivation of,
      238–240
   attacks, xi, 5, 8, 23, 34, 174,
      231, 234
      deaths under, 232
      definition of, 173
      deterrence of, 243–244
      distribution by targets, 236
      involves dissociative
         processes, 177
      motivations for individuals
         to execute, 182
      offensive operation, 18
      symbol of terrorism, 173
      victims unknown to
         killer, 95
   being prepared to, 12–14
   campaign, 18
   categories of, 174–175
   classical categorization of, xvii
   definition of, 176
   deliberations on, 14
   elements of, 182–183
   evolutionary behavioral
      perspective on suicide, 9
   hijackers, 117
   missions, 31, 194, 207
   operations, 30
   social context of, 9–11
   terror, 110
   terrorism, 118, 120, 129–132,
      170, 176, 187
      definition of, 237–238
      group models of, 126–129
      as a group phenomenon,
         180–181
      historical perspective of,
         233–237
      individual models of,
         137–139
      in Islamic context,
         121–125
      and other acts of suicide,
         similarities between, 177
      religious based, 193
      and special forces,
         comparison between, 194
   terrorists, 3–4, 6–8, 54, 69, 72,
      86, 142, 175, 183, 185–186,
      193, 205–206
      characteristics of, 94
      humiliation role in, 182
      motivating factors for, 208
      and other acts of suicide,
         differences between,
         177–179
      personality, 184
   violence, 30
suicide bomb trainer, 127
suicide terrorism, xvii, xviii,
   xi–xiii, 4–7, 9, 37, 76, 85.
   See also communication
   of terrorism; evolutionary
   psychology; Liberation Tigers

of Tamil Eelam (LTTE); social
noise method
definition of, 63
as a phenomenon, xiv, xv–xvi
as a process, xiv, 28–29
as a psychosocial phenomenon
campaigns on suicides,
20–21
multidimensional approach,
27–28
social construction of suicide
bombers, 22–23
social identity matters,
23–27
symptom of social or
psychological
disorders, 19
purpose of, 64
risk factors related to strategic
asymmetric conditions,
29–30
coexistence of several
terrorist or insurgent
groups, 30
cognitive accessibility and
pre-existence of suicidal
terrorist activity, 30–31
feeling of stagnation, crisis
or failure in use of other
terrorist or insurgent
methods, 30
use of explosives, 87
Sunnah, 124n5
supportive social groups,
membership of, 24

Tamil ethnic chauvinism, 100
Tamil insurgency, 101
Tamil National Tigers/Tamil
Tigers, 49, 101, 103, 136. See
also Liberation Tigers of Tamil
Eelam (LTTE)

Tamils in Sri Lanka, discrimination
against, 100
terrorism, xi, xiii, 56, 109–110. See
also social noise method
as a act of violence, 192
as a communication process, 61
definitional issue, 4–5
definition of, 118–120
by US, 192
homicidal killing, 93
killing in, 103–104
psychological effects of, 192
psychology of (see psychology
of terrorism)
selection and recruitment of,
195–196
suicide (see suicide terrorism)
tool in perpetrators hands, 3
training of, 195–196
using of children in, 215–218
way to reframe, 141
weapon of weak, 231
terrorists, 61, 63, 86, 93,
126, 141, 206. See also suicide
terrorism
adversaries and targets,
difference between, 35–36
assassin, 158–159
attacks in 2011, 173
belief, 52–53
campaigns, xi
definition of, 118–120
groups, 127
ideology, 26
minds, 192
psychology, 137
sender of suicide bombers, 154
Third World nations, 12
Tiger Tamils, Sri Lanka, 26
torture, 159–162
training
of special forces, 200–201

SUBJECT INDEX

of terrorists and organizations, 198–200
trauma(s), 151–152
  deficits of psychological assistance for, 167–168
  in non-conflict zones, 169
traumatic
  bereavement, 159–160
  dissociation, 150–151
tribal wars, xi

UNESCO, 128
United Nations, 4, 139
United States Special Operations Command (USSOCOM), 203
USA Patriot Act, 2001, 119
US Army SF, 205

Vietnam War, 104, 120
violence, 97, 192. *See also* war
  as medium itself, 61
  organized (*see* organized violence)

violent conflict, xvi–xvii
violent self-defense, 96, 107
virtues of groups, 52
volunteers for suicide missions, 155
war(s), 95–97. *See also* holy war; jihad
  crimes, 111
  justification for, 108
  killing in, 103–107, 109
  in political theory, 109
  using of children in, 215–218
weapon of mass destruction (WMD), 148
wish to reunite with loved one, 159–160
women suicide bombers, 181
World War II (WW-II), 102, 120, 179

youth use in terrorism, 213, 226